D1279978

MY FELLOW AMERICANS

MY FELLOW AMERICANS

★ ★ ★ ★ ★ ★ ★ ★ ★ ★ ★ ★

SCOUTING, DIVERSITY,

and the U.S. PRESIDENCY

★ ★ ★ ★ ★ ★ ★ ★ ★ ★ ★ ★

DAVID C. SCOTT

FOREWORD BY DOUGLAS BRINKLEY

WIND RUSH
PUBLISHERS

Dallas, Texas

Published by WindRush Publishers
WindRush Publishers and colophon are trademarks of
WindRush Ventures, LLC

First Edition 2014

10 9 8 7 6 5 4 3 2 1

WindRush publications are available at special discounted rates for volume
and bulk purchases, corporate and institutional premiums, promotions,
fund-raising, and educational use. For further information, contact:

WindRush Publishers
P.O. Box 670324
Dallas, Texas 75367
www.WindRushPub.com

Printed and bound in the United States of America.
ISBN-13: 978-0-98590970-3

Cover design, book design, and layout by LandMarc Design learn more at
www.landmarcdesign.com

My Fellow Americans is not an official publication of the Boy Scouts of
America. BSA images are used with permission.

Check out more about this book at: www.MyFellowAmericansBook.com

Get informed and inspired at www.WindRushPub.com

For the young patriots of

BOY SCOUT TROOP 57, GARLAND, TEXAS

and

CUB SCOUT PACK 570, DALLAS, TEXAS
Circle 10 Council, BSA

and

IN MEMORY OF

TEX HIGGINBOTHAM

1998–2014

A fine young Scout who walked the walk.

"*No single movement in our nation has been of greater advantage to our national life than that represented by the Boy Scouts of America.*"

Governor Calvin Coolidge, *February 1919*

CONTENTS

FOREWORD

By Douglas Brinkley

The Boy Scouts of America (BSA) has been a great progenitor of good in our nation since its founding in 1910. Born of changing societal attitudes that aimed to elevate the status of a growing underclass, philanthropic men of means formed BSA to re-mold the active minds of young Americans toward giving service to others. First targeted were the idle Progressive Era boys who seemingly frittered away their days on the nation's street corners making mischief.

This revolutionary program was based on hiking local city-bound lads into the woods surrounding their communities. Once there, the volunteer Scoutmasters would tender valuable lessons on camping skills, campfire cooking, and self-reliance. As a result, thousands of boys excitedly signed up.

Nationally, the organization was run with an iron fist by former YMCA lawyer-turned-Chief Scout Executive James E. West, who set about growing BSA's prestige through tactical endorsements garnered from the titans of industry and legendary statesmen. Of the many affirmations received, the most valuable came from former president Theodore Roosevelt, which started the tradition that remains today: every president since William Howard Taft has served as the Boy Scouts of America's honorary president.

OVER THE PAST FEW YEARS I've been writing *Rightful Heritage: Franklin D. Roosevelt and the American Conservation Movement.* I was astonished to learn what a grand champion of Scouting Roosevelt truly was. Two of his most successful New Deal programs—The Civilian Conservation Corps (CCC) and Civil Works Administration (CWA)—were direct outgrowths of the Scouting Movement. Roosevelt had first become involved with BSA in 1915. By 1921 he ran all Scouting activities in New York City. It was Roosevelt who came up with the idea of a "Water Hike" up the Hudson River from Grant's Tomb to Bear Mountain. Over 5,000 Scouts joined the grand parade.

As America's only four-term president, Roosevelt embraced BSA as an essential component of our nation's democratic spirit. He believed the Scout Oath was the "basis of good citizenship."

What I found most enjoyable about *My Fellow Americans: Scouting, Diversity, and the U.S. Presidency* was the fact that all the sitting 20th and 21st century presidents since Taft praised BSA in a heartfelt and glorious way. Dwight Eisenhower believed that Scouting "merits the unstinted support of every American who wants to make this world a better place in which to live." And Ronald Reagan—at a 1985 White House luncheon—described the importance of earning a BSA honor. "Well," Reagan said, "It's easy to understand why the Boy Scout badge, with the American eagle superimposed on the north sign of the mariners compass, means 'Follow Me, I know the way.' The Boy Scouts of America do know the way, the way to set high standards and how to live by them, and the way to build character, train in citizenship, and foster fitness of mind and body."

David C. Scott dives into Franklin Delano Roosevelt's BSA legacy in *My Fellow Americans* like he does the other 20th century presidents. What impresses me most about his research is his argument that BSA has a tradition of nonpartisan politics. Both Democrats and Republicans have embraced the fundamentals of Scouting over the decades: lifesaving and swimming; animal tracking and using trail signs; woodcraft skills; tree identification; bird and animal ID; star and astronomy knowledge; hiking rules and the ability to march long distances; fire-starting and safety rules, and giving selfless service to others. And, as I've learned from researching *Rightful Heritage*, BSA remains a great teacher of conservation ethics to the young. Whenever a Boy Scout sees trash, he picks it up. Troops spend more time outdoors than indoors. But, most importantly, it's a program for all boys.

From the African American Scouts, who were allowed to join in its first years, to those of American Indian, Hispanic, Asian, Hawaiian, Eskimo, Puerto Rican, Lithuanian, and Italian heritages who joined later, ethnicity was ignored as BSA membership crossed established demographic and racial lines.

By 1913, religious barriers were smashed when Mormon, Catholic, and Jewish boys joined Scouting. "This organization is not Protestant, nor is it

Catholic, nor is it Hebrew," noted West at the time. "It is a character-building organization for boys to be used by all religions and institutions who can see in it a means of helping and assisting the boys of their communities." Eventually, over 35 faith traditions would be recognized within BSA's religious emblems program over the next century.

By the 1960s, BSA had modified its program to better serve both mentally and physically disabled youth, as well as inner city and urban youth.

IN SCOTT'S *MY FELLOW AMERICANS,* we learn anew about how the values of Scouting—America's values—have become part of our nation's intellectual undergirding. And to date, nineteen chief executives agree.

"Clearly, BSA and the U.S. Presidency have shared a special relationship over the past century," Scott writes, "One that surely will continue well into the next."

In keeping with this great Scouting tradition, Scott has rendered a fine public service by writing *My Fellow Americans.* It's an easy to read primer full of fascinating historical anecdotes, excellent pictures, and smart prose.

Every family should own a copy.

Douglas Brinkley
AUSTIN, TEXAS
May 23, 2014

INTRODUCTION

Extending the Hand of Fellowship to All

For the twelve million immigrants (1892 to 1954) who passed through the doors of Ellis Island on the New Jersey side of New York Harbor, perhaps no vision was greater than that of the Statue of Liberty holding aloft her torch of freedom:

Give me your tired, your poor,
Your huddled masses yearning to breathe free,
The wretched refuse of your teeming shore,
Send these, the homeless, tempest-tost to me,
I lift my lamp beside the golden door!

Rising 305 feet into the air from foundation to tip, the first sight of Lady Liberty must have been a momentous experience for those long-suffering refugees of foreign lands, who had risked life and limb to make their way to the "land of milk and honey."

From fifteen-year-old Irish girl Annie Moore, who was the first to pass through the Ellis Island gates in 1892, through Norwegian merchant seaman Arne Peterssen in 1954 (its last), our nation's policy of unapologetically accepting and assimilating foreign peoples into our country is an inherently American phenomenon—one that helped make the United States the greatest and most ethnically diverse nation of freedom-loving people on the face of the earth.

Today, many Americans can trace their roots back to their immigrant ancestors. Beginning with the first permanent colonial settlement in the seventeenth century at Jamestown, Virginia, the next 400 years saw millions of people arrive, bringing with them little more than hope for a better life. These first colonists were renegades, refugees, and adventurers, who became their community's core foundation of builders, innovators, and free-thinkers. And from their work, a civilized society was created, yet constrained by

Immigrants to the United States arrive at Ellis Island in 1910.

the rule of law—mostly foreign law. The first American colonists—all English subjects at the time—conformed to dictates issued by King George III until independence was won with Britain's surrender at Yorktown, Virginia, in 1783.

Afterward, a new government was formed. Preceded in 1781 by the ratification of the Articles of Confederation that formally unified the 13 colonies and served as its first constitution by 49 duly-appointed citizen-delegates, our nation began its pursuit of self-government. With the ratification of the U.S. Constitution at the Constitutional Convention ending in 1789, we gained our current "representative democracy." And from this landmark document came the highest office in the land—the United States presidency.

The Great Experiment had begun.

The first to assume this huge mantle as responsibility was George Washington—former commander of the Continental Army who wielded enough national popularity to declare himself "King of the United States." But by refusing to do so, he established a precedent of leadership as yet unseen in the world—puzzling imperial monarchs across the globe. One of those, King George himself, is fabled to have uttered that Washington's magnanimous action of turning down the crown would make him "the greatest man in the world."

For that (and many other reasons), many consider him just that.

In April 1789, George Washington stood on the balcony of Federal Hall on New York City's famed Wall Street for his inauguration as the United States' first president. Placing his left hand on the Holy Bible and holding his right hand aloft, Washington took the oath of office and assumed the presidential mantle as our nation's first chief executive—becoming the physical embodiment of American ingenuity, leadership, and spirit.

What makes our nation's presidency truly unique is that it's not awarded to the person with the most brute force or military might, it is earned from the power of the civil vote at the ballot box in a peaceful exchange of governmental authority from incumbent to successor. Once in office, this globally recognized "leader of the free world" must rely on the support garnered from the nation's natural-born and immigrant-citizens in order to enact his (eventually her) legislative agenda for the betterment of the country.

FOR THE PAST CENTURY, no national youth organization has helped the U.S. president attain more volunteer-based, service-oriented success than the Boy Scouts of America (BSA).

Since its founding in 1910, BSA has forged the character of many of the great duty-driven leaders of our century by staying true to its timeless values—timeless *American* values—in an all-inclusive program of building duty-driven, citizen-leaders based on out-of-doors activities. Permeating its membership ranks are Americans of virtually every ethnic, religious, and racial strata, who are sponsored by thousands of patriotic, faith-based, fraternal, and civic-minded organizations from across the country. But this amazing assemblage was not forged overnight.

Scouting historian Robert W. Peterson once described the life of an American boy in the early 1900s as being either "idyllic" or one of "drudgery" depending on his financial circumstances. "The families of a handful of industrialists lived sumptuously," he noted, "while four-fifths of the population skirted the edges of poverty or were enmeshed in it."

For the past century, BSA has given guidance to millions of American youth and reinforced the values of honorable living and exceeding one's potential.

BSA, founded by men of both financial means and noble intent, was designed to channel the energies of such young men into a socially productive lifestyle utilizing skills of self-reliance learned in the "classroom of the natural world."

But to get young people outside camping was far easier said than done—especially during a time when many supposedly educated people believed that excessive exposure to nature was unhealthy. Common medical misconceptions at the turn of the twentieth century included the belief that tent camping was intended only for cowboys, the military, or eccentrics, and that the breathing of evening air resulted in cases of malaria.

"Forcing" boys to cook for themselves over an open flame in the woods (when they had a capable mother at home to cook for them) seemed utter nonsense. And the notion of sitting around a smoky campfire was outlandish—everyone knew that all civilized homes had perfectly good kerosene lamps on the walls of their living room. However, that was precisely why Scouting was so appealing to the boys of the early 1900s. They left their homes in droves to live like pioneers and Indians.

But at that time BSA was not the only youth organization to offer this new camping and leadership development program—it was just the best organized and funded. A few years earlier, the Young Man's Christian Association (YMCA) had launched a camping program to promote family unity in the out-of-doors. Quickly, other organizations followed suit, many with little following or success. The Epworth League, the Knights of King Arthur, the Young Crusaders of the Church Temperance League, and the Princely Knights of Character Castle all arose in an attempt to teach moral lessons based on Protestant Christian methodology.

Others like the United States Boy Scouts, the Boys' Brigade, Colonel Cody's Boy Scouts, the National Scouts of America, and the American Boy Scouts were distinctly military-based or quasi-military, and favored technical drilling as the basis for discipline.

"Peace-loving" or nature-based groups like the Woodcraft Indians, the Sons of Daniel Boone, and the Boy Pioneers (all launched by men who would become BSA co-founders) had no official uniforms and were notably non-military.

BSA's first managers, which included businessmen and philanthropists alike, joined forces to create the nation's premier Scouting brand that would ultimately convince its competition to merge their membership under the BSA banner, quickly.

Members of the American Boy Scout organization participate in a military-style drill with dummy muskets in 1910.

But to permanently vanquish all imitators, BSA needed the ultimate national stamp of approval—the recognition and blessing of the sitting president of the United States.

FIRST BROACHING THIS IDEA in August 1910, BSA Managing Secretary John L. Alexander asked BSA co-founder Ernest Thompson Seton to seek the endorsement of the most influential American living at the time, his longtime friend and twenty-sixth president of the United States, Theodore Roosevelt.

Only recently having returned from a year-long hunting and scientific safari into British East Africa, Roosevelt was making a living by churning out political essays and commentary for *The Outlook* magazine in New York City. Seton, the famed author, artist, and naturalist (ultimately to serve as BSA's Chief Scout from 1910–1915), visited Roosevelt's offices in the United Charities Building and asked for his endorsement. Roosevelt answered with a thundering, "Yes."

On a roll, Seton sought Roosevelt's attendance at the upcoming BSA banquet honoring the visiting English founder of worldwide Scouting, Lt. Gen. Robert S.S. Baden-Powell, being held at the posh Waldorf-Astoria

A Scout assists two Gettysburg veterans at their 50-year reunion in July 1913.

Hotel in Manhattan, New York. His attendance would be a highly visible sign of BSA's dominance in the arena of youthful character building—certainly one that would both guarantee positive press coverage and give an immediate national marketing boost.

Roosevelt, however, declined that invitation but rapidly scribbled off a missive for Seton to read at the banquet—one that solidly endorsed BSA's social mission and officially accepted the organization's offer as one of their honorary vice presidents (two years later, he would be named BSA's first and only Chief Scout Citizen). Excitedly, Seton read Roosevelt's letter to the invigorated businessmen assembled at the Waldorf Hotel that evening:

"I should value greatly the chance to meet General Baden-Powell; and I should value even more the chance to identify myself with so admirable a movement as this—the Boy Scouts of America. I believe in the movement with all my heart … I gladly accept the honorary vice presidency."

Instantly, BSA was legitimate and thrust into the national spotlight. But this was just the beginning of the organization's close association with the U.S. presidency.

In October 1910, Lee F. Hanmer, BSA's secretary of the Committee on Organization, contacted the office of current President of the United States William Howard Taft, seeking his acceptance as the organization's honorary president.

As expected, Taft accepted (though, at the time, the president knew little about BSA).

In a briefing made in February 1911 at the White House, BSA representatives informed the president of their pro-youth mission and their goal of developing the nation's future leaders. That day, Taft became a lifetime supporter of the organization and the *Report to the Nation* became an annual event held to this day.

Following that visit, BSA's letterhead included the names of Presidents Roosevelt and Taft (along with those of 75 other men) that marked the official beginning of the organization's long and fruitful association with the nation's most powerful and influential public office holder.

PRESIDENT WOODROW WILSON was BSA's first honorary president to mobilize massive numbers of Scouts in multiple national service projects on the home front during the First World War. Another wartime president, Franklin D. Roosevelt, and future president, Dwight D. Eisenhower, then the Supreme Allied Commander during World War II, both asked the Scouts to help out during that conflict by selling War Bonds and Stamps, planting victory gardens, aiding in the Civil Defense Corps, and collecting essential resources like rubber, paper, and scrap metals.

President Herbert Hoover enlisted Scouting's support for organizations that promoted volunteerism, while President Lyndon B. Johnson requested BSA's aid in the fight against childhood poverty under his "Great Society" initiative.

Later on, Presidents Richard M. Nixon, Jimmy Carter, and Gerald R. Ford called upon the Boy Scouts to lead national efforts on energy and resource conservation service projects, such as Project S.O.A.R.—"Save Our

Boy Scouts participate at the Lincoln Pilgrimage in 1938.

American Resources"—and to participate in the Presidential Sports Award program that encourages young people to be physically fit.

More recently, Presidents George H.W. Bush, William J. Clinton, George W. Bush, and Barack Obama all have asked Scouts to participate in national service organizations like the Points of Light Institute, the Alpha Phi Omega national service fraternity, the Preserve America conservation program, and the America's Great Outdoors initiative.

The funeral services of Presidents Warren G. Harding and Gerald R. Ford included large contingents of Scouts from across the country. Thousands of other Scouts have participated as aides and workers at every presidential inauguration since President Woodrow Wilson's in 1913.

Respectively, Presidents Ronald Reagan and Barack Obama held the office when the 1 millionth and 2 millionth Eagle Scout Awards—Boy Scouting's highest rank—were presented.

Presidents Franklin Roosevelt, Dwight Eisenhower, Ronald Reagan, and Barack Obama respectively presided over the nation when BSA celebrated its twenty-fifth anniversary in 1935, its fiftieth in 1960, its seventy-fifth in 1985, and its centennial in 2010.

Many presidents have visited, addressed, or sent recorded remarks to BSA's 18 National Jamborees. Presidents Calvin Coolidge, Dwight Eisenhower, and George H.W. Bush were fathers of Scouts. President Kennedy was the first former Boy Scout to become the nation's chief executive. Presidents William Clinton, George W. Bush, and Barack Obama were Cub Scouts (Obama in Indonesia), while President Ford is the only president (thus far) to have achieved the rank of Eagle Scout.

President Carter was the first Scoutmaster to go on to serve as president in the Oval Office, while Presidents Franklin Roosevelt, Truman, Eisenhower, Kennedy, Johnson, Ford, and Reagan were adult Scouting volunteers before moving into the White House. Presidents Theodore Roosevelt, Taft, Hoover, Eisenhower, and Ford were Scouting volunteers after their presidential terms ended.

Since BSA's founding in 1910, all presidents with the exception of Theodore Roosevelt, Wilson, Harding, and Kennedy have received the organization's highest volunteer award for dedicated and distinguished service to youth presented by the National Council—the Silver Buffalo medal suspended from a red and white neck ribbon. Theodore Roosevelt, Wilson, and Harding all died before this award was created in 1926; Kennedy was assassinated before he could receive it.

Clearly, BSA and the U.S. Presidency have shared a special bond and relationship over the past century—one that surely will continue well into the next.

This book is a celebration of that special bond.

David C. Scott
Dallas, Texas
May 23, 2014

THEODORE

ROOSEVELT

26ᵀᴴ President of the United States

1901–1909

Born: October 27, 1857, New York City, New York

Died: January 6, 1919, Oyster Bay, Long Island, New York

Wife: (1st) Alice Hathaway Lee (m. 1880–1884)
(2nd) Edith Carow (m. 1886)

Children: Alice, Theodore Jr., Kermit, Ethel, Archie, Quentin

Education: Harvard College (B.A.)
Colonel, U.S. Army (1898)

Honors: Nobel Peace Prize (1906)
Congressional Medal of Honor (posthumous, 2001)

BSA Positions: Hon. Vice President (1910–1917)
Chief Scout Citizen (1912–1919)
Helped form five troops in Oyster Bay, New York
Committee Member, Troop 39, Oyster Bay, New York
(1916–1919)
Scout Commissioner, Nassau County Council, BSA
(1917–1919)

BSA Honors: Theodore Roosevelt Pilgrimage (1920–present)
Theodore Roosevelt Council, New York
Camp Roosevelt (1921–present)
Katahdin Area Council, BSA
Camp Roosevelt/Roosevelt Scout Reservation
(1926 - present)
Gloucester-Salem Council, now Southern
New Jersey Council, BSA
Camp Roosevelt (1919–1969)
Washington, DC Council, (now National Capital
Area Council, BSA)

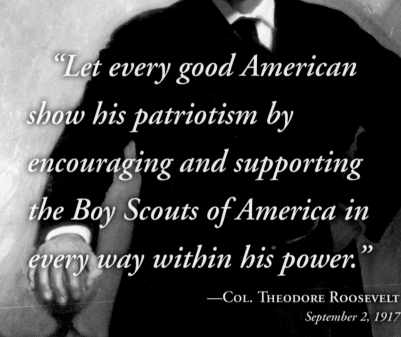

"*Let every good American show his patriotism by encouraging and supporting the Boy Scouts of America in every way within his power.*"

—Col. Theodore Roosevelt
September 2, 1917

CHAPTER ONE

THEODORE ROOSEVELT
The First Vital Volunteer Scouting Leader

*Colonel Roosevelt was the biggest Boy Scout
we ever had in public life.*

—THEODORE E. BURNETT JR.
November 26, 1920

I F THERE WAS ANYONE upon whom BSA could depend, it was the organization's first and only Chief Scout Citizen, Theodore Roosevelt. Born in 1857 with severe asthma that nearly claimed his young life, the sickly Roosevelt grew to manhood determined to defeat his infirmities through physical fitness and strenuous activity. He also trained his mind through the constant reading of books, which filled him with an enormous amount of information and knowledge. Both processes contributed to his legendary moral incorruptibility.

Roosevelt graduated Phi Beta Kappa and Magna Cum Laude from Harvard College and was elected the youngest member of the New York General Assembly. Then, upon the tandem deaths of his young wife and beloved mother on Valentine's Day, 1884, he retreated from New York City to become a cattle rancher in the Dakota Territory. Although Roosevelt ran unsuccessfully for the mayor's office in New York City, he served as a U.S. Civil Service Commissioner, the president of the Police Commission of New York City, the assistant secretary of the U.S. Navy, a Colonel in the 1st United States Volunteer Cavalry, the governor of New York, the vice-president of the United States, and finally, the president of the United States—all accomplished by the age of 42.

While U.S. president, Roosevelt built the Panama Canal, broke-up corporate monopolies and trusts, and federally protected 230 million acres of national parks, national forests, wildlife refuges, and national monuments. He helped build the modern navy, delivered a "Square Deal" to every American family, and was the first American to win the Nobel Peace Prize.

He was the father of six children, the author of more than thirty-five books and hundreds of magazine editorials, a devoted big game hunter, a world-class ornithologist, and the founder of the Boone & Crockett Club—the nation's first fair-hunting and conservation organization.

And more than any other endorsement, the fledgling Boy Scouts of America wanted his.

Roosevelt reviews a Boy Scout troop at his Sagamore Hill estate in 1916.

Roosevelt hosts Troop 1 from Long Island at Sagamore Hill.

AS A VOLUNTEER, Roosevelt served as Scout Commissioner—the precursor to today's council Scout Executive—in charge of expanding membership within his community, which resulted in his founding of five Scout troops near his estate on Long Island. He was a committee member for Troop 39 in Oyster Bay, and hosted reviews and activities for all Scouts at his Sagamore Hill estate. All this must have seemed familiar territory to him because he had been a proto-type Scout leader throughout his adult life.

In the 1890s, Roosevelt led his young children around the woods as an adult leader would guide his (or her) troop today.

"We used to do point-to-point walks where we'd swim ponds, climb bluffs, get over, under or through anything that lay in our way," recalled son Theodore Roosevelt Jr. "Then he would take us camping, as many as a dozen [neighborhood children] at a time, and we would spend that night on the end of some point jutting out into the Sound and sleep soundly to the rustle of the waves on the beach. My father was our Scoutmaster."

During one such outing, a big thunderstorm blew in, but the children remained happy and upbeat. One little boy later confessed to being frightened, but said "confidence in Colonel Roosevelt gave [him] courage to meet the storm." On another trip, Roosevelt took an unexpected tumble into the water. "There goes our daddy," yelled one of the local lads. Every child Roosevelt came into contact with seemed to feel the same way.

IN FEBRUARY 1915, on the fifth anniversary of Scouting in America, the World Film Corporation released a five-reel motion picture titled *The Adventures of a Boy Scout.* Shot as a promotional piece to describe the activities of Scouts, Roosevelt gave it his hearty endorsement.

"I regard it as one of the most important forces telling for our betterment of American citizenship in the future," he lauded. "I am extremely pleased that this picture drama is to appear."

One special guest appearance was made by President Woodrow Wilson, who was filmed reviewing a Scout patrol. Unfortunately, no full copies of the film are known to exist today although twelve promotional photos survive.

Over the next year, the film made its way across the country into local movie houses filled with moviegoers who purchased tickets sold to the public by Boy Scouts to raise funds for their councils and troops. The Scout council in Corpus Christi, Texas, raised $20, enough to help fix up their headquarters, while the Danville, Pennsylvania, unit raised enough funds to expand its troop library.

THROUGHOUT ROOSEVELT'S LIFE, he held keen the belief that all American citizens must be treated with, honor, dignity, and respect—a truism that, in his day, extended throughout a period of extreme racial segregation in national life. While president, to show his disdain for discriminatory policies, he extended the hand of friendship to various minority groups who were patriotic Americans like himself. In doing so, he compromised his political future because many voters and politicians detested those efforts.

Shortly after assuming the office of president after the assassination of President William McKinley in 1901, one of his first invitees to the White

House was Booker T. Washington, an African American orator, author, educator, and presidential advisor. Arriving for dinner, Roosevelt and Washington discussed the issues of the day predicting the firestorm of negative public opinion that would erupt in the nation's newspapers the following day.

"TR was full of chatter and goodwill," described one account, suggesting his ease while entertaining his distinguished guest. Of course, that ease developed into a certain Rooseveltian domination of the "conversation" by the effluent president.

"Hardly an observation was made by anyone else," one guest recalled, "and in fact, it would only have been possible by the exercise of a sort of brutal force."

Nevertheless, an understanding was reached between the two parties because Roosevelt needed Washington's support to get newly-minted African American Republicans into the voting booths to win the South in the 1904 presidential election, as well as gain his advice and counsel on several proposed minority political appointments.

Roosevelt with Troop 4 of Garden City, NY, in May 1916.

This dinner was a watershed moment in the fight for racial equality in America.

In 1906, Roosevelt appointed Oscar S. Straus as the first man of Jewish faith to be placed on the president's Cabinet. Also included were a Catholic, a Protestant, and William Howard Taft, a devout Christian Unitarian.

When these assignments made national news, a predictable outcry occurred and highly critical correspondence arrived daily in the mail. In one famous response, Roosevelt proclaimed, "To discriminate against a thoroughly upright citizen because he belongs to some particular church, or because, like Abraham Lincoln, he has not avowed his allegiance to any church, is an outrage against that liberty of conscience which is one of the foundations of American life."

BSA was lockstep in sentiment. Within a year of beginning operations in June 1910, the organization began welcoming officially recognized units comprised solely of African American boys. And by 1913, they opened their doors to the Catholic Church, Mormon Church, and Jewish faith, and formed the Protestant, Catholic, and Jewish National Religious Committees on Scouting.

In January 1909 with hundreds of national delegates, Roosevelt hosted the first White House Conference on the Care of Dependent Children to discuss federal progress made on the prevention of institutionalizing dependent and abused children. Its organizer and primary advocate was future BSA Chief Scout Executive James E. West.

WHEN THEODORE ROOSEVELT passed away in the early hours of January 6, 1919, the nation mourned. In a memorial service, Franklin K. Lane, Interior Secretary to President Wilson, eloquently summed up Roosevelt's fast-emerging legacy:

We may surely expect to see developed a Roosevelt legend, a body of tales that will exalt the physical power and endurance of the man and the boldness of his spirit, his robust capacity for blunt speech and his hearty comradeship, his live interest in all things living—these will make our boys for the long future proud that they are of his . . . country. And no surer fame than this can come to any man—to live in the hearts of the boys of his land as one whose doings and sayings they would wish to make their own.

Within months of his passing, testimonial and remembrance books appeared in bookstores across the country. Roosevelt was lauded as the "great heart" and the "American prophet." The members of the Boy Scouts of America were especially saddened. In a letter to Edith Roosevelt, his widow, West noted Roosevelt's special significance to Scouts:

"In losing Colonel Roosevelt [he preferred to be addressed by his rank after the Spanish-American War in 1898]," West wrote, "our boys and indeed the whole world have sustained a great loss." West pledged to keep Roosevelt's memory alive to "stimulate the boyhood of our country . . . to better citizenship" through service, informing her that the organization's

A Scout plants a Roosevelt Memorial Tree in 1923.

Executive Board that morning had asked every Scout unit to plant "one or more sturdy trees" in his memory.

Planting trees had become a ritual through which Americans honored their countrymen who had given their lives in World War I. *American Forestry* magazine in 1919 called such trees "a new form of monument—the memorial that lives." So it seemed appropriate to perform such service in honor of the country's leading voice for conservation.

Within days, many of the 16,000 registered Scout troops nationwide announced their intention to plant memorial trees as "a permanent expression of all Colonel Roosevelt stood for to the boys of the nation." Some sought to plant enough trees to form Roosevelt memorial groves, and one group planted 500 seedlings that formed the giant letters "TR." The most prized seeds came from a large black walnut tree shading his grave that provided many bushels of nuts.

In memoriam, BSA's National Scout Commissioner Daniel Carter Beard had hundreds of the nuts collected to "scatter all over the country" in the hands of Scout Executives. But within a few years, this tree could not keep up with the massive demand for its walnuts.

At the dedication of the Roosevelt Memorial Tree in Audubon Park in New Orleans, Louisiana, Governor John M. Parker recalled the time years before when he invited Roosevelt to visit and the great man entertained neighborhood children. In the library at Parker's home, Roosevelt, his sleeves rolled up, at ease on a great wicker chair, regaled the children with an account of his lion hunt in Africa.

At the Audubon Park ceremony, two Scouts approached Parker and saluted. "We will eternally keep watch on that tree," they said, "because we were two of the boys who listened to his splendid story of the lion hunt, which we will never forget as long as we live."

In September 1919, members of the newly formed Roosevelt Memorial Association marched from Buffalo, New York, to his grave at Oyster Bay, Long Island, starting off with an American flag of silk with no stars in the blue union patch. Scouts and high school students escorted the flag most of the way. At each stop, a white star was hand-sewn onto the flag. The forty-eighth and final star was added at Roosevelt's gravesite in Youngs Memorial Cemetery when the memorial flag arrived in Oyster Bay on October 27, which would have been Roosevelt's sixty-first birthday. Dignitaries from around the world attended the ceremony, including King Albert and Queen Elizabeth of Belgium.

Beard, deeply moved, led a small contingent of Scouts to Roosevelt's grave a year later in November as the Roosevelt Memorial Pilgrimage. From a small gathering of Scouts in the first year in 1920, attendance rose to more than 6,000 a decade later. Over the next thirty years, a special Scout memorial program included patriotic songs, recitations, and speeches that the *New York Times* diligently reported on into the early 1950s.

IN THE END, Roosevelt's staunch support of BSA helped the fledgling organization raise much needed funds to achieve financial stability and recruit legions of new leaders and Scouts. From him, the Boy Scouts of America received legitimacy and critical support from a grateful nation. Without him, BSA might not have survived its first decade.

IN HIS OWN WORDS

We Americans give to men [and women] of all races equal and exact justice.

ROOSEVELT, BOSTON, MASSACHUSETTS, NOVEMBER 1893

The Boy Scout movement is distinctively an asset to our country for the development of efficiency . . . and good citizenship.

ROOSEVELT TO JAMES E. WEST, DECEMBER 15, 1915

The movement is one for efficiency and patriotism. It does not try to make soldiers of Boy Scouts, but to make boys who will turn out as men to be fine citizens.

ROOSEVELT TO JAMES E. WEST, JULY 20, 1911

The Boy Scout movement is of peculiar importance to the whole country. It has already done much good, and it will do far more, for it is in its essence a practical scheme through which to impart a proper standard of ethical conduct, proper standards of fair play and consideration for others, and courage and decency.

ROOSEVELT TO JAMES E. WEST, JULY 20, 1911

More and more I have grown to believe in the Boy Scout movement. I regard it as one of the movements most full of promise for the future here in America... It is essential that its leaders be men of strong, wholesome character; of unmistakable devotion to our country, its customs and ideals, as well as in soul and by law citizens thereof, whose wholehearted loyalty is given to this nation, and to this nation alone.

ROOSEVELT TO JAMES E. WEST, DECEMBER 15, 1915

The aggressive fighting for right is the noblest sport the world affords.

ROOSEVELT, BOYS' LIFE, OCTOBER 1936

I earnestly believe in the Boy Scout movement.

ROOSEVELT, FEBRUARY 10, 1911

TAFT

27TH PRESIDENT OF THE UNITED STATES
1909–1913
10TH CHIEF JUSTICE OF THE UNITED STATES SUPREME COURT, 1921–1930

Born: September 15, 1857, Cincinnati, Ohio
Died: March 8, 1930, Washington, DC

Wife: Helen "Nellie" Herron (m. 1886)
Children: Robert, Helen, Charles Phelps

Education: Yale College (B.A.)
            University of Cincinnati (LL.B)

BSA Positions: Hon. President (1910–1913)
               Hon. Vice President (1913–1930)

BSA Honors: Hosted the First Meeting of the Advisory
               Council of the Boy Scouts of America (1st Annual
               Meeting), Washington, DC, February 14, 1911
             23rd Silver Buffalo (1927)

Eagle Scout Awards presented (1910–1912): 23

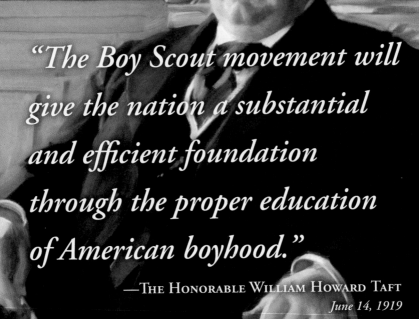

"The Boy Scout movement will give the nation a substantial and efficient foundation through the proper education of American boyhood."

—THE HONORABLE WILLIAM HOWARD TAFT
June 14, 1919

CHAPTER TWO

WILLIAM HOWARD TAFT
"Big Bill"

"A lifelong open heart and a devotion to boys."

—PRESIDENT HERBERT HOOVER
March 10, 1930

WILLIAM HOWARD TAFT WAS NOT A SMALL MAN—far from it. Standing at just under six feet and weighing 330 pounds, "Big Bill's" girth exceeded that of a baby elephant, making him the heaviest Chief Executive in American history. Perhaps attempting to exorcise the spirit of predecessor Theodore Roosevelt, the so-called "apostle of the strenuous life," Taft expanded the White House's West Wing and built today's Oval Office over Roosevelt's tennis court.

Albeit blessed with a jovial temperament, Taft may have smarted nonetheless at the many jokes aimed at his expansive waistline. "He looks like an American bison, a gentle, kind one," declared American newspaper editor Arthur Brisbane.

"Taft is the politest man in Washington," acknowledged U.S. Supreme Court Associate Justice David Josiah Brewer. "The other day he gave up his seat in a streetcar to *three* ladies."

The reality was even worse—Taft once became stuck in a bathtub on the second floor of the White House and several maintenance workers were summoned to pry him loose.

Those embarrassments aside, William Taft navigated his presidency courtesy of a quality legal brain.

TAFT WAS BORN in 1857 to a Cincinnati judge who once had served in the cabinet of President Ulysses S. Grant. From the Cincinnati public school system, Taft ascended to the hallowed halls of Yale University in New Haven, Connecticut, graduating second in his class in 1878. Returning home, Taft studied law at the University of Cincinnati and was admitted to the Ohio Bar in 1880.

Engaged as Hamilton County assistant prosecutor, he rose to a judgeship on the Cincinnati Supreme Court and into the office of Solicitor General of the United States in 1890. From there he progressed to a seat on the U.S. Sixth Circuit Court, in 1900 becoming dean of the Cincinnati Law School.

His meteoric rise did not go unnoticed, and after the successful conclusion of the Spanish-American War in 1898, President William McKinley appointed Taft chief civil administrator in the Philippines—part of the

Taft with Robert Baden-Powell (left) and Archibald Butt (right) at the White House in February 1912.

spoils of war. Taft was a smart and humane manager who was sympathetic to the needs of the Filipinos. He built roads and schools, encouraged citizens to participate in government, and jump-started the economy through local product development and trade.

"Under him the islanders are now taking the first steps along the hard path that ultimately leads to self-respect and self-government," wrote Vice President of the United States Theodore Roosevelt in *The Outlook* magazine in 1901. "The material uplifting of the people must go together with their moral uplifting."

Although some colonists on the island considered the native Filipinos to be "inferior," wife Nellie Taft recalled, "We insisted upon complete racial equality. ...We made it a rule from the beginning that neither politics nor race should influence our hospitality in any way."

Some years later while First Lady, Nellie Taft appointed African Americans to the White House staff to help elevate their stature at the time. She also helped fund a local kindergarten for African American children.

In preparation for the impending presidential election of 1908, Booker T. Washington was named as one of Taft's advisors. Washington suggested planks for the Republican platform with regard to African American relations. As president, Taft would publicly endorse and affirm Washington's plan for "uplifting the black race," which would include increased educational opportunities and the need for entrepreneurship in the African American community.

Likewise, BSA approved the creation of sanctioned units within minority populations throughout the nation and its international territories. The first official African American troop was loosely formed in the modest community of Evanston, Illinois, north of Chicago, under African American Scoutmaster A.H. Edmonds in mid-1911. It began officially santioned operations on May 6, 1912 just after receiving its certified BSA charter of organization.

As described in the *Chicago Defender* newspaper, "Word received this morning [May 3] by A.H Edmonds from the executive council of the Boy Scouts of America, stated that the application for membership made by the troop of local colored boys has been accepted."

Their troop's charter was signed by Chief Scout Ernest Thompson Seton, Chief Scout Executive James E. West, President Taft, and BSA honorary vice president Theodore Roosevelt.

The *Defender* later editorialized, "We are endowed with the honor of having the only troop of colored Boy Scouts in America, yet we do not appreciate the fact to any great event."

The U.S. territories of Hawaii, Porto Rico (now spelled Puerto Rico), and the Philippine Islands hosted a number of new troops—8 in Hawaii, 12 in Porto Rico, and 14 in the Philippines.

"For the first time in this generation a Hawaiian boy—a Scout—has made fire without matches," writes BSA Scout Commissioner James Wilder, "using only Hawaiian material from the native wilderness."

Scout authorities also reported that in the two other Hawaiian locales, "the boys are passing the various tests with interest and great enthusiasm." Around the same time, BSA executives initiated a formal partnership with the Catholic Church (a religious minority) to sponsor Scout troops throughout the nation beginning with New York State.

The agreement was immediately supported by His Eminence Cardinal Farley, who let it be known that the Scouting movement was "favored by

Sen. Robert Ogden (far left), Taft, Booker T. Washington (right), and Andrew Carnegie (far right).

Taft reviews a Boy Scout troop in 1912.

Catholic boys under the leadership of Catholic Scoutmasters and under Catholic Scout leaders."

With Roosevelt's support, Taft succeeded him to the presidency in March 1909—although reluctantly. "Taft did not want to be president," writes biographer Michael Benson. "Although he agreed that it was for the best. His heart was not in it."

Taft, himself, commented discordantly during the March blizzard that enveloped his Inauguration, "I always said it would be a cold day when I got to be president of the United States."

Initially President Taft pledged to continue Roosevelt's progressive social policies, leading critics to suggest that "TAFT" actually stood for "Taking Advice From Theodore."

That opinion would soon change.

As president (and completely antithetical to his predecessor), Taft supported high tariffs on Canadian goods. He sacked U.S. Chief Forester Gifford Pinchot and Secretary of the Interior James R. Garfield, both of whom had been appointed by conservation-minded Roosevelt, in moves that ultimately reversed three million acres of protected government land back into private hands. Taft's Justice Department filed an antitrust suit against the nation's largest company, U.S. Steel, which had acquired a Tennessee company during the previous administration. Roosevelt, himself, was named as a defendant as the acquisition had been consummated during his presidential tenure. Even though this charge was leveled at Roosevelt, it was done without Taft's knowledge, and permanently crushed their once warm relationship.

Taft was caught between liberal Republican Progressives and traditional Republican "machine politicians" who supported his rejection of the Rooseveltian agenda of social reform. As a result, progressive Republicans ceased their support of Taft in the upcoming presidential election of 1912 and set up Roosevelt's run as the "Bull Moose" Party candidate after the GOP convention in Chicago—ultimately securing victory for the Democratic challenger, Governor Woodrow Wilson of New Jersey.

But despite its loss of their former champion, the Progressive Era continued. In June 1910, the progressively inspired and funded Boy Scouts of America (BSA) opened its first office in the YMCA building at 124 East 28th Street, Manhattan, with a secretary and one lone stenographer to manage the fledgling social reform organization.

By 1911, BSA had expanded into larger offices at 200 Fifth Avenue with a paid executive secretary in the person of Washington lawyer James E. West and a handful of administrative staff. Supported by donations from many of the most influential national reform-minded organizations of New York City (such as the Russell Sage Foundation that funded the construction of the YMCA building on East 28th Street), BSA's executive board sought Taft's presidential endorsement.

His secretary, Charles D. Morton, responded to West: "The president directs me to say that he will accept the Honorary Presidency of the National Council of the Boy Scouts of America, and thus sustain a similar relation to the movement in the United States as does King George [V] to a similar movement in England, and Lord Gray in Canada." And so BSA's honorary presidency began.

A year later in April 1912, President Taft would create the "Children's Bureau" within the Department of Commerce and Labor. Led by social reformer Julia Lathrop (the first woman ever to run a U.S. governmental bureau), it was the first governmental agency assigned solely to the protection and advocacy of American women and children.

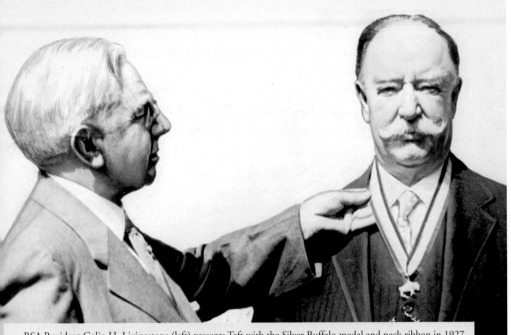

BSA President Colin H. Livingstone (left) presents Taft with the Silver Buffalo medal and neck ribbon in 1927.

IN NOVEMBER 1910, BSA's stationary letterhead featured the names of only thirty-five eminent men who made up the National Council. By February 1911, that list had ballooned to seventy-five and included the Honorable William H. Taft and Col. Theodore Roosevelt.

West, desiring to make the most of Taft's endorsement, wished to present the National Council's first *Annual Report* directly to the president in the Oval Office. National Executive Board member Lee F. Hanmer made the arrangements, and on February 14, 1911, BSA's delegation convened at the Willard Hotel at 14th Street and marched the two blocks to the White House, thus beginning a tradition that continues to this day.

However, Taft had not been briefed in advance, and at the time, had little idea regarding what BSA had been formed to do. As a result, upon the delegation's entrance, he failed to make any comment or opening remarks and a deafening silence ensued. Sensing awkwardness, Hanmer rattled off a statement that at once reported BSA's institutional progress and explained to the president the purpose of the organization.

"It is a broad non-sectarian movement for the making of the boy," Hanmer told Taft, "and we invite every man interested in the American boy to help us in this movement." He diplomatically continued: "You are probably familiar with the chief aims of our organization, but I will state, in brief, that to have 300,000 boy pledges to the one purpose of doing at least one good turn every day for somebody, without looking for a reward, is a thing we are proud of."

Presumably, Taft was pleased with what he heard because his association with BSA continued for the rest of his life.

After leaving the presidency and its pressures in March 1913, Taft resolved to lose much of the excessive weight that undermined his health. In the following years, he shed more than eighty pounds, relieving his sleep apnea and extending his life.

He continued to speak on the importance of BSA's program and objectives and in 1927 the National Council presented a physically fit Taft with BSA's highest award for a volunteer, the Silver Buffalo, "in recognition for his services" to the nation's youth—only the 23rd issued to date.

Big Bill was living a Scouting life.

IN HIS OWN WORDS

The progress which the [African American] has made in the last fifty years…is marvelous, and it furnishes every reason to hope that in the next twenty-five years a still greater improvement in his condition as a productive member of society.

INAUGURAL ADDRESS, WASHINGTON, DC, MARCH 4, 1909

I have come across [the Boy Scouts of America's] beneficial effect in my constant travel all over the country and every addition to the thoroughness of its organization and efficiency is to be encouraged.

"BOY SCOUT WEEK NET GOOD RESULTS," *New York Times,* JUNE 11, 1919

I am very glad to give my sympathy and support to such a Movement as this. Anything that directs the boy's spirit in the right channel for usefulness and for the making of manly men should be encouraged."

AS QUOTED IN MURRAY'S *History of the Boy Scouts of America*

Education alone, without the instilling of moral principle and without the strengthening of that morality with religious spirit, may often prove to give to citizens a knowledge without the moral impulse to use it properly.

AS QUOTED IN MURRAY'S *History of the Boy Scouts of America*

I am here as Honorary President of the Boy Scouts of America to bear witness to the usefulness of the organization. Scout training will be of lasting benefit to the youth of America, which means the betterment of the country as a whole. We occupy boys in school a few hours a day and they have a great deal of leisure time. We don't work boys hard enough. Now the Boy Scouts movement is one of those steps of improvement that keeps a boy busy most of the time.

It takes away the improper development of the boy through too much leisure. It teaches the joy of service and takes away selfishness that leisure gives him. Take care of the boy and we can leave the men to themselves. There are not more boys in this organization because its scope of activities has been limited through the lack of funds. There are not enough funds to carry on the work, to buy uniforms which add so greatly to the spirit for the work, and to pay for many other items incidental to the running of the association. The Boy Scouts movement will give the nation a substantial and efficient foundation through the proper education of American boyhood.

"To Extend Drive for Scouts Here," *New York Times*, June 14, 1919

Boys, you and I are members of the same great organization and I am very proud of my membership, as I am sure you are. You have demonstrated today that you are prepared, and efficiently prepared, to render aid to others who may be greatly in need of assistance. This is the great underlying purpose of the Boy Scouts of America organization, that boys may be trained to help others, and the officers and the men, who are at the head of the movement desire above all else that this spirit may dominate every boy in this great country of ours. We have reason to be very proud of you boys...for the splendid work that you have [done]. May God bless you every one.

Address, San Francisco, CA, September 1915

WOODROW

WILSON

28TH PRESIDENT OF THE UNITED STATES

—— 1913–1921 ——

Born: December 28, 1856, Staunton, Virginia
Died: February 3, 1924, Washington, DC

Wife: (1st) Ellen Axson (m. 1885–1914)
(2nd) Edith Bolling Galt (m. 1915)
Children: Margaret Woodrow, Jessie Woodrow, Sayre, Eleanor R.

Education: Princeton University (B.A.)
Johns Hopkins University (Ph.D.)

Honors: Nobel Peace Prize (1919)

BSA Positions: Hon. President (1913–1921)
Hon. Vice President (1921–1924)

BSA Honors: Signed BSA's Federal Charter (1916)
Namesake for Woodrow Wilson Reservation for Boy Scouts/
Camp Wilson Scout Reservation (1924–1969),
Washington, DC Council (now National Capital Area
Council, BSA)

Eagle Scout Awards presented (1913–1920): 1,956

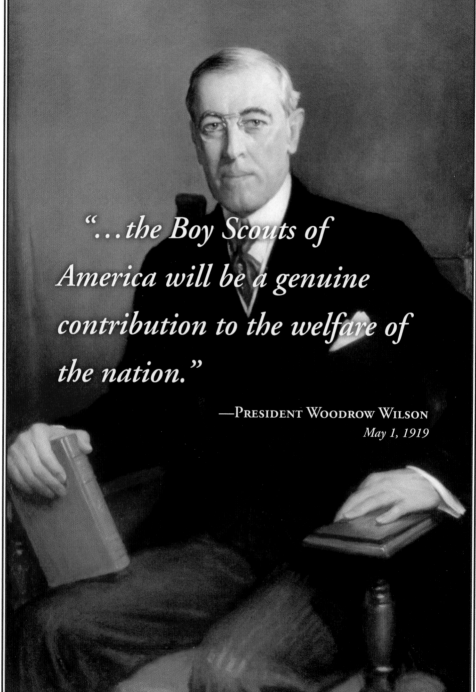

"…the Boy Scouts of America will be a genuine contribution to the welfare of the nation."

—President Woodrow Wilson
May 1, 1919

CHAPTER THREE

WOODROW WILSON

Calling All Scouts

"A man whose heart was always young."

—*Boys' Life*, MARCH 1924

YOUNG TOMMY WILSON SEEMED SLOW. As a ten-year-old boy in 1866, Thomas Woodrow Wilson could not read though he very much wanted to. Growing up in Georgia as the third child of Presbyterian minister Joseph Ruggles Wilson (a first-generation Irish American), at home the Word of God was revered and read constantly. A pious man of letters, the "thrifty and enterprising" Reverend Wilson excelled at taking Biblical lessons and applying them to the concerns of his congregation. And if judged by weekly attendance, he was quite effective. But amid the fiery passions of the learned Reverend's temperament, Tommy's inability to comprehend the written alphabet confounded and depressed him.

In a later age, clinicians would have concluded that Tommy suffered from dyslexia—the inability to interpret letters as whole words and sounds, sometimes popularly referred to as *word blindness*. Reverend Wilson believed his son's disability could be overcome with diligent work, but not necessarily with reading alone.

So from an early age, Reverend Wilson took his son aside and spent many hours teaching him the fine art of debate and logical thinking—a critical skill that would take the boy far in life, exceeding his father's expectations. According to historian Jay Winter, "Wilson's father would give him an idea that the true test was making the world a place where justice, and goodness had a better and bigger place than it had before he came on the scene."

"When [Tommy] finally did decode the alphabet and enter the priesthood of the literate," relates biographer H.W. Brands, "he felt an exhilaration that stayed with him his whole life."

Wilson shakes hands with Scout Frank Reed before a message relay to Chicago in June 1913.

AFTER MOVING TO North Carolina, the seventeen-year-old Tommy enrolled briefly at Davidson University in nearby Wilmington. But family financial difficulties—and perhaps his lack of interest—led him to withdraw, spending his days in Wilmington reading and working on his written composition skills. He later recalled, "I like nothing so well as writing and talking."

During this break from academics, the young Wilson's interest in college studies revived. In his travels, Reverend Wilson had met the president of the College of New Jersey (now Princeton University as it was officially renamed in 1896). When the College's chief made a recruiting swing through the Carolinas, Tommy gained admittance and in September 1875 set out on a train heading north.

"[Tommy] helped organize the Liberal Debating Club, whose members held forth on crucial questions of the day," Brands writes. "He competed in public-speaking contests. He joined the staff of the [newspaper], becoming editor his senior year." Excelling in oratory, Wilson became involved in politics, drafting position papers and debating the critical issues of the time.

He commented to his college classmates: "My judgment of this place is that it is a splendid place for the education of the *mind*, but no sort of place for the education of the *man*." He admired various British statesmen and wrote a well-received essay published in the *International Review* maintaining that the English parliamentary system was superior to the American model because of the problems of U.S. machine politics and corruption.

Upon graduation from the College of New Jersey in 1879, Wilson entered the University of Virginia to study law but found it "a hard taskmaster." After eighteen months and pleading ill health, he returned home but heeded his father's advice to "stick to the law and its prospects be they ever so depressing or disgusting." Thereafter he studied law on his own.

For diversion and training, Wilson made extemporaneous addresses "to the empty benches of my father's church ... in preparation for the future," read history, and wrote with a passion. He even took voice lessons to strengthen his auditory impact.

"My topics are mostly political," he later told a college friend. "And I can sometimes almost see the benches smile at some of my opinions and deliverances."

In the autumn of 1883, Wilson entered a new university in Baltimore funded by entrepreneurial tycoon Johns Hopkins, earning a Ph.D. in "governmental studies past and present." His dissertation, published in 1885 under the title *Congressional Government*, emphasized "constitutional theory at the expense of legislative practice."

In 1890, Dr. Wilson was back at the College of New Jersey as a professor of jurisprudence and political science, progressing over the years into the presidency of Princeton University in 1902. At this time he began using his middle name, Woodrow, rather than Thomas, explaining to the curious that he did so "to honor his mother's special request" as it was her maiden surname. Although old friends still called him "Tommy," all others addressed him as the more prepossessing "Woodrow."

By 1910, Wilson's reputation as a first-class educator had caught the attention of the New Jersey Democratic Party. After he won the governorship, the Democratic political bosses expected him to accommodate their interests. Instead, Wilson pushed through a progressive agenda of reforms that included the establishment of a system of state primaries that virtually eliminated the political party boss from local politics, revamped the state's

(Above and Right) Wilson inspects a Boy Scout troop at the White House around 1914.

public utility systems, and introduced worker's compensation, winning national visibility in the process.

With the 1912 presidential election looming, Wilson was tapped on the forty-third ballot at the Democratic National Convention to challenge Republican President William Howard Taft, and Progressive Party nominee, former president Theodore Roosevelt. Ultimately, Roosevelt's inclusion on the ballot would split the Republican vote and ensure Woodrow Wilson's election as the 28th president of the United States.

The Boy Scouts of America (BSA) made a formidable impression at President Woodrow Wilson's inauguration in March 1913. Expecting a march by suffragettes, five thousand Boy Scouts toting six-foot-long wooden walking sticks formed a crowd control barrier by interlocking their staves in a long line down the procession route. One thousand Scouts surrounded and protected the reviewing stand while another three hundred Scouts performed first aid where necessary.

"The greatest heroes of all were those [Scouts] who volunteered for service, [although it] kept them from seeing the parade," one observer recalled.

"THE FIRST TWO years of Wilson's first term are one of the most remarkable moments in modern politics," says historian David M. Kennedy.

"There's more reform agenda accomplished in that brief moment than in virtually any other two year period in the 20th century."

Wilson created the Federal Reserve System in 1913, lowered tariffs on imported foreign goods—with the loss of income leading to the passage of the 16th Amendment that authorized a federal income tax—and curtailed child labor with the Keating-Owen Act of 1916.

On January 28, 1916, President Wilson nominated Louis D. Brandeis as the first Jewish member of the Supreme Court. Although bitterly contested during the confirmation hearings in Congress, Brandeis was confirmed five months later and remained on the bench for 23 years. During his career, Brandeis championed the minimum wage for women factory workers as well as "holding business and political leaders accountable to the public."

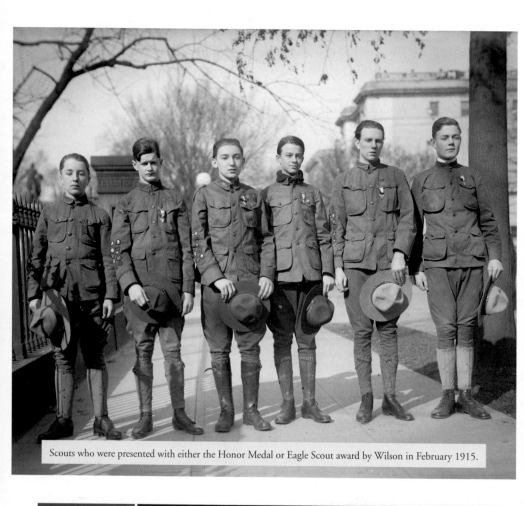

Scouts who were presented with either the Honor Medal or Eagle Scout award by Wilson in February 1915.

"Brandeis was a militant crusader for social justice whoever his opponent might be," writes his successor Associate Justice William O. Douglass. "He was dangerous not only because of his brilliance, his arithmetic, his courage. He was dangerous because he was incorruptible."

During the Wilson Administration, BSA formally published its first Religious Policy declaring "Scouting presents greater opportunities for the development of the boy religiously than does any other movement instituted solely for the boys."

It further stated, "Boy Scouts of America, as an organized body, therefore, recognizes the religious element in the training of a boy, but it is absolutely non-sectarian in its attitude towards that religious training."

In 1912, the Roman Catholic Church formed its first Catholic Committee of Scouting. It was followed quickly by the Church of Latter Day Saints ("Mormon" Church) through its Mutual Improvement Association that "took up the Scouting program" for its 1500 member groups. Having much success, administrators reported "the boys have been doing [Scouting] with much enthusiasm."

The nation's first Jewish troop was formed in New York City in 1913 at the 92nd Street Young Men's Hebrew Association (YMHA). Today that unit is known as Troop 635.

As the majority of BSA's sponsoring organizations practiced Christianity, in 1915, national executives authorized the production on an official BSA version of several versions of the Bible and Testament. In addition to scripture, it contained "full information as to how a boy may become a Scout."

IN JUNE 1916, Wilson signed BSA's federal charter granting it the congressional protection it had sought since April 1910 when BSA co-incorporator, William D. Boyce, originally filed a national charter request. Now, BSA was the only organization legally authorized to use the word "Scout" and "Scouting."

But Wilson's greatest test was to be the First World War, sparked by the assassination of Archduke Franz Ferdinand, heir to the Austro-Hungarian throne, in Sarajevo in June 1915.

Under Wilson's leadership, the U.S.'s policy was to stay out of the brutal conflict, which quickly ground down into barbaric trench warfare from the North Sea to Switzerland. When the British ocean liner *Lusitania* was sunk by German torpedoes off the coast of Ireland, many Americans were among the 1,198 dead in the disaster. Wilson knew that the country eventually would have to enter the war—but when?

For the next two years, German submarines attacked vessel after vessel, sinking seven U.S. merchant ships on the high seas. Finally, in April 1917, Wilson called for war on Germany and the United States entered the conflict in Europe.

Yet it would be Germany's eventual defeat in November 1918 (with terms of surrender decided upon at the Paris Peace Conference of 1919) that would propel Wilson into an undeniable global leadership position: he proposed a peaceful "League of Nations" (the precursor to the United Nations) to promote international equality among nations to commence operations at the Conference's end in January 1920.

"There is one thing that the American people always rise to and extend their hand to, and that is the truth of justice and of liberty and of peace," Wilson said. "We have accepted that truth and we are going to be led by it, and it is going to lead us—and through us the world—out into pastures of quietness and peace such as the world never dreamed of before."

IN ORDER FOR the United States to wage war on Germany and her allies, national industrial production had to be converted to a war footing. The president called on BSA, now boasting over 575,000 members, to help in the home-front effort.

Scouts sold Liberty Bonds and War Savings Stamps during five campaigns that contributed nearly $400 million dollars (the equivalent of $7.1 billion today) to the country's war chest. Scouts collected used tires and metal scrap. They inventoried the national supply of black walnut trees whose wood went into airplane propellers and gun stocks. Scouts planted and tended to "victory gardens" that made more food available for America's soldiers overseas (known as *doughboys*).

Writing to BSA president Colin H. Livingstone, Wilson declared that "the service rendered by the boys has been greatly appreciated by the whole nation." Ultimately, BSA volunteers sold $354 million in Liberty Loan bonds, distributed $43 million in War Savings Stamps, rounded up 21 million board feet of black walnut trees, and distributed over 30 million pieces of government literature to encourage public support of the war effort.

Scouts harvest corn on a Scout farm during the First World War.

In the aftermath of the First World War, BSA members were being called upon by federal authorities to promote the concept of "Americanism" by assisting the U.S. Bureau of Naturalization in the distribution of thousands of invitations to "foreign-born citizens to attend classes for preparation of naturalization." And through 1919, Scouts distributed some 400,000 cards throughout 471 cities. But their war and post-war services did not end there.

Scouts served in naturalization ceremonies by presenting certificates of citizenship to the happy recipients and acting as ushers at numerous mass Americanism rallies.

"Boy Scouts helped in maintaining the 'melting pot' for the foreign-born just as they form and maintain the all-American 'melting pot' among the youth of America," exclaimed delighted BSA executives. "But perhaps even more important in the work of Americanization, which is going on within Scout troops, is that the boys of foreign parentage are being taught loyalty to the best American traditions. Through these young Americans their parents also are being reached to a degree hardly realized because it's incalculable."

In appreciation, Wilson issued a *Proclamation* in May 1919 that recognized the national wartime service performed by its legion of Boy Scouts. On the basis of that, BSA issued certificates to individual Scouts and leaders

Scouts present a BSA memorial wreath during the funeral of Wilson in February 1924.

attesting to that effort in "having manifested a desire to have a part in the nationwide effort pursuant to *Proclamation by the President of the United States* to strengthen and extend the influence of the Boy Scouts of America in carrying out its program with the boyhood of our country."

Each recipient was enrolled as an "Associate member of the National Council, Boy Scouts of America" in "Character Building," "Citizenship Training," and "Americanization" for the year ending June 30, 1920.

By then, the Boy Scouts of America was a popular and highly appreciated player on the national stage, having been recognized for its ability to mobilize and perform much-needed national service projects.

Its transformation into a national icon had begun.

We opened our gate to the world and said: "Let all men who wish to be free come to us and they will be welcome." We said, "This independence of ours is not a selfish thing for our own exclusive private use. It is for everybody to whom we can find the means of extending it."

ADDRESS, PHILADELPHIA, PA, JULY 4, 1914

Anything that is done to increase the effectiveness of the Boy Scouts of America is a genuine contribution to the welfare of the nation.

AS QUOTED IN *Boys' Life*, NOVEMBER 1932

It is fine to have the boys of the country organized for the purposes the Boy Scouts represent, and whenever I see a group of them I am proud of their manliness and feel cheered by the knowledge of what their organization represents.

LETTER, WILSON TO BOY SCOUTS OF AMERICA,
New York Times, DECEMBER 3, 1915

My earnest wish is that every Scout leader gives every Boy Scout an opportunity to take a definite part in this practical method of giving expression to his Scout obligation of service to our country.

LETTER, WILSON TO COLIN H. LIVINGSTONE, SEPTEMBER 20, 1917

The fine efficiency of the Boy Scouts of America in serving the country must, of course, be maintained ... I hope that all who can make gifts to the organization or serve as Scoutmasters will feel it their duty to help to organize the hundreds of thousands of boys who need the leadership and the impulse of the Boy Scouts in order that the nation may have their intelligent service.

LETTER, WILSON TO COLIN H. LIVINGSTONE, JANUARY 14, 1918

My warmest greetings to the boys on their return to school. May the year bring them every good thing and strengthen them in all the ideals of their service. It is a pleasure to me to be their chief because I know that good citizens without number will come out of their ranks to counsel and serve the country we love.

TELEGRAM, WILSON TO *Boys' Life*, AUGUST 1, 1918

I beg every member of the Boy Scouts of America to realize that the service rendered by the boys has been greatly appreciated by the whole nation.

LETTER, WILSON TO COLIN H. LIVINGSTONE, AUGUST 23, 1918

I wish to convey to your parents, your community and your Boy Scout organization my appreciation of the training that has developed in you, such a fine spirit of wholesome and loyal citizenship.

"WILSON PRAISES SCOUTS FOR WAR STAMP SALES," *New York Times*, NOVEMBER 5, 1920

WARREN G.

HARDING

29TH PRESIDENT OF THE UNITED STATES

1921–1923

Born: November 2, 1865, near Blooming Grove, Ohio
Died: August 2, 1923, San Francisco, California

Wife: Florence Kling (m. 1891)
Children: Marshall Eugene DeWolf (stepson)

Education: Ohio Central College (B.S.)

BSA Positions: Hon. President (1921–1923)

BSA Honors: Harding (Membership Growth) Award (1923)
Harding Area Council, Ohio
Harding Area District, Heart of Ohio Council, Ohio
Harding Pilgrimage, Marion, Ohio

Eagle Scout Awards presented (1921–1923): 5,503

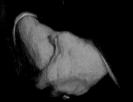

"I am with the Scout movement heart and soul."

—PRESIDENT WARREN G. HARDING
November 1920

CHAPTER FOUR

WARREN G. HARDING

Our Friend

"What Lincoln was to the older men, Harding is to us."

—Boy Scout Stephen Lowe, *Boys' Life*,
October 1923

In August 1923, twelve-year-old Stephen Lowe was a Boy Scout in Kearney, Nebraska. A Scout for less than a year, Stephen nonetheless was about to undertake the most important task of his Scouting career—represent his council to a nation in mourning.

Stephen recently had impressed the local Scout Executive through his pursuit of a notably Scoutlike life. Thus, he was assigned to pick wild prairie flowers from Kearney and present them at the funeral train for the late President Warren G. Harding, whose flag-draped casket was to arrive at the local depot on August 5.

Harding, 29th president of the United States, had expired just days before in San Francisco, California, suffering an unexpected heart attack in the middle of a conversation with the First Lady.

Stephen understood the importance of his assignment: to pick the most beautiful flowers his state had to offer.

"I went at it with a will," he told a reporter. "After getting the flowers, I placed them in a large basket, all ready for the train."

But events were not cooperating.

The Harding funeral train prior to departure from San Francisco in August 1923.

"The telephone rang and [Scout Executive] Joy said that the funeral train would not stop at Kearney, [and] that I must go 50 miles [east to Grand Island] where the train would change engines."

Driven to Grand Island by his father, young Stephen, dressed in full Scout uniform, arrived at the depot. With basket in hand, he approached the presidential railroad car, *Superb*, and saw the soldier assigned to guard the President's casket. Brimming with emotion, the Scout handed the container of flowers to the soldier, then snapped to attention, saluted, and stood there silently until the train pulled out of the station bound for Washington.

"What Lincoln was to the older men," recalled Stephen Lowe, "Harding is to us."

EARLIER THAT JUNE, President Harding and his wife, Florence, sensing that their image had been tarnished by scandals rocking Washington, decided to reconnect with the national populace through a "handshakes and speeches" tour and put a problematic presidency behind them.

Dubbed the "Voyage of Understanding," the Hardings sought their escape from the damning national headlines that accused the affable president of utter stupidity when dealing with his immoral friends assigned by him to administration positions.

For example, after his untimely death the Teapot Dome scandal came to light. It involved the illicit leasing of federal petroleum reserves to private companies in exchange for large sums of Liberty War Bonds and "loans" orchestrated by his Secretary of the Interior Albert B. Fall. Jail time ensued making Fall the first sitting cabinet member ever to be convicted of bribery. Other less egregious (yet still illegal) activities preceeded this heinous scandal, however.

As a presidential favor, Harding's former campaign manager, Albert D. Lasker, was put in charge of the U.S. shipping board, although he had no previous experience in the area. As a result of having no appraisal done, he allowed a valuable steel cargo ship worth $200 per ton to be sold for $30 per ton to a private American shipping company. Lasker resigned two years later after a congressional investigation had begun.

The official in charge of the government's Office of Alien Property, Thomas W. Miller, was convicted of accepting bribes and was stripped of his U.S. citizenship and given 18 months in prison.

Charles R. Forbes, Harding's director of the Veteran's Bureau, disregarded the needs of First World War soldiers and lined his own pockets in exchange for offering insider information to his co-conspirators regarding the awarding of lucrative governmental contracts before they were announced via published public notice. It is estimated that he defrauded the government in blatant overcharges by $28.5 billion in today's currency.

As this era was distinguished by alcohol prohibition, Harding's Prohibition Commissioner Roy Asa Haynes ran a highly corrupt operation with his agents earning a year's worth of federal salary in one month worth of bribes received from bootleggers to "look the other way." Also, he made the market for the sale of "B permits" for legal liquor to the highest bidder on the black market—effectively making them a "negotiable security."

In addition, Harding's own Attorney General Harry M. Daugherty was put on trial (and twice acquitted by a hung jury when he blamed all illegal actions on a recently deceased Justice Department aide) for taking bribes from bootleggers and general corruption charges in March 1924.

Harding, when answering journalist William Allen White regarding his presidential worries, exasperatingly lamented, ""I have no trouble with my enemies, but my damn friends; they're the ones that keep me walking the floor nights!"

WITH ALL DUE RESPECT to Doris Kearns Goodwin's Pulitzer Prize-winning book documenting Abraham Lincoln's presidency titled *Team of Rivals*, a future Warren Harding biography could be titled appropriately, *Team of Criminals*. However, some of his appointments were well thought out like New Orleans born, African American businessman Walter L. Cohen. He served honorably as Harding's Comptroller of U.S. Customs. As one of the first African American men to hold a federal office, Cohen was a highly regarded Catholic politician and businessman, who accepted the post believing it to be one of the "most lucrative federal offices in the South."

Harding also appointed men like Jewish Rabbi Joseph S. Kornfeld and Catholic priest Father Joseph M. Denning to foreign diplomatic positions. Kornfeld served as the U.S. Minister to Persia (now Iran) in the Middle East, while Denning was the American Ambassador to the Vatican in Rome.

Harding greets Scouts who biked to the White House from Columbus, OH, in June 1921.

Harding poses with BSA's *Annual Report* delegation at the White House in February 1922.

As mentioned previously, Harding's 1920 presidential campaign manager was a man of Jewish faith named Albert Lasker, who also was known as the father of modern advertising as well as the architect of Harding's landslide victory before serving as the president's inept head of the U.S. shipping board.

Like President Wilson before him, Harding was in favor of a Jewish homeland in Palestine.

"It is impossible for one, who has studied the service of the Hebrew people, to avoid the faith that they will one day be restored to their historic national home," he wrote, "and there enter into a new and yet greater phase of their contribution to the advance of humanity."

In October 1921, Harding visited Birmingham, Alabama, and made the first speech heard in the South on racial equality.

"Partnership of the races ... must be there," he declared, "if humanity is to achieve the ends which we have set for it."

A month later, the president signed the Sheppard-Tower Maternity Act into law making it the nation's first major social reform program. It automatically funded 3,000 health centers across the country and encouraged preventative and pre-natal care for women. It also paid for a legion of child welfare workers to go into the field and investigate family conditions of care.

Considered to be a highly important piece of legislation for the empowerment of women (as they had just been given the right to vote in

August 1920) the law was sponsored by Julia Lathrop of the U.S. Children's Bureau established in 1912 under President William Howard Taft.

INTERNATIONALLY, BSA MEMBERS and officials were asked to travel to France and help revive the French Scouting tradition. To do so, BSA members sponsored special camps to re-train adult Frenchmen on how to be, once again, Scoutmasters of quality and "serve boys of their home communities as leaders."

Although both Hardings had health problems, the president's probably were exacerbated by the criminals in his administration. So surely a

Harding greets Washington, DC, Eagle Scouts during BSA's *Annual Report* presentation in February 1921.

Harding meets with Scouts in 1923.

presidential train trip on board the *Superb* to the Western states and Alaska would be the ticket back to good health.

On a bright sunny day in Washington, DC, the train pulling *Supurb* left Union Station. Glancing back at the nation's capital quickly disappearing behind the horizon, Harding hardly could have known that it would be his last view of Washington.

The *Superb* made planned stops in cities and towns across the heartland of America, where Harding took time to step out of his car and mingle with thousands of citizens before taking a podium to deliver the kind of oratory expected of a "popular" sitting president.

When the train reached Kansas City, the Hardings had the first of two opportunities to reconnect with their beloved Boy Scouts of America—

Mrs. Harding presented Letters of Commendation to two Scouts (Damon Boss and Russell Dennis) who had performed heroic actions that resulted in the saving of lives.

Second, in Butte, Montana, the president presented six Honor Medals in heroic lifesaving to five Boy Scouts (Omar Bradford, Wilbur Marvin, John McCarthy, Willard Murrey, and James Weal) and the Scout Executive of the Butte Council. The president acknowledged their exemplary heroism exhibited on a hike up the 10,000-foot-high Devil's Peak, where tragedy occurred when lightening struck the patrol during a storm as they descended. The hikers were hurled down a portion of the steep slope—all temporarily unconscious—with some having severe burns to their legs and back.

Eleven miles from any help, two Scouts were sent by Scout Executive Benjamin Owen down the mountain. They traveled without the aid of a compass, which had been demagnetized by the lightening strike. Performing emergency first aid on the Scouts who could no longer walk, several delirious boys were loaded onto the backs of others and carefully carried down the zigzagging slope.

Off the mountain by midnight, the group was met by the rescuers alerted by the two Scouts who traveled the eleven miles back to civilization in less than two hours.

"You are a fine example and inspiration to your fellows," Harding told them. "I am proud of you as President of the Republic."

Boys' Life magazine called Harding's address "one of the finest tributes ever paid to Boy Scout heroism."

Returning to the *Superb*'s rear platform, the president gave a final wave to the gathered thousands. They cheered frantically. And with the presidential train slowly gaining speed, the whistle blew, and the Hardings continued their course westward toward Alaska.

From station to station and speech after speech, one journalist traveling with the First Family marveled at Harding's "continuous salute and smile for the sturdy little lads in [Boy Scout] khaki."

Sadly it all would end tragically.

In retrospective comments published in *Boys' Life* magazine after his death, the author scribed, "When his train stopped to let him alight to visit your city, you were on hand, Scouts, by special request, to be part of his bodyguard. The bodyguard of a President! What an honor!"

Harding speaks at the Honor Medal presentation in Butte, MT, in July 1923.

SHORTLY AFTER HIS inauguration in March 1921, Harding accepted the role of Honorary President of the Boy Scouts of America. BSA executives sought to capitalize on his happy-go-lucky reputation, his jovial personality that made all who came into contact with him feel as though they were his closest friends.

Arriving at the White House on a bright Wednesday afternoon in April, a delegation led by Chief Scout Executive James E. West and BSA President Colin H. Livingstone included eight recipients of the Eagle Scout award from the local Washington, DC, Council.

"The Boy Scouts have done a useful work," pronounced Harding. "I shall be very proud to serve as honorary president of the organization."

By the end of 1922, BSA had incorporated the Harding Award into its program as a recruitment tool. The prize was presented to a Troop or a Council that increased membership at least 25 percent over the previous year. A council that earned the award was recognized as "First Class," and a letter from the president of the United States was sent to its Scout Executive.

In 1923, 302 Councils earned Harding Awards, while 5,058 red, white, and blue Harding Award silk flag streamers were earned by Troops that had

Theodore Roosevelt Jr. attaches the Harding Ribbon to troop flagpoles in December 1923.
BSA's Harding Ribbon for membership recruitment (below).

met the recruiting requirement. BSA's national enrollment increased reg-
istrations by an additional 81,000 Scouts and 20,000 volunteer leaders,
taking total membership to half a million members.

Harding's endorsement had greatly benefited BSA but his untimely
death quickly shortened his influence.

DURING THE INITIAL funeral procession through San Francisco,
twenty Eagle Scouts marched in his cortege. Two hundred Scouts and
leaders met Harding's train at the Salt Lake City station—directed by
the general in charge of Infantry to keep the 25,000 mourners at bay
by encircling the train and performing police duties by interlocking
walking staves.

As the Harding rail procession rattled on, more and more
Scouts stood at attention along the route and saluted as it passed—

obviously heeding the request of Chief Scout Executive James E. West to have Scout representatives at "every station … regardless of the hour or whether or not the train stops."

West had written in a memo to members across the country that, "Scouts should be present as Guards of Honor. Standing at attention and whenever the train should stop, a Scout [will] put aboard it a tribute of wild flowers, representative of the outdoor spirit of the Movement."

With this dictate, Harding's memory belonged to the Boy Scouts, "heart and soul."

ONE HUNDRED SCOUTS and 15,000 citizens gathered at Kearney, Nebraska, to witness the train pass by. Impressed, Mrs. Harding commented about "the humanizing effect that Boy Scouts have upon a crowd."

In Omaha, the mourners on the presidential train witnessed hundreds of Scouts—some with bugles blowing "Taps" and others gathered in Troops—all standing at attention and saluting respectfully.

In Washington, the National Council's delegation, which included Chief Scout Executive West, BSA President Livingstone, and ten specially selected Scouts wearing black neckerchiefs, presented a floral wreath, while a chorus of Scouts and children expressed their grief in song.

Soon, the funeral train left for Harding's hometown of Marion, Ohio, where legions of Boy Scouts again lined the route, standing at attention, "paying their last respects to a fallen comrade till the end of the journey."

Through the pages of *Boys' Life* and *Scouting* magazines, West encouraged Scouts and units across the nation to plant Harding Memorial Trees at "appropriate places and participate in a national Good Turn."

But the most lasting tribute paid to the fallen president was the convocation of a "National Memorial Meeting" by all troops to be held on a date near November 2—the president's birthday.

Out of this seed sprang the Harding Memorial Pilgrimage to his tomb held annually in Marion, Ohio, since 1932.

I want to see the time when black men will regard themselves as full participants in the benefits and duties of American citizenship.

ADDRESS, BIRMINGHAM, ALABAMA, OCTOBER 26, 1921

The future of America depends upon the boys of America living up to the ideals encompassed in the Scout Oath.

AS QUOTED IN *Boys' Life*, OCTOBER 1923

The Boy Scouts have done a useful work, and the readiness and efficiency with which they did it, particularly during the war period, justifies our earnest hope that their usefulness may be continued and enhanced in the future. I shall be very proud to serve as Honorary President of the organization.

LETTER, HARDING TO COLIN H. LIVINGSTONE, MARCH 17, 1921

I am with the Scout Movement heart and soul. It is an organization teaching the spirit of service and honor which we must always have in our citizenship. It is a school of our democracy because in it standing is won only by taking the equal opportunity given all individuals to show their own merit, capacity, and worth. I wish every boy in our America could have the advantage and the honor of being in the Boy Scout organization and of learning therein that co-operation, justice, the customs of fair play and the gentleness of good manner make for peace and growth, as distinguished from the results of disorganization and selfishness and cowardice, which leads to contentions and conflict.

TELEGRAM, HARDING TO THEODORE ROOSEVELT JR., NOVEMBER 1920

I want to take advantage of this occasion to express my continuing interest in the Boy Scout Movement and my hope that you may have all success in your effort to multiply the membership. You inform me that the membership now stands at 409,537 and that you are undertaking a campaign which aims to bring it into the millions. The Boy Scout Movement has now been in progress so long that nobody at all familiar with its results could possibly doubt its excellent influence upon both the boys who constitute the membership and the men who generously give of their time, efforts and means to its maintenance. It has been especially gratifying to me that this Movement has proved itself strong enough to maintain enthusiasm and effective work since the close of the war and that its present outlook is so promising.

LETTER, HARDING TO JAMES E. WEST, AUGUST 1921

CALVIN

COOLIDGE

30TH PRESIDENT OF THE UNITED STATES

1923–1929

Born: July 4, 1872, Plymouth Notch, Vermont
Died: January 5, 1933, Northampton, Massachusetts

Wife: Grace Goodhue (m. 1905)
Children: John, Calvin Jr.

Education: Amherst College (B.A.)

BSA Positions: Hon. President (1923–1929)
Hon. Vice President (1929–1933)
National BSA Leader's Conference host (1927)
Presidential Conference on Outdoor Education host (1924)
Father of two Boy Scouts

BSA Honors: Presented the first class of Silver Buffalo Award recipients
at the 1926 Annual Meeting
37th Silver Buffalo (1929)
Calvin Coolidge Council, BSA, Bellows Falls, Vermont
(1936 – 1965)
Calvin Coolidge District, Green Mountain Council (VT),
BSA (1972 – current)

Eagle Scout Awards presented (1924–1928): 24,179

"*No organization is doing better work in developing noble virtues and strong character in our youth. This service is of incalculable value.*"

—PRESIDENT CALVIN COOLIDGE

CHAPTER FIVE

CALVIN COOLIDGE

Silent Cal

"He was ever ready to serve the interests of youth."

Boys' Life
March 1933

THE CALVIN COOLIDGE STORY is one about quality, not quantity.

The year was 1928 and President Coolidge was passing through Fort Lauderdale via the Florida East Coast Railway. As the train pulled to a stop, a mass of eight thousand citizens—including many Girl Scouts—waved and shouted to him.

"Say something to the Girl Scouts!" screamed their enthusiastic leader.

Coolidge paused for a second, raised his head, and eloquently spun off a welcoming speech consisting wholly of the salutation: "Hello, Girl Scouts." After lowering his hand, he turned around.

At a White House reception, the president was approached by a society matron who announced a wager with an attending gentleman that she could get Coolidge to say more than three words to her. His laconic response: "You lose."

Asked by a former classmate to send greetings to their college reunion, Coolidge agreed. At the event, the master of ceremonies announced that he had received a telegram from the institution's most famous alumnus.

Coolidge meets with BSA's *Annual Report* delegation in February 1925.

Thunderous applause rang out. Then, with a large gesture from the speaker, the room went silent. The emcee carefully opened the envelope and read its entire contents in a loud, clear voice: "Greetings. Calvin Coolidge."

His last will and testament was just twenty-three words long. He advised his successor, Herbert Hoover, on how to deal with the garrulous Washington elite by saying, "If you keep dead still, they will run down in three or four minutes."

He wasn't known as "Silent Cal" for nothing.

But when it came to the Boy Scouts of America (BSA), Calvin Coolidge was a passionate and vocal supporter—at least by his standards.

BORN ON THE FOURTH of July 1872 in Plymouth Notch, Vermont, John Calvin Coolidge Jr. descended from hardy European stock that had settled Massachusetts and Vermont beginning in the 1630s.

His birth "did not cause banks to close or business to be tied up, for that was a country of farmers only," recalls one Coolidge biographer. "However, the little stranger, with a foresight sound and characteristic, had chosen as the day of his advent, one which the neighbors were bound to celebrate."

Known as a hard worker from the beginning, young Calvin seemed to live life according to an adage from a bygone era:

The bee gains little from the flower,
A stone a day will raise a tower.
Yet the hive is filled, the tower is done.
If steadily the work goes on.

Coolidge grew up a Vermont farm boy with simple values. He considered himself born with two ears and one mouth, and so he listened much more than he spoke. His father recalled never having to tell Cal what to do. He looked, listened, learned, and acted, especially with regard to his responsibilities.

"He's always been that and I guess he always will be. He wasn't extraordinary. He did his work at school," recalled his father, John Coolidge Sr. He did his work at home as well.

"When a small boy, he got up in the middle of the night," notes another biographer, "for he remembered that he had not filled up the wood bin, one of his duties."

His life became one of two things "work or recuperation from work." With that spirit, he gained an education.

Calvin lost his mother in 1884 when he was twelve years old, and his sister died six years later. Suddenly it was only he and his father.

In 1891, Cal entered Amherst College where he made friends slowly and methodically. He addressed fellow students by their full given names. Entering the room of a fellow student commonly addressed as Bill at eight in the evening, Coolidge forced out a, "Hello, William," opened a book, and read silently until eleven. When exiting for the night, he offered, "Goodnight, William," and left the room.

Such was an evening of conversation with the future president.

"He never spoke unless he had something to say," writes biographer W.R. Washburn. "The country needs men like him, not men who can talk, but men who can listen and act, deeds, not words."

When moved to write, his theses were outstanding. Coolidge won a prize of one hundred dollars for an essay titled "The Principles of the Revolutionary War." His father was little surprised at his son's academic success after witnessing the college student amidst books and papers in the family's sitting room during Cal's first summer out of Amherst.

Coolidge graduated with honors in 1895. One of his classmates was the future Standard Oil Company executive and BSA executive board member, George D. Pratt.

Coolidge was admitted to the Massachusetts bar in July 1897 without ever attending law school: he simply clerked in local legal firms as was commonly done in those days. Two years later he entered public life as an unpaid member of the Northampton (Massachusetts) City Council. After his advancement to the post of the city solicitor in 1900, one unfriendly councilman attested that *he* had not voted for Coolidge. To which Solicitor Coolidge replied: "Somebody did."

In late 1905, Coolidge took a wife, the former Grace Goodhue, who worked as a teacher at the Clark School for the Deaf. They met when she strolled past his bachelor quarters one day and spotted Calvin shaving while wearing his derby hat: she started laughing hysterically. Seeing Grace, Coolidge made it a point to meet her, and by October, they were husband and wife.

Everyone asked what she saw in him.

"Certainly no Prince Charming or knight in shining armor," recalled mutual friend Alfred Pearce Dennis. "She saw…that unseen thing which we call, for want of a better name, character."

Within three years two sons arrived: John in 1906 and Cal Jr. in 1908.

In 1910 Coolidge was elected mayor of Northampton, and in January 1914, he took his newly won seat in the Massachusetts State Senate. His letter of introduction read, "Like a singed cat, he is better than he looks."

Voted Senate president, he accepted the post in a stirring speech consisting of forty-four words.

"I don't like to speak. It's all nonsense," recalled Coolidge some years later. "I'd much rather be at home doing my work."

Next he was elected lieutenant-governor of Massachusetts, then its governor. By 1921, Coolidge was U.S. vice president and upon the death of Warren G. Harding on August 2, 1923, Calvin Coolidge became president of the United States, sworn into office at 1 a.m. in Plymouth Notch, Vermont, by his father, the local notary public.

After the brief ceremony at the family farm, he "trudged through the black Vermont night to visit his mother's grave," writes biographer David Pietrusza. "He wanted her to know."

Coolidge accepts a Tate McKenzie statue at the White House in 1927.

That same day, the president's son, Cal Jr., was working diligently at his job in a tobacco field. When his employer ran up to him and announced that President Harding had died making his father the nation's new chief executive, young Cal Jr. replied, "Yes, I suppose he is president. Which shed shall I work in?"

In the Coolidge family work was work, no matter what the level.

PRESIDENT CALVIN COOLIDGE was a strong proponent of the equality of all people. Writing in his compilation book of speeches, *Foundations of the Republic*, he expressed abhorrence at the suggestion that certain races not run for elected office, as well as the exclusion of certain faiths, like Catholics, from governmental posts.

"Our Constitution guarantees equal rights to all our citizens, without discrimination on account of race or color," he exclaimed. "I have taken my oath to support that Constitution."

Coolidge so strongly supported the rights and fair treatment of American Indians that he formalized it with the signing of the Indian Citizenship Act on June 2, 1924. It granted full U.S. citizenship to all Native Americans.

Coolidge meets with 1500 Scouts from New York, New Jersey, and Connecticut at the White House in 1927.

The President and Mrs. Coolidge accept a pony from a Scout at the White House circa 1928.

Furthermore, it allowed them the right to retain their "tribal lands and cultural rights." As a lasting image, the president was photographed in a native Indian headdress to express his solidarity with them.

BSA had similar inclusionary intent.

In 1924, the organization formed its Division of Church Relations that would evolve into the Religious Relationships Committee of today. A year later, the Interracial Work Committee was formed to formalize BSA's support and endorsement of all African American and other minority-based Scouting units. Conceptualized a decade earlier by national Scout executives Bolton Smith and Stanley A. Harris, this committee was funded quickly by the Laura Spellman Rockefeller Memorial Foundation and immediately commenced operations.

Initially, their goals were to educate local councils and their executive boards on the importance of taking Scouting to all local youth, as well as to take a census of all African American troops currently in existence. They found that there were currently 248 operating African American troops that touted 4,923 boys under African American leadership. Louisville, Kentucky, had 30 troops, followed by Chicago with 26, Washington, DC, with 10, and 8 in Brooklyn, New York.

Importantly, it was the Chicago Council that broke BSA's employee color barrier by employing the first full-time African American district executive in the nation to service that growing Scouting population. And African American youths flocked to the program.

It is generally regarded (though not proven definitively) that Edgar Cunningham of Troop 12 in Waterloo, Iowa, was the nation's first African American Eagle Scout. He earned the award on June 8, 1926, and received a handwritten letter from President Coolidge congratulating him on his accomplishment.

In 1928, the "younger Scout" experimental program known as "Cubbing" (for boys between the ages of 9 and 11) was born. By the time it was approved for a national rollout a short time later, women were allowed to join BSA's leadership ranks as Cub Den Mothers.

But starting out in 1928, women were strictly members of local mother's committees, who were tasked with recruiting both boys and the older Boy Scout lads who would serve as their youthful examples of American boyhood—the Den Chiefs. By mid-1938, over 1,000 women had signed up to lead Cub units.

As a social reformer, President Coolidge embraced the values of the Boy Scouts of America, as his two sons were the first Scouts to reside in the White House. Inspired by their devotion to the program, President Coolidge became a vocal supporter of BSA.

"Both my sons are Scouts and my observation of the benefits they have derived from their affiliation has strengthened my conviction of the organization's usefulness," he stated soon after arriving in the Oval Office. "I shall be glad to render any proper service I can to the organization at any time."

But tragedy would soon strike.

Sadly, in July 1924, Cal Jr. developed a blister on the toe of his right foot after a strenuous tennis match with his brother, John, on the White House tennis court. The next morning, the sixteen-year-old "awoke with a stiff and painful leg." A septic infection took his life by the end of the week in those days before antibiotics.

A grieving president lamented in his memoirs, "I do not know why such a price was exacted for occupying the White House." A memorial tree was planted on the White House grounds in honor of his Scout son.

Native Americans pay a visit to Coolidge on the White House's south lawn in February 1925.

In sympathy, BSA managers sent a large floral arrangement in memory of Cal Jr. On the day of his burial, a number of Washington, DC, Scouts formed a barrier outside from the White House to Union Station to protect the Coolidge family from the gathering crowds, as they removed their son's body to Vermont for burial. In tribute, Boy Scouts carried the casket to the burial plot and, as the service ended, each Scout filed by the grave and dropped in a rose in honor of "one of their own."

President Coolidge remained faithful to BSA and in 1926 issued a stirring statement on the importance and meaning of the Scout Oath and Scout Law:

"It is a wonderful instrument for good," he declared. "It is an inspiration to you whose duty and privilege it is to widen its horizon and extend its influence."

In 1929, President Coolidge was honored as the 37th Silver Buffalo recipient for "his sympathy and interest in the Scout Movement, the pres-

Scouts Robert Fulton (left) and Louis Paulin deliver BSA's funeral wreath to the White House in honor of Calvin Coolidge Jr. in July 1924.

tige of the friendship, [and] his unfailing insight into the real objectives of character building and citizenship training."

As biographer Claude Feuss notes: "Calvin Coolidge had character—and in the long run character outruns what is temporarily spectacular."

How right he is.

Our Constitution guarantees equal rights to all our citizens, without discrimination on account of race or color. I have taken my oath to support that Constitution.

CALVIN COOLIDGE, *Foundations of the Republic*

No organization is doing better work in developing noble virtues and strong character in our youth. This service is of incalculable value.

As quoted in Murray, *History of the Boy Scouts of America*

Please extend to the Boy Scouts of America my greetings and good wishes. The future of the country is in the hands of the boys of today and I believe that the Scout Movement with its ideals of service and honorable conduct help to make the future secure.

AS QUOTED IN *Boys' Life*, JULY 1924

The program [of the Boy Scouts of America] is a means to an end. Its fundamental object is to use modern environment in character building and training for citizenship.

ADDRESS TO THE NATIONAL COUNCIL, BSA, MAY 1, 1926

[The Boy Scouts of America] is one of the growing institutions by which our country is working out the fulfillment of an eternal promise.

ADDRESS TO THE NATIONAL COUNCIL, BSA, MAY 1, 1926

Scouting very definitely teaches that rewards come only after achievement through personal effort and self-discipline. ... Not only does one learn to do things, but in many instances he learns what he can do best.

ADDRESS TO THE NATIONAL COUNCIL, BSA, MAY 1, 1926

The boy learns "to be prepared." This is the motto of the Scouts. They are prepared to take their proper place in life, prepared to meet any unusual situation arising in their personal or civic relations.

ADDRESS TO THE NATIONAL COUNCIL, BSA, MAY 1, 1926

There has been no single Movement in our nation that has been of greater advantage to our national life than that represented by the Boy Scouts of America. It has started at the very foundation of our citizenship and has trained the boys at a time when their minds were in their best condition to receive it. The training given has been very wisely and excellently planned and developed. On many occasions I have noted with pride the manner in which the Boy Scouts have acted, and it speaks more eloquently than words of the security of the future of our United States.

GOVERNOR COOLIDGE OF MASSACHUSETTS, FEBRUARY 1919

The more I have studied this movement, its inception, purposes, organization, and principles, the more I have been impressed. Not only is it based on the fundamental rules of right thinking and acting, but it seems to embrace in its code almost every virtue needed in the personal and social life of mankind. It is a wonderful instrument for good. If every boy in the United States could be placed under the wholesome influences of the Scout program, and should live up to the Scout Oath and rules, we would hear fewer pessimistic words as to the future of our nation.

AS QUOTED IN MURRAY, *History of the Boy Scouts of America*

HERBERT

HOOVER

31ˢᵀ President of the United States

1929–1933

Born: August 10, 1874, West Branch, Iowa
Died: October 20, 1964, New York City, New York

Wife: Louise "Lou" Henry (m. 1899–1944)
Children: Herbert Clark Jr., Allan Henry

Education: Stanford University (B.S.)

BSA Positions: Hon. President (1929–1933)
Hon. President, Indiana Council, BSA (1931)
Hon Vice President (1933–1964)
Father of a Boy Scout

BSA Honors: 44ᵗʰ Silver Buffalo (1930)
Honorary President, Indiana Council (1931)
Medal, Indiana Council, BSA (1931)
President Hoover (Membership Growth) Award (1932)
Herbert Hoover Historic Trail & Medal, Cedar Valley, Iowa
Medal, Buffalo Bill Council, BSA (1960)

Eagle Scout Awards presented (1929–1932): 32,857

"*I do not know of any form of Americanism that so produces a real American citizen as the Boy Scouts.*"

—THE HONORABLE HERBERT HOOVER
1920

CHAPTER SIX

HERBERT HOOVER
The Father of Volunteerism

"His work in feeding the hungry expressed the care and generosity of all Americans, regardless of political differences."

PRESIDENT HARRY S. TRUMAN
June 1965

ONE OF THE FINEST SERVICE PROJECTS carried out by the Boy Scouts of America (BSA) each year is the Scouting for Food campaign. Annually, Scouts across the nation canvass their neighborhoods collecting canned goods for local food banks. Though this program is relatively new to Scouting, the idea of helping feed the nation goes back to the beginning of the Scouting Movement. BSA has President Herbert Hoover to thank for formalizing this type of service project on a national scale.

Most commonly remembered as the nation's chief executive during the Great Depression—the greatest economic downturn in American history—Hoover was once known as the "Great Humanitarian" for feeding the war-ravaged countries of Europe during the 1920s following the First World War. Based on that alone, he rightfully claimed the title of "Father of Volunteerism."

Born in August 1874 and orphaned at the age of ten, the young Iowa native was sent to live with his uncle, who was determined to improve the youth's life. His uncle's emotional support helped young Herbert earn good grades in school, where he excelled at math and science. Eventually, he gained entry to the new university in the community of Palo Alto, California, endowed by railroad tycoon and former governor of the state, Leland Stanford Jr.

At Stanford University, Hoover studied geology and graduated in 1895 with a degree as a mining engineer. Hoover traveled the world and mastered his profession. International assignments gave him perspective on many other countries and societies, their natural resources, and their food supplies.

The young geologist started in Australia but soon moved to China as a mining consultant to the Chinese emperor. At the outbreak of the First World War, Hoover and his wife, the former Louise "Lou" Henry, were living in London. They started helping Americans trapped in the country without passage back to the United States.

Scouts present the gift of a buffalo horn to Hoover in honor of his 56th birthday in August 1930. (far right) BSA's Hoover Ribbon for membership recruitment.

Seeing that food shortages were emerging in Belgium as the German army advanced upon France, Hoover accepted the chairmanship of the Commission for Relief in Belgium "to get food to the starving people." Under his leadership, volunteers fed some 11 million Belgian citizens between 1914 and 1919. His duties included raising money to support those feeding programs as well as finding ways to get food shipments past German blockades.

When the United States entered the war in 1917, President Woodrow Wilson asked the forty-three-year-old "Boy Wonder" to return to America to solve *this* country's mounting food supply problems as his U.S. Food Administrator. Hoover's responsibilities included monitoring national food supplies, making sure U.S. citizens remained nourished, and ensuring a constant supply of food to American and other allied troops fighting in Europe.

Hoover threw himself into the work.

As chairman of the Committee on Food, Hoover's first challenge was to convince Americans to *conserve* food. He created innovative programs like "Meatless Mondays" and "Wheatless Wednesdays" to promote sustainability and a sense of national unity. But, to make it work, he had to get the word out to the population fast. To help in this, BSA was asked to perform one of its first national services on the home front: distribute literature to promote the careful use of domestic food resources.

By late 1917, a half million Boy Scouts were working on war service projects at the request of Administrator Hoover and President Wilson. Hoover's main food program was to encourage the creation of "War Gardens" and "Victory Gardens," where Scouts tended to fruits and vegetables planted and grown at home and in their communities.

"The goal of this campaign was to get every Scout to conserve food and start a garden of his own," writes historian Mitch Reis. "Scouts who could not start a garden were encouraged to help someone else with theirs. Many troops and councils started large gardens in which all local Scouts worked together."

Under the slogan, "Every Scout to Feed a Soldier," these "Grub Scouts" across the country participated in a national food crusade. Their first challenge was to increase the American bean crop for overseas shipment.

"Let the Boy Scouts see to it that beans are planted everywhere," cabled Hoover to Chief Scout Executive James E. West, "so that the biggest bean crop ever known shall be the war contribution of the Boy Scouts of America and her allies."

West told Hoover there were hundreds of thousands of Scouts ready and willing to serve as "your aides, as producers and conservers of food, as service to our country."

BSA President Colin H. Livingstone, having no backyard of his own, plowed up his entire front yard and put in multiple vegetable crops—as did BSA Treasurer George D. Pratt, and National Scout Commissioner Daniel Carter Beard.

"I have been particularly pleased with the keen interest which you have displayed in the work of the Food Administration," Hoover wrote to West. "[I am] gratified by the assistance which you have rendered our Nation during the past season in many ways as aides."

By the end of the war, West could report that more than 12,000 Boy Scout War and Victory Gardens had been planted with plots of 200 to 300

Hoover meets with a Scout delegation around 1931.

Hoover inspects a Boy Scout troop around 1932.

acres designated as communal Boy Scout Farms. These gardens included large crops of corn, beans, and potatoes. Hoover lauded Scouting's efforts, "In that splendid service, they showed a spirit that covered the entire population during the war. It is the spirit that rests in the entire Boy Scout Movement."

Hoover's great success propelled him to higher political office. He moved into the position of director-general of the American Relief Administration, to the chairmanship of the President's Conference on Unemployment, had a seat on the World War Foreign Debt Commission, and on to the executive committee of the American Red Cross. By 1927, he was directing the Great Mississippi Flood Relief program that oversaw massive federal relief efforts in ten states. And just eighteen months later, Herbert Hoover was elected the thirty-first president of the United States.

AS PRESIDENT, HOOVER attacked corruption across the nation. Most notable was his prosecution of Chicago gangster Al Capone on tax evasion charges. Hoover had established the antitrust division of the Justice Department soon after taking office in 1929 to "prosecute unfair competition and restraint of trade cases," and proposed federal loans to improve urban slums. He granted tax cuts to low-income Americans and created the Veterans Administration, effectively doubling the number of current veterans hospitals. Hoover endorsed the Children's Charter at his White House Conference on Child Health and Protection in April 1931 that advocated the protection of every American child from harm as their "first right of citizenship," regardless of race or gender.

As a conservation-minded chief executive, Hoover added an additional 3 million acres to America's National Parks and 2.3 million acres to the National Forests. He submitted legislation to Congress to create massive water dams in the Tennessee Valley and central California.

Former U.S. Senator and Senate Majority Leader Charles Curtis was Hoover's vice president. Making this pick especially notable was Curtis' heredity—he was the first man of "significantly" non-European ancestry to occupy such an office—being three-quarters American Indian on his maternal side (Kaw, Osage, and Pottawatomie). As a youth, Curtis had grown

Hoover inspects Florida Scouts around 1930.

up living with his maternal grandparents on the Kaw Nation's reservation in Kansas.

In 1928, President Hoover appointed Charles J. Rhodes as commissioner of Indian Affairs to "accelerate the assimilation of American Indians into the general society."

BSA, by that time, had created a committee dedicated to recruiting Native American youth at the request of President Hoover's secretary of the Interior secretary, Ray Lyman Wilbur.

Unlike African American Scouts at the time, Native American boys could be placed into any existing troop of white Scouts and given immediate exposure to jamborees, campouts, and other friendship-building experiences. Additionally, the Indian Lore merit badge was created a short time later with requirements specifically designed to teach all Scouts about the heritage, games, and skills of Native American tribal culture.

Also, foreign-born youths were to be aggressively recruited for the first time. Identified for inclusion were boys of Spanish-American (Hispanic) descent, as well as those of Polish, Lithuanian, and Italian ancestry. Importantly, all promotional literature for these ethnic groups was to be printed in their home language to facilitate their membership.

BSA made the most headway by partnering with established advocate agencies like the Latin Union League of American Citizens that promoted Scouting heavily among their Hispanic membership. Likewise, the Catholic Church assisted with recruiting this ethnic group as well with many troops being formed quickly within the boundaries of San Antonio's Alamo Area Council.

Further developments included a new training course for Hispanic troop leaders and its promotion through the church that established "small revolving funds" for assisting slim troop budgets.

Additionally by 1931, BSA finalized a formal arrangement with Chicago's Polish National Alliance to sponsor its 300,000 youth members in BSA.

First Lady Lou Hoover made headlines when she invited the wife of the nation's first African American Congressman, Oscar S. DePriest of Illinois, to have tea with Congressional wives.

President Hoover appointed African American Benjamin O. Davis Jr. to the U.S. Military Academy at West Point when only one other African American line officer previously had attended—Davis' own father. The younger Davis went on to fly with the famed Tuskegee Airmen during World War II and ultimately rose to the rank of a four-star general in the U.S. Air Force (retired) under President William J. Clinton.

But with the Depression coming down on the country, such accomplishments could not relieve the mounting number of homeless people living in so-called "Hoovervilles" around Washington, DC—shanty towns filled with out-of-work veterans and their financially broke families (one Hooverville even popped-up just west of the White House).

"We were heroes in 1917," exclaimed one bitter former soldier, "but we're just bums now."

Leaving the presidency as a defeated man in 1933, Hoover threw himself into his volunteer work with wife Lou.

Lou, an enthusiastic supporter of the American Girl Scout movement, joined her husband in supporting other organizations that would improve the quality of national life—particularly among children. In doing so, they recognized, "the imperative need of this nation at all times is the leadership of Uncommon Men or Women."

Previously in 1930, national BSA managers had recognized President Herbert Hoover's service to the youth of America with the awarding of its 44th Silver Buffalo medal. As stated in his citation: "[Hoover's] sympathy with the Scout movement and his intelligent interest in its citizenship and character-building program has given fresh impetus to public interest in Scouting."

In retirement, the Hoovers spent their lives serving the youth of America.

Hoover meets with Scouts at the White House in 1931.

IN HIS OWN WORDS

I want a square deal ... not unjust discriminations between special groups.
Veto of HR 10381, June 26, 1930

I do not know of any form of Americanism that so produces a real American citizen as the Boy Scouts.
"A Message from Mr. Hoover," *Boys' Life,* June 1920

If we could have eight million Boy Scouts from one generation, we would no longer have an Americanization problem.
"A Message from Mr. Hoover," *Boys' Life,* June 1920

[The Boy Scouts of America] is highly important, particularly in these times, that the support of the public be maintained for our educational, social and character-building agencies and I am confident that your fine record will contribute to this end.
LETTER, HOOVER TO BSA PRESIDENT WALTER W. HEAD, MAY 16, 1932

It is most important at this time that the activities of the Boy Scouts of America and indeed the activities of all of our character-building agencies, should be maintained... This will not only bring to thousands of additional boys the joys and satisfactions of the Game of Scouting, but make the character-building and citizenship results a vital factor in advancing our democracy.
LETTER, HOOVER TO BSA PRESIDENT WALTER W. HEAD, JULY 26, 1932

The first test of democracy is that each individual shall have the opportunity to take that position of leadership in the community to which his character, his ability, and his ambition entitle him; . . . the progress of our country is thus directly related to the training in leadership we can give the youth of the nation. In meeting the vital need that when the oncoming generation takes over our national affairs it shall be a generation bulwarked with character, the Boy Scout movement plays a most useful part.

Boys' Life, JULY 1932

The Boy Scout movement has opened for him the portals to adventure and constructive joy, by reviving the lore of the frontier and the campfire; by establishing contacts with the birds and sometimes with the bees; by matching his patience to the deliberate character of fish; by efficient operations of the swimming hole; and by peeps into the thousand mysteries of the streams, the trees, and the stars.

Boys' Life, JULY 1932

FRANKLIN D.

ROOSEVELT

32ND PRESIDENT OF THE UNITED STATES

1933–1945

Born: January 30, 1882, Hyde Park, New York
Died: April 12, 1945, Warm Springs, Georgia

Wife: Anna Eleanor Roosevelt (m. 1905)
Children: Anna, James, Elliott, Franklin Delano Jr., John Aspinwall

Education: Harvard College (B.A.)

BSA Positions: Hon. President (1933–1945)
              Member, Special Committee on Nautical Scouting (1915)
              Chairman, Scout Committee of Greater New York (1921)
              President, Boy Scout Foundation of Greater New York
                (starting 1922)
              Developed the Ten Mile River Scout Camp (1924–1928)

BSA Honors: 46th Silver Buffalo (1930)
              Roosevelt Efficiency Award Ribbon (1933)
              Order of the Arrow membership (1933)
              Received the 5 millionth Boy Scout Handbook (1935)
              Attended the 1st BSA National Jamboree, Washington, DC
                (1937)
              Camp Roosevelt, Ocean County Council (1954–1955)

Eagle Scout Awards presented (1933–1944): 105,179

"*I firmly believe that the Boy Scout movement represents a new era of moral force in America.*"

—President Franklin D. Roosevelt
June 2, 1933

CHAPTER SEVEN

FRANKLIN D. ROOSEVELT
The Amiable Boy Scout

"His life and his work are an inspiration to all of us."

—Winston S. Churchill
ca. 1955

WHEN PULITZER PRIZE-WINNING POLITICAL COMMENTATOR Walter Lippman described Franklin D. Roosevelt as "a kind of amiable Boy Scout," the United States was deep into the Great Depression.

Elected to the presidency in November 1932 on the promise of a "New Deal" to put Americans back to work, Roosevelt's new programs included the Civilian Conservation Corps (CCC) and the Works Progress Administration (WPA), both of which created temporary manual labor jobs for unskilled workers, and the National Recovery Administration (NRA) created to regulate fair pricing practices.

Lippman may have recognized Roosevelt's Scoutlike demeanor and generally affable personality, but he also recognized that the New Deal's back-to-work programs resembled a series of Boy Scouting service projects.

The CWA, where formerly unemployed men and women would "shovel snow, rake leaves, and clean up through the winter," may have been short-lived, but it was effective at putting paychecks into the hands of struggling American workers (at least for as long as it was in existence).

Maybe Roosevelt's years of exposure to the Boy Scouts of America's (BSA) core values and ideals influenced the development of these programs; (although first volunteering in 1915), from 1921 on, he was the consummate Scouting volunteer.

HAVING ENJOYED CONSIDERABLE success in New York State politics, Franklin Roosevelt was jolted by unexpected defeat in 1920 as the vice presidential running mate of Democratic presidential candidate James M. Cox, the sitting governor of Ohio. Seeking another activity to take his mind off of defeat, Roosevelt began working diligently with his local Scouting council. In witnessing their explosive growth since first volunteering with the New York Sea Scouts some six years prior, Roosevelt accepted an offer to expand the Scouting program in his home state as the chairman of the Scout Committee of Greater New York.

Roosevelt meets with BSA's *Annual Report* delegation at the White House in February 1937.

Roosevelt inspects the Bear Mountain Scout Camp in 1921. This was the last photograph of him walking unassisted.

Assigned to organize any and all program activities in the city, Roosevelt threw himself into his volunteer work. Scouting had put on a national service effort during the First World War that President Woodrow Wilson had described as "splendid," enticing Roosevelt to help expand its local reach. In summer 1921, he organized New York City's large celebration called the "Water Hike."

With some 5,000 Scouts taking part, festivities began with a visit to the General Grant National Memorial in Manhattan (better known as Grant's Tomb) and a parade review led by New York City Mayor John Francis Hylan. Afterward, selected Scouts set off on an all-day trip up the Hudson River to Bear Mountain Scout Camp with Scout officials and friends of the Boy Scouts of America to inspect the eighteen campsites that served 2,100 local Boy Scouts.

To get there, Roosevelt's volunteers chartered the largest boat in the "White Fleet" of the Hudson Navigation Company. Upon docking, the contingent walked up to the Bear Mountain camp. Leading the reception committee was Roosevelt himself with Chief Scout Executive James

E. West, BSA Executive Board member George D. Pratt, and *New York Evening Mail* publisher Henry L. Stoddard.

Throughout a day filled with speeches, parades, demonstrations of knot-tying, a bonfire, and a fried chicken dinner, Chairman Roosevelt "led his guests around the camp, hiking through campsites, talking about their Scouting activities, and showing off the numerous teepee tents resting on built-up wooden platforms."

After a wonderful and successful event, he departed for New York City, and then, one week later, for the family vacation home on Campobello Island in New Brunswick, Canada, just over the American border.

But at Campobello tragedy struck.

Soon after arriving, Roosevelt greeted his five children with an afternoon of activities that included a cruise on his sailing boat in the Bay of Fundy. Strangely, he began to show poor muscle coordination, suddenly slipping off the side of the boat. Undaunted, Roosevelt returned to the house and retired for the evening.

The next morning, he felt strange. An odd chill ran through his body, regardless of whether he was in motion or sitting, and he felt extremely tired. When Roosevelt awoke the following day, he was unable to walk—his left leg buckled under him—and he was running a fever of 102 degrees Fahrenheit. Unknowingly, Franklin Roosevelt had contracted either the Guillain-Barre Syndrome virus (a disease that causes the body's cells to attack themselves resulting in lost muscle control) or the poliomyelitis virus, known then as infantile paralysis, but today as polio.

His life had changed forever.

The following years would greatly try his spirit as he struggled to accept his disability and life in a wheelchair. Though it was not easy, the future 32nd president of the United States maintained his association with BSA by continuing to do volunteer work as president of the Boy Scout Foundation of Greater New York and helping to establish the Ten Mile River Scout Camp.

Roosevelt re-entered politics in dramatic fashion during the 1928 Democratic National Convention. Selected to nominate "Happy Warrior" Alfred E. Smith as the nominee for president against Republican Herbert Hoover, Roosevelt decided he would walk to the podium at all cost. With help from son Elliott, he did just that—with smiles and waves to distract the attention of convention-goers (and the press) from missteps.

That year, Roosevelt was elected 44th governor of New York, setting the stage for his eventual run for the presidency against Hoover four years later.

Resulting from his inward courage and devoted service to Scouting over the previous 15 years, BSA managers presented him with the 46th Silver Buffalo Award in 1930—the same year President Hoover was so honored.

AT ROOSEVELT'S PRESIDENTIAL Inaugural celebration on March 4, 1933, in addition to the thousands of Scouts requested to be present at the ceremonies, the president-elect requested four specially selected Eagle Scouts to be with him on the reviewing stand as well as "on the plaza in front of the Capital." To comply, BSA's proud Chief Scout Executive James E. West sent word out to all the council presidents to send their best Scouts to Washington regardless of race, religion, or creed for the grand service project.

Franklin Roosevelt was pleased as he believed in human equality as well. Later as the nation's chief executive, Roosevelt appointed the first Jewish Secretary of the Treasury in the person of Henry Morganthau Jr., the son of the prominent New York real estate mogul and diplomat. Morganthau's most significant contribution was the formulation, sale, and marketing of War Bonds to finance America's entry into World War II.

In July 1938, Roosevelt nominated another man of Jewish faith, jurist Felix Frankfurter, to the position of Associate Justice of the U.S. Supreme Court. Frankfurter was known for his assistance in founding the American Civil Liberties Union. At the time, a staggering 15 percent of President Roosevelt's high office appointments were Jewish, compared to only 3 percent of the American population practicing that faith.

On June 25, 1941, Roosevelt signed Executive Order 8802 that created the Fair Employment Practices Committee—now regarded as one of the most important pieces of legislation for civil rights since the end of the Civil War and the ensuing Reconstruction period in American history. In declaring racial discrimination in the defense industry as patently illegal, it was the first piece of federal action that promoted equal opportunity in the workplace.

"There is evidence available that needed workers have been barred from industries engaged in defense production solely because of considerations of race, creed, color or national origin, to the detriment of workers' morale and of national unity," it read. "I do hereby reaffirm the policy of the United States that there shall be no discrimination in the employment of workers in defense industries or government because of race, creed, color, or national origin, and I do hereby declare that it is the duty of employers and of labor organizations, in furtherance of said policy and of this order, to provide for the full and equitable participation of all workers in defense industries, without discrimination because of race, creed, color, or national origin."

IN 1934, A NATIONAL BSA COMMITTEE was formed to manage Scouting's growth among Japanese immigrants on the West Coast as well as with the national Native American and Hispanic programs.

"A great number of very excellent troops are organized under Japanese leadership," declared BSA's executive board in the 1934 *Annual Report,* "and a considerable number of Japanese boys are found in troops with white boys"—another remarkable revelation at the time.

The nation's Chinese American Scouts were added to the committee's oversight the following year.

By that time, BSA was intensely aware of the importance of recruiting minorities as suggested in a report commissioned by national Scout executives from 1934–35 in "making careful study and considerable experimentation on the best methods of developing work among [these] nationality groups." It was decided that emphasis would be put on developing the parents of "foreign-born" boys as well as the sons born of "foreign-born" parents to promote the values of Scouting through distinctive leadership training opportunities designed especially for each ethnic group.

For example, BSA's national office offered accolades to a troop of Native American boys from the Theodore Roosevelt Council in Arizona that made the long train ride to the 1937 BSA National Jamboree in Washington, DC. Additionally, Scout executives from BSA's Region IX were proud to showcase their Hopi teepees and "colorful" costumes brought and displayed by them. But a few years later, the nation's social fabric changed for the worst although Scouting's remained steady.

On December 7, 1941, the United States entered World War II after the Empire of Japan attacked American warships in Pearl Harbor. Some immediate actions called for by President Roosevelt included the mandatory rounding-up

Roosevelt accepts the 5 millionth copy of BSA's *Handbook* at the White House in February 1935.

of all Japanese citizens living in the United States and moving them to special internment camps. BSA's goals, however, remained unchanged.

Throughout 1942, top Scouting managers moved the program into those camps and expressed its importance to Japanese American boys—now more than ever.

"A significant piece of work is being done in Japanese relocation centers," it was written in BSA's *Annual Report* of 1942, "with fine cooperation on the part of Government leaders and Japanese leaders."

Another positive Scouting development at the time was the creation of BSA's Religious Emblems program as its first faith—Catholic and its Ad Altare Dei medal—was accepted. Although the Ad Altare Dei medal was first awarded in 1926 to Los Angeles Boy Scouts, BSA approved it for official uniform wear in 1939—a highly successful move that resulted in the program's expansion to the Lutheran medal in 1943, the Jewish medal in 1944, and several other Protestant denomination medals a year later.

As president, Roosevelt supported BSA through an annual radio declaration in celebration of Scouting's birthday. Nearly every February during his administration, Roosevelt offered his glowing congratulations for the accomplishments of Scouting and offered his best wishes for its continuation as America's most successful youth development organization.

"I hope that the people who are listening to my voice will give careful heed to this Scout Oath," Roosevelt told the nation in February 1935. "It is the basis of good citizenship."

A few months later, Roosevelt and the nation's capital prepared to open its proverbial doors to the national and international delegates for BSA's first National Jamboree. But when sudden polio contagion fears emerged in the city, the landmark event was cancelled and rescheduled for the summer of 1937.

FROM JUNE 30 through July 9, 1937, Washington, DC, was abuzz with activity as the nation's capital played host to the 25,000 Scouts that had descended upon the city in celebration of youth and leadership.

Roosevelt being inducted into BSA's national honor society, the Order of the Arrow, at Camp Man of the Ten Mile River Scout Reservation in August 1933.

Roosevelt admires the Eagle medal of Franklin St. John of New York during the 1st National Jamboree in July 1937.

As reported in the event's official history book, the base of the Washington Monument featured "Scouts from everywhere [who] met each other all together for the first thrill of such a meeting."

Two days before the jamboree ended, on July 7, organizers staged a parade that included President Roosevelt himself, Chief Scout Executive James E. West, and National Scout Commissioner Dan Beard, escorted by specially selected Eagle Scouts. With all three dignitaries riding in the back seat of an open-air automobile, they greeted the throngs of Scouts, Scouters, and visitors with waves and salutations.

Roosevelt, donning a light-colored jacket and white hat, reveled in the adulation. His participation launched a tradition that continues today — formal presidential recognition of BSA's National Jamboree through official communication or personal attendance.

THE YEAR 1942 brought a new set of challenges that BSA had not experienced since 1917—supporting a second national war effort. In response to Japan's bombing of Pearl Harbor in December 1941, Roosevelt called on all Americans to work together for victory. Eagerly coming to the aid of the country were 1.5 million Cub and Boy Scouts. West pledged to Roosevelt "the full and whole-hearted co-operation of our organization."

Once again, BSA became the primary means of leaflet and poster distribution for the Office of War Information Department as no one knew their communities better than the legions of local Boy Scouts. Furthermore, these boys were clean-cut and polite, and, thereby, could easily convince business owners to participate. As a result, thousands of posters went up in storefronts nationally to recruit new soldiers and promote valued material collection drives. Every two weeks, new posters went out to replace the old ones and Boy Scouts led the charge.

Among other national service projects, Boy Scouts and Cub Scouts led drives to collect aluminum and other scrap metals, waste paper, clothing, and rubber. They planted trees and tended to gardens. They served as local messengers and dispatch bearers, sold Defense Bonds and Stamps, and collected musical instruments for servicemen in Army camps.

Though President Roosevelt did not live to see the end of World War II, he witnessed first-hand the power of the Scouting Movement.

"I have always been a staunch believer in Scouting," he declared in 1943. "Now, in time of war, as your honorary president, I urge everyone connected with Scouting, boys and men, to see to it that Scouting is maintained at its full strength and effectiveness as a practical contribution to the war effort."

The Boy Scouts of America was entering its golden age.

Industry must take the initiative in opening the doors of employment to all loyal and qualified workers regardless of race, national origin, religion, or color.

MEMORANDUM, JUNE 12, 1941

I firmly believe that the Boy Scout Movement represents a new era of moral force in America.

FRANKLIN D. ROOSEVELT, WASHINGTON, DC, JUNE 2, 1933

[The Boy Scouts of America] is based on cooperation—you know what that means. It is based on the spirit of service.

ADDRESS, TEN MILE RIVER SCOUT CAMP, NEW YORK, AUGUSET 23, 1933

When you get right down to it, the National Recovery Act (NRA) is based on the same fundamentals that Scouting is based on. In other words, trying to do something for the other fellow and not trying to do somebody wrong.

Boys' Life, FEBRUARY 1934

This is what Scouting achieves:

It inculcates in the boy a definite sense of civic responsibility.
It develops respect for the rights of others.
It places the interest on honor and decency.
It is constructive prevention.
But is not prevention rather than correction the solution of the crime problem?
GIVE THE BOY SCOUTING!

Boys' Life, FEBRUARY 1934

Summed up in one sentence, the aim of Scouting is to build up better citizenship. I believe that we are contributing greatly to that objective.

RADIO ADDRESS, WASHINGTON, DC, FEBRUARY 10, 1934

The ideals of Scouting are not simply ideals for boys. They are ideals for men. For the ideal of service to others can never be outgrown, however often it may be lost sight of by some.

ADDRESS, "INVITATION TO THE BOY SCOUT JAMBOREE,"
WASHINGTON, DC, FEBRUARY 8, 1937

As one who has been interested in Scouting over many years, it has been most heartening to have so many evidences of the practical values of Scout training. We must remember that next to active military service itself, there is no higher opportunity for serving our country than helping youth to carry on in their efforts to make themselves physically strong, mentally awake, and morally straight, and prepared to help their country to the full in time of war, as well as in time of peace. We must make sure that those volunteer agencies, which are supplementing the church, the home, and the school by providing programs that will help equip the present generation to cope with life problems in the difficult days ahead, are maintained to their maximum capacity and effectiveness.

AS QUOTED IN MURRAY, *History of the Boy Scouts of America*

The future basis of international goodwill must rest on mutual understanding and loyalty to high [Scouting] ideals.

LETTER, FRANKLIN D. ROOSEVELT TO BSA PRESIDENT WALTER W. HEAD,
"FOURTH WORLD JAMBOREE," JULY 20, 1933

Ours is the duty to inculcate in the Scout mind those simple but fundamental principles which embrace strength of body, alertness of mind and, above these and growing out of them, that sense of moral responsibility upon which all sound character rests.

RADIO ADDRESS, WASHINGTON, DC, FEBRUARY 8, 1939

I like to think that faithful observance of the Scout Oath constitutes an excellent preliminary training in the duties of citizenship. I like to think of the entire Scout training as an apprenticeship for the mastery of civic duties.

RADIO ADDRESS, WASHINGTON, DC, FEBRUARY 8, 1939

TRUMAN

33RD PRESIDENT OF THE UNITED STATES

1945–1953

Born: May 8, 1884, Lamar, Missouri
Died: December 26, 1972, Kansas City, Missouri

Wife: Elizabeth Virginia "Bess" Wallace (m. 1919)
Children: Mary Margaret

Education: Independence High School, Missouri
         No college degree

BSA Positions: Hon. President (1945–1953)
             Hon. Vice President (1953–1972)
             Volunteer, Missouri

BSA Honors: Harry S. Truman Reservoir at the H. Roe Bartle Scout
             Reservation, Heart of America Council, BSA,
             Kansas City, Missouri
             172nd Silver Buffalo (1950)
             Attended the 2nd BSA National Jamboree, Valley Forge,
             Pennsylvania (1950)
             Harry S. Truman Trail & Medal, Independence, Missouri

Eagle Scout Awards presented (1945–1952): 84,540

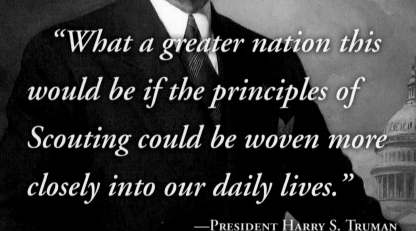

"*What a greater nation this would be if the principles of Scouting could be woven more closely into our daily lives.*"

—PRESIDENT HARRY S. TRUMAN
June 30, 1950

CHAPTER 8

HARRY S. TRUMAN
Valley Forge or Bust

"His fortitude never wavered, and his faith in America never flagged."

—PRESIDENT RICHARD M. NIXON
December 26, 1972

O N THE EVENING OF JUNE 30, 1950, the 47,000 Scouts attending the Boy Scouts of America's (BSA) 2nd National Jamboree at Valley Forge, Pennsylvania, were abuzz with anticipation of the arrival of the president of the United States. The last jamboree had been held thirteen years earlier, but due to the outbreak of World War II and the aftermath of reconstruction, the second muster had been delayed.

Boys themselves wondered if Truman actually would come to their massive campsite. Only four days before, President Truman had ordered U.S. air and sea forces to the Korean Peninsula to aid South Korea in its defense against the Communist forces of North Korea, which had invaded across the 38th Parallel—the line of demarcation established as the post-World War II border between the two Koreas.

The president's schedule filled-up quickly with meetings with members of the Joint Chiefs of Staff, Congress, and international advisors. But even in the midst of a new war, President Truman left the White House at the end of that week and boarded a train at Washington's Union Station that would take him to Valley Forge and thousands of waiting Boy Scouts.

Truman arrived at the campground at 9 p.m., took the stage five minutes later, and addressed the boys. Beginning with a brief account of George Washington's encampment in Valley Forge during the winter of 1777, the president alluded to the aggression taking place overseas.

"If we are to succeed in our common struggle for peace," he said, "we must know and work with these freedom-loving people of other countries."

He hoped this jamboree would encourage "cooperative human action" among nations.

Truman speaks to Scouts at the 2nd National Jamboree in June 1950.

Truman meets with BSA's *Annual Report* delegation in February 1952.

At 9:45, Truman climbed back aboard the presidential train and left for Philadelphia's Municipal Station, where he stepped off and motored to the Philadelphia Naval Yard for his return to Washington aboard the *USS Williamsburg.*

Truman's undaunted visit underscored the positive impact Scouting was having on the nation's youth. He understood as had the presidents before him that within BSA's membership rolls were assembled the best young men that the country could produce.

But Truman's appreciation of the Boy Scouts had began many years earlier when he was a candidate for county judge in his home ground of eastern Missouri after his haberdashery business (a men's clothing store)— failed.

Had Truman been a better entrepreneur in 1921, he might never have been approached by the Pendergast brothers (the political bosses of Jackson County and Kansas City) to run for office. By the 1920s, they controlled the entire political machine for the election of local Democratic politicians with Michael Pendergast in the eastern portion of Jackson County and Thomas Pendergast in the west. Having an open judgeship to fill, the brothers made an unexpected call on a clothing salesman, who was standing alone in his empty shop.

HARRY TRUMAN WAS an intuitive and honest gentleman from the rural portion of the county, who understood what his fellow farmers wanted in their officials: independence.

"He was a Baptist and Mason and former farmer who had spent most of his life in the country," writes biographer Robert H. Ferrell. "[He] had relatives there and was well known."

Truman also was a veteran, which carried political weight in the period following the First World War. The brothers believed veterans would support his candidacy, which would make up the bulk of his base of support. Agreeably, in March 1922 Truman announced his candidacy for county judge in front of the Robert M. Clure Post of the American Legion near Independence, Jackson County, Missouri.

By law he was allowed to spend a maximum of $800, of which $525 already had been spent on fifteen thousand Jackson County maps. To raise larger crowds, candidate Truman depended on local Boy Scouts—especially John Woodhouse, the chief bugler of the local Boy Scout Drum and Bugle Corps.

Woodhouse earned two dollars a night for six bugle performances over a two-week span. Candidate Truman would transport him and a second Scout to and from rallys.

According to eyewitness accounts, the two uniformed Scouts would start at one end of the town and march through to the other with Woodhouse blowing "First Call," followed by "Reveille," "Mess Call," "Assembly," and finally, "To the Colors." The second Scout walked behind bearing sandwich boards that announced the time and venue of Truman's next stump speech—usually at a "schoolhouse or Methodist church." Typically, he met the boys at a predetermined spot along the route and all three finished the march together.

Once elected to public office, Truman was a man of principle, integrity, and weighed both sides of an issue before rendering a decision.

Acceding to the presidency upon Franklin Roosevelt's death in April 1945, Truman concerned himself with civil rights, and even sent a civil right agenda to Congress for passage into law in February 1948. It laid the base for future executive orders for the uplifting of the nation's minority citizens.

Through Executive Order 9981, issued on July 26, 1948, President Truman desegregated the U.S. Armed Forces with the calculated sweep of his pen that sent shock waves across the country and initiated the civil rights movement of the 1950s and 1960s.

A following Executive Order made it a crime to discriminate against a person solely based on their race, when applying for a civil service job.

Executive Order 10308 issued on December 3, 1951, created the Committee on Government Contract Compliance that oversaw the non-discriminatory nature of race when involved with awarding of federal defense contracts.

All three Orders eventually helped create the legal base for governmental enforcement for those seeking to obtain equal rights under the law during the Civil Right Movement. To BSA's credit, it already was a racially diverse organization dating back to its earliest years, a fact not lost on Truman.

Regularly, the president welcomed BSA's delegation of Scouts that presented the organization's *Annual Report to the Nation*, as well as inviting special Eagle Scouts to participate in the lighting of the National Christmas Tree in Washington.

Seeking re-election during the 1948 presidential race, Truman invoked the organization in local speeches. Arriving by train for a campaign stop in Idaho Falls, Idaho, Truman was greeted by one of the town's "impressive" Eagle Scouts.

"He has all the merit badges that it is possible to get, I think," Truman said. "He is a fine looking young man."

And in giving a boost to the upcoming Scout Rally and Circus show to be held in Idaho Falls, Truman reminded his audience that he was very proud to be the Honorary President of the Boy Scouts of America.

AT THE TIME, BSA was entrenched in advancing minority Scouting opportunities utilizing strategic partnerships and basic grassroots recruiting.

In 1947, Region IX executives held its first Annual Negro Scouters' Conference in Dallas, Texas, with several hundred men attending. Three years later, Region IX awarded its first Silver Antelope medal "for outstanding regional service to boyhood" to an African American Scouter in Texas. Only eight years prior in 1932, the first African American Scouter had received a Silver Beaver award for outstanding service to youth on a council level.

By 1952, BSA managers expressed a clear desire to take Scouting even further by modifying the program to include "handicapped" boys and "underprivileged" boys. These handicapped lads had received much attention from their impressive service performed during the national "Get Out to Vote" National Good Turn—over 300 special units had provided Scouts for the cause making it "a happy and worthwhile experience."

Also occurring this year, BSA altered Eagle Scout requirements for these young men by allowing certain substitutions with regard to capabili-

Truman meets with BSA's *Annual Report* delegation in the Oval Office in February 1951.

Truman meets with BSA's *Annual Report* delegation at the White House in February 1950.

ties but holding strong that such action never implied "any lack of ability on the part of the Scout to take care of himself and serve others."

The so-called "underprivileged" boy program received attention as well, as many former Scouts were returning home and "assuming leadership in the organization of Scouting in their own neighborhoods."

Now dubbed "Rural Scouting," it expanded from "underprivileged" youth into society-labeled "juvenile delinquents" and "socially slow" young men in need.

BY THE TIME Truman's second term began in 1949, BSA was well into its two-year campaign to promote the organization's Fortieth Anniversary bearing the slogan "Strengthen the Arm of Liberty" referring to the right arm of the Statue of Liberty holding aloft her flaming torch of freedom.

From 1949 to 1952, Scouts, Councils, and townships across the United States raised money to purchase and dedicate some 200 copper, 8-foot-tall, miniature statues known as "Little Sisters of Liberty." Manufactured at a cost of about $3,500 apiece, these replicas of the Statue of Liberty standing in New York Harbor began popping up in public squares across the country—especially in the Midwest.

"This should be a proud day for Wyoming," shouted Governor Arthur Crane in the state capital of Cheyenne during an unveiling ceremony. "First, there are patriotic citizens who voluntarily give of their time to guide and direct the Scouts of Cheyenne and vicinity. Secondly, there are youthful citizens faithfully following the Scout Oath. Thirdly, they have chosen the objective for the year, 'Strengthen the Arm of Liberty.'"

IN RECALLING TRUMAN'S campaign speech in Nampa, Idaho, in 1950, Truman declared: "I understand today the Boy Scouts are sponsoring the dedication of a replica of the Statue of Liberty in Nampa. That is a wonderful thing—that is a wonderful thing."

"In this fortieth anniversary of Scouting in America," the president continued, "It is certainly fitting that the Boy Scouts are carrying on a crusade to 'Strengthen the Arm of Liberty.' I congratulate you on your enterprise that you are putting on here."

He advised the Nampa crowd that he was unsure if he could make the upcoming 2nd BSA National Jamboree that summer since "the president never can tell where he will be."

But he did.

And as a token of gratitude from BSA, President Harry S. Truman was awarded the 172nd Silver Buffalo award on that evening of June 30 in Valley Forge—an acknowledgment of his longstanding and immeasurable service to Scouting.

Discrimination, like a disease, must be attacked wherever it appears.
LETTER, TRUMAN TO CHARLES G. BOLTE, SEPTEMBER 4, 1946

The Boy Scouts of America, since it was founded in 1910, has contributed greatly to the character training of our youth. What a greater nation this would be if the principles of Scouting could be woven more closely into our daily lives.
ADDRESS, VALLEY FORGE, PA, JUNE 30, 1950

Boy Scouts of America is making a vital contribution to the character-building of our boys and young men. Let us work together to make the program of the Boy Scouts available to every American boy.
ADDRESS, VALLEY FORGE, PA, JUNE 30, 1950

I have said to the [Boy Scouts] that come to see me … that I would give anything in the world if I were a 16-year-old boy now, because then I could live to see the next 50 years. We think we have done great things in the last 50 years, but it will be nothing compared with what will be done in the next 50 years.
ADDRESS, WASHINGTON, DC, FEBRUARY 13, 1952

If we can impress upon our youth principles of friendliness and mutual respect, we shall go a long way toward establishing a better understanding among the nations of the world.
AS QUOTED ON WWW.SCOUTING.ORG

DWIGHT D.

EISENHOWER

34ᵀᴴ PRESIDENT OF THE UNITED STATES

1953–1961

Born: October 14, 1890 Denison, Texas
Died: March 28, 1969 Washington, DC

Wife: Mary Geneva "Mamie" Doud (m. 1916)
Children: Doud Dwight, John Sheldon Doud

Education: U.S. Military Academy (B.S.)
Supreme Allied Commander in Europe (1943–1945)
General of the Army (1944)

BSA Positions: Hon. President (1953–1961)
Hon. Vice President (1961–1969)
BSA Executive Board (1948–1969)
National Court of Honor member (1951–1969)
Father of one Boy Scout

BSA Honors: General Eisenhower Waste Paper Campaign Medal (1945)
General Eisenhower Unit Award (75mm shell container
from the European battle field) (1945)
Gold Medal for the Waste Paper Campaign (1946)
137th Silver Buffalo (1946)
Attended 2nd BSA National Jamboree, Valley Forge, PA
(1950)
Sent Recorded Message to the 3rd BSA National Jamboree,
Irvine Ranch, California (1953)
Sent Written Message due to illness to 4th BSA National
Jamboree, Valley Forge, Pennsylvania (1957)
Attended the 5th BSA National Jamboree, Colorado
Springs, Colorado (1960)
President Eisenhower Jubilee Streamer (1960)

Eagle Scout Awards presented (1953–1960): 125,692

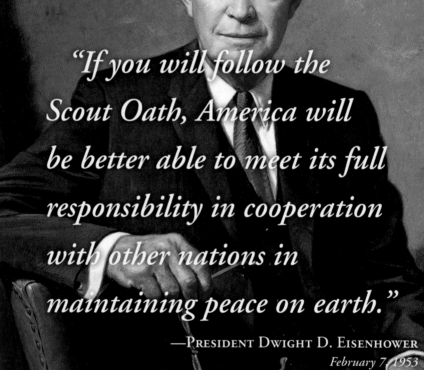

"If you will follow the Scout Oath, America will be better able to meet its full responsibility in cooperation with other nations in maintaining peace on earth."

—PRESIDENT DWIGHT D. EISENHOWER
February 7, 1953

CHAPTER NINE

DWIGHT D. EISENHOWER

We Love Ike

"As long as men cherish their freedom, Dwight Eisenhower will stand with them."

PRESIDENT RICHARD M. NIXON

March 28, 1969

G ENERAL DWIGHT D. EISENHOWER, the Supreme Commander of Allied Forces in Europe during World War II, was the most popular American alive in 1945. He was so beloved that President Harry S. Truman offered to stand down as the Democratic nominee for president and run for vice president on Eisenhower's ticket should the general enter the race for the White House as a Democrat.

Putting off that decision until 1951, Eisenhower won election as a Republican under the slogan, "I Like Ike." But to Boy Scouts across the

nation, they preferred "We Love Ike" because he was "one of them."

As a duty-minded man who answered his country's call to war, General Eisenhower became partners with the Boy Scouts of America (BSA) to get much-needed supplies to his troops overseas. The result was the General Eisenhower Waste Paper Campaign Medal and

Eisenhower meets with BSA's *Annual Report* delegation in February 1955.

the General Eisenhower Unit Award—two powerful symbols of Scout volunteerism in the mid-1940s.

In the April 1945 issue of BSA's official magazine, *Boys' Life*, the organization announced its intent to collect 150,000 tons of waste paper for the war effort but they gathered more than twice that amount as a result of the Eisenhower Medal campaign's 300,000 recipients. At the time, any Boy Scout, Senior Scout, or Cub Scout who collected a half ton (1,000 pounds) of scrap paper qualified for the award.

"This is an individual award for an outstanding personal achievement," declared *Boys' Life*.

Scout units that met the requirements received a spent shell casing container made from collected waste paper that had been used in the European theater of war and a printed citation from Eisenhower himself that read,

> *To the Boy Scouts of America –*
>
> *You were asked by the War Production Board to do a vital job and you have come through like a real soldier. My sincere thanks to every Scout and Cub.*
>
> *Signed, Dwight D. Eisenhower*
> *General of the Army*
> *Supreme Allied Commander*
> *30 April 1945*

Eisenhower greets the crowd at the 1960 National Jamboree.

Described as "a thrilling type of permanent display in your meeting place," thousands of Scout units began collecting waste paper in March and April 1945. An appreciative BSA presented the general with a gold medal of thanks later in December.

"I accept this medal from all the Boy Scouts of America," he wrote. "And I shall cherish it."

That would be the first award of many that BSA would present him over the coming years.

At BSA's thirty-sixth National Annual Meeting held at the Hotel Jefferson in St. Louis, Missouri, on May 17, 1946, national Scouting managers awarded Eisenhower the 137th Silver Buffalo Medal for his work with youth, that included his notable membership on BSA's Executive Board.

Yet Eisenhower's association with BSA was just beginning.

By 1950, Eisenhower was a member of the BSA National Court of Honor. As an admired supporter of the program, he was asked to address Boy Scouts at their 2nd National Jamboree at Valley Forge, Pennsylvania.

As a tactical military expert, he recognized the gravity of the situation shaping up on the Korean Peninsula and used the international jamboree platform to promote national patriotism and condemn the advance of the Northern Communist forces of North Korea into the South.

"The American flag represents what the multitudes of humanity have yearned for through the ages—friendship among men, liberty for men, justice toward men," he extolled. "America, under God, is a way of life ruled by the eternal truths of human brotherhood, human dignity, human rights."

Scouts and their leaders rose to their feet in support of his remarks, confirming his popularity among some of the best and most loyal workers in the country. Eighteen months later, Dwight D. Eisenhower was elected the 34th president of the United States.

AT HIS FIRST State of the Union address to Congress in 1952, President Eisenhower announced his intention to solidly enforce former President Harry S. Truman's Executive Orders desegregating the nation's capital and the U.S. military stating, "I propose to use whatever authority exists in the office of the President to end segregation in the District of Columbia, including the Federal Government, and any segregation in the Armed Forces."

Within Washington, DC, the president requested that two additional District Commissioners of color be added to the city's governing body "to broaden representation of all elements of our local population."

Another time when challenged by South Carolina Governor James F. Byrnes regarding racial *inequality*, Eisenhower responded, "I believe it is incumbent upon us to make constant and distinct progress toward eliminating those things that all of us would class as unjust and unfair. In this category there clearly falls, to my mind, the right to equal consideration in Federal employment, regardless of race or color."

On September 9, 1957, President Eisenhower signed the nation's first Civil Rights Act into law. As the first since the nation's post-Civil War Reconstruction period, it worked as a voting rights bill. Eisenhower also set up the Civil Rights Division in the Justice Department as well as the Commission of Civil Rights in the office of the U.S. Attorney General. They oversaw the enforcement of this legislation without regard for one's race, color, faith, or national origin.

Within three weeks, Eisenhower's dedication to desegregation was tested again with the integration of Little Rock's (Arkansas) Central High School for nine black students (one of which was African American Eagle Scout Ernest Green). As mob rule took over the city in protest of the legal decision, Eisenhower sent in federal troops to ensure the desegregation action was upheld as declared by the Supreme Court in 1955's landmark ruling in *Brown v. Board of Education*.

"A foundation of our American way of life is our national respect for law," Eisenhower announced to the nation on September 24, 1957.

On September 25, rising civil rights leader Martin Luther King Jr. sent the president a telegram offering his "sincere support" to "restore law and order in Little Rock." Eisenhower responded, "I share your confidence that Americans everywhere remain devoted to our tradition of adherence to orderly processes of law."

Three years later on May 6, President Eisenhower signed the Civil Rights Act of 1960, thereby eliminating loopholes contained in the earlier law.

OVER THE SAME time period, BSA was performing great deeds as well. Now truly focused on providing a quality program to special-needs boys, the National Council touted those that had advanced to the rank of Eagle Scout utilizing appropriately substituted requirements.

"Fourteen Life Scouts became Eagles under this plan in 1953," crowed top BSA officials, "and in most cases the substitute requirements exceed the regular requirements in difficulty."

A few years later in its January 1955 issue, *Boys' Life* published a story titled, "Lion Hearts in Iron Lungs," about boys living in iron lungs that refuse to give up on their Scouting goals.

And in another success, the well-known African American magazine, *Ebony*, endorsed BSA as its managers allowed 1,000 African American Scouts to attend its 3rd National Jamboree in 1953.

"Through Scouting activities," declared *Ebony*, "a lot is done toward bettering relations between people of different races, creeds, and religious faiths."

By 1954 (and way ahead of the nation) there were several racially integrated Boy Scout troops—mostly in the north but inclusive of one located in the deep south. Effectively, the southern dubbed "separate but equal" rule had fallen within the ranks of the Boy Scouts of America. However, full southern state troop integration would have to wait until 1974.

In 1958, further work within the Native American population allowed BSA to receive an enthusiastic endorsement from the Navajo Tribal Council as their boys had had "a very successful experience … with Scouting."

Reported BSA officials, "Representatives of the two largest Sioux tribes, the Oglala Sioux and the Rosebud Sioux of South Dakota, expressed the hope that these groups might cooperatively be able to develop resources necessary to make similar projects possible with their people."

Further BSA activities included the formation of the Buddhist Relations Committee at national BSA headquarters, as there were currently 67 troops chartered to the Buddhist church with "a manual on the subject of Scouting" being produced for them.

As Alaska became the 49th state in January 1959, the Interracial Service Division was expanded to include the development of Scouting for Eskimo boys.

BSA's 1959 *Annual Report* also published a story about a Yakima Indian medicine man, Nipo Strongheart, who was a great supporter of Scouting and its national honor society, the Order of the Arrow, that was based on Indian lore and its study.

"I'm glad that my white brothers are helping to maintain the Indian culture my people have been striving to keep for many years," he said.

The membership and popularity of the Order of the Arrow had been expanding yearly since its establishment in 1915 but especially since its official adoption and endorsement by BSA's executive board in 1948. As such, specially chosen Boy Scouts were dressing, dancing, and performing the Order's induction ceremonies attired as Native American figures.

By the golden anniversary National Jamboree of 1960 that was held in Irvine, California, "the great national denominations of America and many of the smaller denominations conducted religious services there"—thus formally reinforcing Scouting's devotion to one's religious independence and its importance. On the Sunday of the Jamboree, over twelve thousand Catholic boys attended services while thirty thousand Protestant boys did the same.

INSPIRED BY SCOUTING'S own pledge to promote human equality and national duty, Eisenhower availed himself to Boy Scout representatives

Eisenhower laughs with Scouts at the 1950 National Jamboree.

each year. Every February, specially selected BSA members, one from each of the organization's 12 Regions, made their annual pilgrimage to the Oval Office to deliver BSA's *Annual Report to the Nation*. Performing the ceremonial acceptance task eight times, the president enjoyed making a glowing statement each occasion in support of Scouting—all of which would be published in the BSA's bound copies of their *Annual Report.*

"Self-development and service to others, independence and good citizenship, a sense of brotherhood and responsiveness to spiritual values—these qualities which Scouting fosters mean much to America," he wrote in his 1955 annual message.

During Eisenhower's last full year as president (1960), BSA celebrated its Fiftieth Anniversary, putting the proverbial exclamation point on its incredible membership explosion during the Eisenhower Administration. And when Eisenhower left office, BSA rolls approached the four-million-member mark.

AS BSA'S HONORARY PRESIDENT, Eisenhower spoke at the fifty-year celebration banquet on June 1, 1960, held at the Sheraton-Park Hotel in Washington, DC—just weeks before the opening of the 5th National Jamboree in Colorado Springs, Colorado.

Addressing the packed banquet room, President Eisenhower discussed his Scouting experiences with his son, John, and spoke about how important he believed it to be for the health of the republic.

"Scouting is indeed doing something for all of us that is not only necessary but I would say vital to our vigor as a nation based upon a religious concept, but is ready to take on its own shoulders its duty with respect to itself, with respect to those that are less fortunate," he said. "Only in this way, in my opinion, is America going to be able to lead the way to that goal that mankind has sought so long, and so far so futilely, a peace with honor and with justice."

TODAY, MANY YEARS after President Dwight D. Eisenhower's death, his Presidential Library and Museum in Abilene, Kansas, runs a program in support of the core values that he and Scouting strove to uphold. Their character-building program centers on the Eisenhower Leadership Patch, which can be earned by both Cubs and Boy Scouts. The Cub objective focuses on character building, while the Boy Scout objective centers on developing quality citizenship.

Composed of a central patch surrounded by six programmatic designs, the Leadership Patch has been earned by thousands of Cub Scouts striving for honesty, respect, responsibility, perseverance, courage, and cooperation. Their Boy Scout counterparts have demonstrated knowledge, dispositions, preparation, participation, protection, and perpetuation.

With each topic lesson tied to some event in Eisenhower's life and career, the patch can only be earned while visiting the Eisenhower Presidential Library and Museum.

IN HIS OWN WORDS

A cardinal ideal in this heritage we cherish is the equality of rights of all citizens of every race and color and creed.

ADDRESS, "STATE OF THE UNION," WASHINGTON, DC
FEBRUARY 2, 1953

I urge you all to live up to the high ideals for which Scouting stands—your duty as patriotic citizens. If you will follow the Scout Oath, America will be better able to meet its full responsibility in cooperation with other nations in maintaining peace on earth.

LETTER, "MESSAGE TO THE BOY SCOUTS OF AMERICA
ON THEIR 43RD ANNIVERSARY," FEBRUARY 7, 1953

The Boy Scout Movement continues to make progress. It yearly enriches our nation, and contributes generously to the economic, physical, and spiritual resources of the country. So I am particularly glad to send congratulations to all of you responsible for this great achievement.

RECORDED MESSAGE, 3RD NATIONAL BOY SCOUT JAMBOREE, IRVINE
RANCH, CA, JULY 17, 1953

America is … grateful for the work of those respected and beloved leaders who, giving freely of their time, transmit to our youth values basic to good citizenship.

ANNUAL MESSAGE TO THE BOY SCOUTS OF AMERICA,
FEBRUARY 1954

I submit that it would be difficult for any political party or any government to state its purposes, at home or abroad, in better terms than mere serious, earnest repetition of the Scout Oath—To do my duty to my God and country.

ADDRESS, THE 44TH NATIONAL COUNCIL MEETING OF THE BOY SCOUTS
OF AMERICA, WASHINGTON, DC, MAY 29, 1954

Self-development and service to others, independence and good citizenship, a sense of brotherhood and responsiveness to spiritual values—these qualities which Scouting fosters mean much to America.

ANNUAL MESSAGE TO THE BOY SCOUTS OF AMERICA, FEBRUARY 1955

Founded on obedience to God and guided by the principles of good citizenship, the Boy Scouts of America have long contributed to the welfare of the land by building young lives strong in body, mind, and spirit.

ANNUAL MESSAGE TO THE BOY SCOUTS OF AMERICA, FEBRUARY 6, 1958

The Boy Scouts play an important part in the life of the national community.

ANNUAL MESSAGE TO THE BOY SCOUTS OF AMERICA, FEBRUARY 5, 1959

Scouting gives training in character. The greatest qualification that any individual can have is to have it said of him, "He's a man of integrity and of real character."

ADDRESS, PENNSYLVANIA STATE UNIVERSITY, JULY 6, 1961

The Boy Scout Movement merits the unstinted support of every American who wants to make his country and his world a better place in which to live. Its emphasis on community service and tolerance and world friendship promotes a speedier attainment of the enduring peace among men for which we all strive. By developing among its members both a spirit of sturdiness, self-reliance, and a realization of the need for cooperative effort in every major enterprise, the movement is a prime force in preparing tomorrow's men for their duty to themselves, their country, and their world. Here in the United States, the Boy Scouts of America have accomplished much in its years of service. But today, more than ever before, we need expansion of its membership and influence.

AS QUOTED AT WWW.SCOUTING.ORG

JOHN F.

KENNEDY

35TH PRESIDENT OF THE UNITED STATES

1961–1963

Born: May 29, 1917 Brookline, Massachusetts
Died: November 22, 1963—Dallas, Texas

Wife: Jacqueline Lee Bouvier (m. 1953)
Children: Caroline Bouvier, John Fitzgerald, Jr., Patrick Bouvier

Education: Harvard College (B.S.)

BSA Positions: Hon. President (1961–1963)
Star Scout, Troop 2, Bronxville, New York
Volunteer, Boston Council, BSA (1946–1955)
District Vice Chairman
Executive Board member (4+ years)
Vice President (1 year)
National Council Representative (2 years)

Eagle Scout Awards presented (1961–1963): 78,246

"*Training and associations of Boy Scout life are invaluable to the individual development of young men and to the quality of community life.*"

—PRESIDENT JOHN F. KENNEDY
February 1962

CHAPTER TEN

JOHN F. KENNEDY

The Boy Scout in Camelot

"John F. Kennedy has fought the good fight for the God-given rights of his fellow man."

CARDINAL RICHARD CUSHING
November 25, 1963

THE YEAR 1961 OPENED with enormous promise for the United States of America. The previous November, voters had elected a forty-two-year-old senator from Massachusetts as their next president. With youthful vigor and a glamorous family, John F. Kennedy's era in the White House became known as "Camelot," harking back to the mythical days of Arthurian legend when knights adorned in shining armor fought man and beast in defense of honor, virtue, and integrity.

But for the Boy Scouts of America (BSA), the election of John F. Kennedy marked a watershed moment in its history—a former Boy Scout now occupied the Oval Office. Until then, no elected president ever had participated in BSA as a youth because most had come of age before its founding in 1910.

Henceforth, this would not be the case.

Recognizing the impact of Scouting across the nation, Kennedy authorized a select group of Boy Scouts to take part in his inauguration ceremonies that January 1961. BSA called it an "historic event" as 2,200 Boy Scouts, Explorers, and leaders stood along the parade route.

"Scouts served in the inaugural route as ushers and grandstand supervisory personnel," lauds BSA's 1961 *Annual Report*. "[Scouts served as] honor guards at the presidential reviewing stand, as orderlies for key government personnel at the presidential balls and other pre-inaugural and inaugural events."

Kennedy meets with BSA's *Annual Report* delegation at the White House in February 1961.

The letter young Jack Kennedy wrote to his father in 1929 asking for a raise in his allowance.

The news anchors of a television network covering the festivities had a 20-minute discussion on the relevance of the Scouting movement and of the new president's long-time Scouting membership and volunteerism. Even the Scouting résumé of Vice President Lyndon B. Johnson was discussed, along with others of similar experience in Kennedy's first cabinet.

"It is a matter of satisfaction to me that all of my cabinet and official family were Scouts as boys with the exception of two who later served in Scouting as Scouters," Kennedy would later say.

Nearly three years later in the months following his untimely assassination in Dallas, Texas, on November 22, 1963, Chief Scout Executive Joseph A. Brunton Jr. would write about Scouting's impact on Kennedy.

IN 1929, TWELVE-YEAR-OLD John "Jack" Kennedy wanted to be a Boy Scout but insisted on paying his own way. Joseph Kennedy, his father, who always expected his children to develop self-sufficiency at an early age, must have been pleased to receive this note from his son.

"My recent allowance is 40 cents. This is used for aeroplanes and other playthings of childhood," wrote Jack, the newest member of Troop 2 in Bronxville, New York. "But now I am a Scout and I put away my childish things ... I have to buy canteens, haversacks, blankets, searchlights, poncho—things that will last for years and I can always use it while I can't use chocolate marshmallow ice cream sundaes and, so I put in my plea for a raise of thirty cents for me to use for Scout things and pay my own way more around."

There is no a record as to whether Joseph Kennedy granted his son's request. But it is plausible that Scouting certainly had a positive impact on the future president.

"Did the fact that young John Kennedy was a Scout make a difference to him—and perhaps to the world?" queries Chief Scout Executive Brunton some years later. "Did the teamwork he learned in his patrol and in his troop make him better able to get along with other people, better prepared to accept responsibilities and carry them out?"

Undoubtedly, Kennedy's early years as a Boy Scout must have helped.

Within two years of joining, Kennedy advanced through the rank of Star Scout before other interests drew him away from the program. But even after leaving the movement, Scouting values stayed with him—especially those of bravery and courageousness in the face of opposition.

In 1957, then Senator Kennedy of Massachusetts won the Pulitzer Prize for literature with his book, *Profiles in Courage*. It recounts vignettes of eight former U.S. senators who showed "extraordinary political courage" during their careers. Citing legendary American writer Ernest Hemingway's concept of "grace under pressure," Kennedy crafted his book through which "honor under pressure" would become a literary classic.

"In a democracy, every citizen, regardless of his interest in politics, 'holds office'; every one of us is in a position of responsibility; and, in the final analysis, the kind of government we get depends upon how we fulfill those responsibilities," writes Kennedy. "We, the people, are the boss, and we will get the kind of political leadership, be it good or bad, that we demand and deserve."

Such important lessons in integrity would propel him into the White House in 1961.

By mid-year, *Profiles in Courage* would be released in a Young Readers Edition, as the lessons that he detailed for adults were just as important to youth—especially Boy Scouts. The September 1961 issue of *Boys' Life* advertised its usefulness in character building to its readership.

"This is about politicians ... who were failures," writes Kennedy in the new edition. "Each had some principle or idea he believed in, and each choose to act according to his beliefs even though to do so meant criticism and often defeat in election."

Today, in celebration of the principles of honor and courage detailed in that book, the John F. Kennedy Presidential Library Foundation presents the Profiles in Courage Award annually. President Gerald R. Ford—the only president to date to earn the Eagle Scout rank—received the award in 2001 for his leadership during the Watergate scandal that resulted in the fall of the Nixon Administration.

WHILE CAMPAIGNING FOR the presidency, Kennedy was a vocal supporter for racial equality and made a point to call on civil rights leader Martin Luther King Jr.'s wife, Coretta, to proclaim his support for her husband's work when he had been arrested for participating in a peaceful demonstration at a department store lunch counter. In an attempt to gain King's release, Kennedy's brother and the nation's attorney general, Robert F. Kennedy, called Georgia Governor Ernest Vandiver to plead the case—an effort that helped shore up the African American voting block for brother John in the 1960 presidential election.

On November 20, 1962, President Kennedy signed Executive Order 11603 that "prohibited the act of racial discrimination in federally supported housing or related facilities."

Executive Order 10980 established the Presidential Commission on the Status of Women to bring notice to issues pertaining to women. The Commission was led by former First Lady Eleanor Roosevelt. In her report issued in October 1963, it noted that women were experiencing workplace discrimination as well as social and cultural barriers. One result was the founding of the National Organization for Women (NOW). Another was the Equal Pay Act of 1963 that made wage disparity illegal based upon gender.

IN 1961, BSA's multi-ethnic Interracial Service Division changed its name to the Urban Relationship Service, as the Scouting movement was now fully engrossed in racial integration and it began to focus on appealing to low-income, low-opportunity inner city youth.

Internal numbers established by BSA's executive board revealed that "72 percent of all the non-white population in America now lives in urban America and 66 percent of America's Spanish-speaking population lives in urban centers. This new approach will continue Scouting's outreach to these groups." Further analysis showed that more Scouting within these areas would combat "growing problems of congested central city districts and slum acres."

The result was a partnership with President Kennedy's Urban Renewal Administration aimed at getting boys living in federal housing

Kennedy meets with BSA's *Annual Report* delegation in February 1963.

Kennedy meets with the "Scouting Family of the Year" in February 1962.

projects to join BSA. The first states addressed were New York and New Jersey. The program was expanded to 37 states by 1962 and "most encouraging results have been reported"—including funding provided by the Sears-Roebuck Foundation for a new national executive to run the national Central City service area.

WHEN KENNEDY RECEIVED BSA's 51st *Annual Report* in February 1961, the organization operated under the slogan, "Strengthen America: Character Counts." There were 1.3 million adult volunteers serving 3 million Scouts across the country. And the national organization was seeking to improve in five areas: expanding boys' opportunities, improving professional leadership, forging more effective districts, generating greater financial support, and improving the service of units.

These objectives matched up well with Kennedy's own belief that modern-day goal-setting could help solve the nation's problems. President Kennedy engaged the Commission on National Goals, which had been set up only a year earlier by President Dwight Eisenhower.

At Kennedy's direction, the Commission acted to "guard the rights of the individual, to ensure his [or] her development, and to enlarge his [or] her opportunity." The report went on to say that the nation was in "grave danger" with Communism expanding around the globe and with one third of the global population already under its control.

Kennedy wanted BSA to promote patriotism and loyalty among Americans, thereby strengthening the country.

BSA resolved to: *Build* a stronger America by leading boys to "good character, participating citizenship, and physical fitness; to *Serve* the cause of democracy by helping boys expand their knowledge and love for country; and to *Achieve* the purposes of Scouting by leading boys to self-sufficiency and a reverence for God.

By the end of the Kennedy Administration in November 1963, 527 local Scouting councils with 1.5 million adult volunteers were serving over 4 million Scout youth.

By emphasizing emergency preparedness in a developing nuclear world, the Kennedy presidency sought to train a new generation of leaders who would take charge in national emergencies. But it also sought to re-invigorate the American spirit of exploration and reinforce the nation's superiority in technological development. The result was the creation of the National Air and Space Administration (NASA), where some of the greatest alumni of American Scouting would proudly serve their country.

The cruel disease of discrimination knows no sectional or state boundaries. The continuing attack on this problem must be equally broad. It must be both private and public—it must be conducted at national, state and local levels— and it must include both legislative and executive action.

ADDRESS, WASHINGTON, DC, FEBRUARY 28, 1963

Training and associations of Boy Scout life are invaluable to the individual development of young men and to the quality of community life. More than 30 million persons have taken an active part in the Scouting movement since its founding. It has been a most valuable influence in our Nation's life, and I know that future energies of the Boy Scouts will add even more to the vigor and strength of our Nation.

LETTER, KENNEDY TO JOSEPH A. BRUNTON JR., FEBRUARY 1962

We are very proud of the Boy Scouts and I am particularly glad that we have so many of them in West Virginia, so many of them in the country. I can't imagine better training for our younger citizens and I hope that this impressive evidence this morning of their strong patriotic feeling will be an inspiration to thousands of other young boys who, themselves, can become Scouts and demonstrate their desire for citizenship and also their strong love of their country.

ADDRESS, "THE WEST VIRGINIA CENTENNIAL CELEBRATION,"
MAY 20, 1963

For more than 50 years, Scouting has played an important part in the lives of the Boy Scouts of this nation. It has helped to mold character, to form friendships, to provide a worthwhile outlet for the natural energies of growing boys, and to train these boys to become good citizens of the future.

AS QUOTED AT WWW.SCOUTING.ORG

In a very real sense, the principles learned and practiced as Boy Scouts add to the strength of America and her ideals.

AS QUOTED AT. WWW.SCOUTING.ORG

LYNDON B.

JOHNSON

36ᵀᴴ President of the United States

1963–1969

Born: August 27, 1908, Stonewall, Texas

Died: January 22, 1973, Stonewall, Texas

Wife: Claudia Alta "Lady Bird" Taylor (m. 1934)

Children: Lynda Bird, Lucy Baines

Education: Southwest Texas State Teachers' College (B.S.)

BSA Positions: Hon. President (1963–1969)

Hon. Vice President (1969–1973)

Volunteer, Capital Area Council, Austin, Texas

Volunteer, National Capital Area Council, Washington,
DC (1959 – 1963)

Founder, Explorer Post 1200 (Chartered by U.S.
House of Representatives for Congressional pages),
Washington, DC

BSA Honors: 296th Silver Buffalo (1964)

Attended the 6th BSA National Jamboree, Valley Forge,
Pennsylvania (1964)

Eagle Scout Awards presented (1964–1968): 143,286

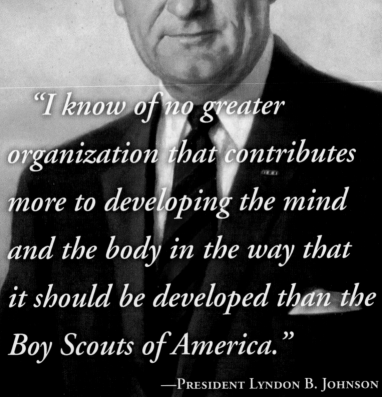

"I know of no greater organization that contributes more to developing the mind and the body in the way that it should be developed than the Boy Scouts of America."

—PRESIDENT LYNDON B. JOHNSON
February 8, 1967

CHAPTER ELEVEN

LYNDON B. JOHNSON
Strengthening America's Heritage

"His immense efforts to help the poor, the sick, and the oppressed stand out as landmarks of America's concern for those too weak to help themselves."
—U.S. SENATOR EDWARD M. KENNEDY
January 23, 1973

"S EE WASHINGTON FIRST" was the cry of Troop 1 of Burlington, New Jersey, in 1913. Their town, situated just 150 miles from the nation's capital, boasted an aggressive unit of twenty-six boys and a Scoutmaster of similar mind. A man of action, Carleton E. Sholl considered Washington as the place for Scouts to vacation due to the "wonderful opportunities for an enjoyable and instructive summer outing at a very small cost."

More importantly, Scoutmaster Sholl, a thirty-year-old real estate agent, who had helped prepare the canoeing section of the 1912 Boy Scout *Handbook*, wrote that the organization should "strive to establish a national Boy Scout memorial of some nature that will give every Scout some special center of interest while visiting the headquarters of the country's government."

Forty-six years later, Sholl's vision became reality.

On July 28, 1959, the Senate of the United States, led by majority leader and long-time Scouting volunteer, Lyndon Baines Johnson, passed Public Law 86-11, authorizing the Boy Scouts of America "to erect a memorial on public grounds in Washington, DC."

The memorial, a tribute to Scouting's promotion of leadership among the nation's young people, was to be erected by friends of the Scouting movement and members past and present by accepting donations of "dimes and nickels and pennies," representing Boy Scouts of America's (BSA) spirit of service to the nation.

By early 1961, BSA's artist search committee had decided on the famed sixty-three-year-old American sculptor, Donald DeLue, whose past work had earned him a commission from the Philadelphia Post Office and two prestigious awards from the National Sculpture Society.

Dedicated on November 7, 1964, the Boy Scout Memorial sits on a site selected by the National Park Service—also the location of the 1st National

Johnson speaks to BSA's *Annual Report* delegation in February 1967.

Johnson accepts a citation in February 1964.

BSA Jamboree held in Washington in 1937. (It is one of a handful of monuments in our nation's capital that commemorates a living *cause* rather than a person or event, and the only one that was paid for solely by private funds.)

In addition to the 5,000 Scouts, Scout leaders, BSA national headquarters staff, and prominent governmental officials, one eminent public servant showed up as well: Associate Supreme Court Justice Tom C. Clark. Clark, appointed by President Harry S. Truman and a long-standing member of the Court, chose this event to celebrate the fiftieth anniversary of his achieving the rank of Eagle Scout in Dallas, Texas, in 1914.

In watching the unveiling team, Justice Clark noted it was "comprised of a Boy Scout, a Cub Scout, and an Explorer," and was especially moved to emotion that day.

The 14-foot-high statue itself is of a Boy Scout walking in front of two large figures, one of a man and one of a woman. The Scout represents "the aspirations of all past, present, and future Scouts throughout the world." The large male figure is the embodiment of physical, moral, and mental fitness along with love for country, loyalty, honor, and courage. He holds a helmet symbolizing masculine work and attire.

The female figure symbolizes "enlightenment with the love of God and fellow man, freedom, and democracy." She bears the eternal flame of God's Holy Spirit. Inscribed upon the statue's large pedestal, set in President's Park on the Ellipse near 15th Avenue and Constitution Avenue next to a reflecting pool, is the Scout Oath and the list of donors.

Though Senator Johnson had ushered through the federal authorization for the memorial through Congress, his impact on Scouting would be much greater in time.

After the assassination of his predecessor, President John F. Kennedy, Vice President Johnson took the reins of office with the intention of bringing his own brand of "fairness" into the Oval Office, which included complete racial equality patterned after current legislation.

Johnson signed into law the Civil Rights Act of 1964 on July 2 that made gender discrimination illegal as well as racial, ethnic, national, and religious discrimination. Voting rights were strictly enforced, and racially segregated facilities were ended in schools, workplaces, federal facilities, and public accommodations.

The Voting Rights Act followed in 1965, which outlawed "discriminatory voting practices," such as having to pass literacy tests in order to become registered voters, that had essentially "disenfranchised" certain African Americans from their right to express their opinion at the ballot box.

Along with appointing of African American lawyer Thurgood Marshall to the U.S. Supreme Court in 1967, President Johnson signed the Civil Rights Act of 1968 (also known as the Fair Housing Act) that ended any type of racial, gender, ethnic, national, or religious discrimination in the process of renting, purchasing, or the financing of a home.

Johnson also felt that BSA held these same beliefs.

FOLLOWING THE LEAD of President Johnson's Great Society program, BSA further embarked on servicing the inner city and rural areas that they considered full of boys that were "seriously disadvantaged." National Scouting managers formed the new Inner City-Rural Program that would be a co-operative effort between the National Council and select local councils with each council having to develop a project "especially designed for service to disadvantaged boys" through innovative and creative proposals with common objectives in mind.

First, each project had to broaden the basis upon which Scouting penetrated the current market and provide maximum effectiveness within individual neighborhoods and communities. It would utilize modified methods

Johnson receives a copy of the new *Handbook* during the delivery of BSA's *Annual Report* in February 1966.

to expand Scouting's appeal within those areas, and it had to "thoroughly document" all actions and outcomes. The result was Scouting's expansion into government sector housing projects and low density urban districts.

In 1968, the BOYPOWER '76 national membership recruitment campaign was launched in an attempt to recruit an additional two million Scouts to its rolls. In the program's first years, membership numbers grew steadily. However, with the release of the 1972 Boy Scout *Handbook*, which contained revised (and ultimately unpopular) Eagle Scout requirements, BSA's membership dropped precipitously. But the news was not all bad.

BSA formed a partnership with the American Foundation for the Blind in 1965 and, for the first time, produced an audio recorded version of the *Handbook*. It also released a large-print format for less visually impaired Scouts. Furthermore, "talking-book" versions were created for each merit badge pamphlet and a Braille edition of each *Boys' Life* magazine monthly issue was published as well.

BSA produced a special program guide for the leaders with mentally disabled young men. Deaf Scouts received special materials as well.

Johnson receives gifts after speaking at BSA's National Jamboree in 1964.

FURTHER INROADS WERE made into Scouting for Native American boys with the holding of the Ninth Tribal Leaders' Conference in 1966 at Fort Collins, Colorado. And additional co-operation was pledged by the National Congress of American Indians to BSA at their annual meeting in Oklahoma City that year.

As tradition dictated, President Johnson received his first BSA *Annual Report to the Nation* in February 1964. At the appointed time, BSA delegates entered the Oval Office and presented the president with, not only the bound *Report*, but also a large model of a covered wagon. It suggested BSA's new national theme of "Strengthen America's Heritage" that would take center stage at the upcoming 6th National Jamboree at Valley Forge, Pennsylvania, that summer. BSA rolls now stood at about five million members and its popularity was increasing.

As declared in the 1964 *Annual Report*, "While the Scouting program is based on action and doing, the objective of these activities of its program is the building of character, citizenship, and personal fitness in the boy."

Under the heading of "Citizenship" was a deeper emphasis on a new nationalism, whereby a Scout and his unit could embark upon a program to "preserve our freedom through reverent, resolute, responsible patriotism." And President Johnson was to become a part of it at the National Jamboree.

As the event's special guest speaker on July 23, President Johnson took the stage in front of 52,000 Scouts and leaders.

"The America that you will build and live to see will be far different from the America of today," he began. "You will see wonders and participate in achievements of which we older Americans can only dream."

He was right.

Taking President Kennedy's lead, Johnson pushed forward with the Space Program that soon would take Americans to the moon and back. Of the 312 pilots and scientists to travel into space between 1959 and 2010, 207 had been Scouts. Of the twenty-seven men who would travel to the moon, twenty-four were former Scouts. And of the twelve moonwalkers, eleven were once Scouts. And the first person to tread on the lunar surface, Neil A. Armstrong, was an Eagle Scout.

Before leaving the Jamboree, President Lyndon B. Johnson was presented with the 296th Silver Buffalo Award in recognition of his dedicated and unwavering service to youth.

To shatter forever not only the barriers of law and public practice, but the walls which bound the condition of many by the color of his skin. To dissolve, as best we can, the antique enmities of the heart which diminish the holder, divide the great democracy, and do wrong—great wrong—to the children of God.

ADDRESS, WASHINGTON, DC, JUNE 4, 1965

I know of no greater organization that contributes more to developing the mind and the body in the way that it should be developed than the Boy Scouts of America.

COMMENTS, "RECEIVING THE REPORT TO THE NATION," FEBRUARY 8, 1967

This is one of the truly fine organizations in our country and it has been my pleasure to advance the cause of your organization upon several occasions, and I sincerely hope that I may be of further service to the Boy Scouts in the future.

REP. LYNDON B. JOHNSON

It is always a pleasure to hear about Scouting.

COMMENTS, "RECEIVING THE REPORT TO THE NATION," FEBRUARY 9, 1966

We hope that all the other young people in America, as they come along, will want to emulate you.

COMMENTS, "RECEIVING THE REPORT TO THE NATION," FEBRUARY 8, 1967

RICHARD M.

NIXON

37ᵀᴴ PRESIDENT OF THE UNITED STATES

1969–1974

Born: January 9, 1913 Yorba Linda, California

Died: April 22, 1994 New York City, New York

Wife: Thelma Catherine "Pat" Ryan (m. 1940–1993)

Children: Tricia, Julie

Education: Whittier College (B.A.)

Duke University (LL.B)

BSA Positions: Hon. President (1969–1975)

Executive Board member, Crescent Bay Council, BSA (1961–1966)

National Explorer's Presidential Conference host, Washington, DC (1971)

BSA Honors: Silver Buffalo (1971)

Attended as U.S. vice president the 3rd BSA National Jamboree, Irvine Ranch, California (1953)

Attended as U.S. vice president the 4th BSA National Jamboree, Valley Forge, Pennsylvania (1957)

Eagle Scout Awards presented (1969–1974): 203,921

"*I strongly believe that Scouting offers an exceptional opportunity to learn about good citizenship by being a good citizen.*"

—PRESIDENT RICHARD NIXON

CHAPTER TWELVE

RICHARD M. NIXON

Exploring the Nation

"He was the grocer's son who got ahead by working harder and longer than everyone else. How American."

U.S. SENATOR BOB DOLE
April 27, 1994

On March 21, 1971, Senator Edmund Muskie of Maine took the floor in a hearing room in the Hart Building on Capitol Hill to address his colleagues on behalf of the Boy Scouts of America (BSA) and House Congressional Resolution 255.

"I submit, for appropriate reference a concurrent resolution commemorating the first annual National Explorers Presidents Congress," he began. "This Congress will take place in Washington from June 2 to June 6 and is expected to bring together between 4,000 and 5,000 young people from Explorer posts around the country."

Although the Exploring program began in 1959, the Boy Scouts of America established the Exploring division at their National Office in New Jersey a decade later to provide an intensive worksite-based program of vocational training for older Scouts. Organized throughout the country in "posts," Scouts were trained at police and fire stations, and professional buildings "from hospitals to space-science companies to law offices."

Different from the original Boy Scouting program dating back to 1910, BSA again proved it was ahead of societal evolution, when in 1969 it began allowing girls to join the Explorer division as "Explorer Participants" provided they were members of the Girl Scouts of America or Camp Fire Girls. Two years later, young women could join Exploring outright without having a prior affiliation. Although some joined because they saw their brothers "having all the fun," others simply found the vocational training exciting and challenging.

And parents agreed.

By 1971, over 23,000 Exploring posts boasted 350,000 members, a figure that was expected to rise to 1 million by the nation's bicentennial in 1976 (but it did not).

"Exploring is everywhere for reasons which should hearten Americans," declared *Reader's Digest*. "It is having its way. Upcoming generations—the ones we are always prone to despair over—will make tomorrow's America better than ever."

Vice President Nixon cooks with Scouts at the 1953 National Jamboree.

Vice President Nixon presents the Eagle Medal around 1958.

PROPOSED IN 1970, the first annual National Explorers Presidents Congress was to take place on the South Lawn of the White House at the invitation of President Richard M. Nixon the following year. The youthful presidents of all national divisional posts were invited to represent each local community post. The goal in Washington was for these representatives to receive experience in the democratic process and elect their national leadership.

There would be a vote for a national president and twelve regional vice-presidents—one representative for each of the twelve BSA national regions. Elected to one-year terms, they would become members of the Adult National Explorers Committee of the Boy Scouts of America.

According to the Muskie resolution, the gathering would reflect "their daily avocational and vocational interests, community participation, and youthful concern with today's national issues and problems." When the vote was taken on April 1, H.R. 255 passed and, eventually, Congress would congratulate these impressive young people for being the "future leaders of our Nation."

Late on the afternoon of June 2, 1971, President Richard M. Nixon left the White House for the South Lawn to address the 2,000 assembled delegates representing the Exploring program throughout the country. Not

Vice President Nixon speaks at the 1953 National Jamboree.

surprisingly, the youthful teenage men and women represented a cross section of American citizenry.

At the time, the nation was embroiled in the highly unpopular Vietnam War, so the president fully understood the gravity of what he was about to say to these young citizens. It had to reinforce in them a sense of national patriotism and devotion to community.

"I just want to tell you that I have a great deal of faith in not only this country but in you," he implored. "And one of the reasons I have faith in this country is because of my faith in you and in your generation. Let me put it in this context: At the present time, I think that your generation, the generation from 14 to 21, has the best chance of any generation in this century to enjoy what we have not had in this century in America—a full generation of peace."

He concluded, "I simply want to say to you: Don't lose faith in your country. I know that you love it; otherwise, you would not be in this great organization. Keep your faith in America."

After long applause, Nixon returned to the Oval Office to finish his day, confident that the first National Explorers Presidents Congress would be a success.

It was. And it would be held annually for the next 26 years, ending with the advent of Venturing.

As Scouting began to recruit more members from the inner cities, Nixon believed their principles of racial equality to be the same as his own.

A YEAR EARLIER in March 1970, the Nixon Administration began its first large-scale desegregation policy of the public school system.

"This issue is not partisan. It is not sectional," the president declared in a speech to the nation. "It is an American issue, of direct and immediate concern to every citizen."

His edict to permanently end schoolhouse segregation was designed to reinforce the landmark 1954 Supreme Court decision of *Brown v. Board of Education* as being constitutional in both "constitutional and human terms," and that a commitment to his policy would secure the "achievement of a free and open society."

Additionally, Nixon implemented his "Philadelphia Plan" (initially conceived but not yet enacted during the Johnson Administration) within the Department of Labor in September 1969, which marked the beginning of the nation's first federally mandated affirmative action program. It "set a range of percentages of minority hirings with which contractors would be required to make a 'good faith' effort to comply."

Other actions included the 1969 federal hate crimes law that made it illegal to harm someone "motivated by a victim's actual or perceived gender, sexual orientation, gender identity, or disability," the Rehabilitation Act of 1973 that served as a "Bill of Rights" for disabled citizens, and his endorsement of the Equal Rights Amendment for women after it cleared both houses of Congress and went to the states for ratification in 1972. They all have made a positive difference in American life today.

BSA RESPONDED TO calls for women's rights in its own way in 1971 with the first presentations of the Silver Fawn award. Conceived as the equivalent to the Silver Beaver award that recognized a man's outstanding service to boyhood within a local council, the Silver Fawn recipients were rewarded for their work within the local Cub Scout program only. The medal was eventually discontinued in 1974 after 2,455 presentations had been made. Future awardees would receive the Silver Beaver medal and neck ribbon.

In 1973, BSA's national executive board elected its first two women members in the persons of Elizabeth Augustus Knight (wife to John S. Knight, the founder of the Knight-Ridder newspaper conglomerate) and LaVern W. Parmley (the editor of *Children's Friend* magazine).

Vice President Nixon receives a framed Norman Rockwell print during BSA's 50th Anniversary celebration in 1960.

Further diversity advancements were made with the creation of the Relationships Division in 1974. It was tasked with promoting, maintaining, and overseeing the chartered organization system of unit sponsorship. Included was the monitoring of faith-based and fraternal organizations, education and civic groups, as well as the inner city, rural, and handicapped programs. This Division also would help to determine the "purpose of the Boy Scouts of America so every region, area, and council might better understand the concept of Scouting as a resource program for community organizations."

The result was the creation of an Annual Service Plan that would examine sponsoring organization relationships in time increments of 30, 60, 90, and 120 days.

EARLIER IN 1971, national Scouting managers had adopted a new slogan to empower the nation's youth: "America's Manpower Begins With Boypower." BSA's national office also had another top initiative to push forward—Project SOAR, which stood for "Save Our American Resources." It sprang out of the national "Keep America Beautiful" project launched the year before by the federal government.

As *Boys' Life* pointed out, SOAR was "BSA's nationwide effort to battle pollution of air, water, and soil, and to teach others the meaning of saving our natural wealth." Initiated at the request of Nixon (and as BSA's national Good Turn), SOAR organized millions of people who volunteered many millions of man-hours to clean up the environment.

"SOAR is probably the greatest thing that had happened in contemporary Scouting," said Ted Petit, BSA's manager of conservation services at the time. "We knew Scouts would respond but, even in our greatest expectations, no one could imagine how overwhelming the response would be."

By 1971, BSA had 1.2 million members participating in clean-up projects along 132,059 miles of highways and streams and in 282,508 acres of public areas, removing 669,924 tons of trash and debris.

By 1972, BSA membership had expanded to four million youth and adult volunteers cleaning 470,000 miles of highways and waterways and 1.3 million acres of public lands, and disposing of 1.5 million tons of litter.

Today, while Project SOAR is no longer a part of the National Good Turn, many councils still perform projects in its name, which continue to benefit the country.

A president can ask for reconciliation in the racial conflict that divides Americans. But reconciliation comes only from the hearts of people.

ADDRESS, MIAMI BEACH, FLORIDA, AUGUST 8, 1968

I welcome your determination to seek out new members in our great and growing cities, as well as throughout rural America. For through Scouting, many of these young citizens can more fully develop their potential for public service, and become effective leaders in their communities and in our nation.

AS QUOTED ON SCOUTING.ORG

I strongly believe that Scouting offers an exceptional opportunity to learn about good citizenship by being a good citizen, and I am glad to hear that we can count on you to carry on the very important work . . . in encouraging America's boys to make themselves into the men our country needs.

AS QUOTED ON SCOUTING.ORG

GERALD R.

FORD

38ᵀᴴ PRESIDENT OF THE UNITED STATES

1974–1977

Born: July 14, 1913 Omaha, Nebraska
Died: December 26, 2006 Rancho Mirage, California

Wife: Elizabeth Ann "Betty" Bloomer (m. 1948)
Children: Michael Gerald, John Gardner, Steven Meigs, Susan Elizabeth

Education: University of Michigan (B.A.)
              Yale Law School (LL.B.)

BSA Positions: Hon. President (1975–1977)
              Hon. Vice President (1977–2006)
              Boy Scout, Troop 15, Grand Rapids, Michigan
              Volunteer, Grand Valley Council, Grand Rapids, Michigan
                (1945–1948)

BSA Honors: Silver Buffalo (1975)
              Scouter of the Year (1974)
              Distinguished Eagle Scout Award (1970)
              Eagle Scout, Class of 1927
              Gerald R. Ford Chapter, National Eagle Scout Association,
              Gerald R. Council, Grand Rapids, Michigan
              Gerald R. Ford Council, BSA, Grand Rapids, Michigan
              President Ford Trail & Medal, Grand Rapids, Michigan

Eagle Scout Awards presented (1975–1976): 48,972

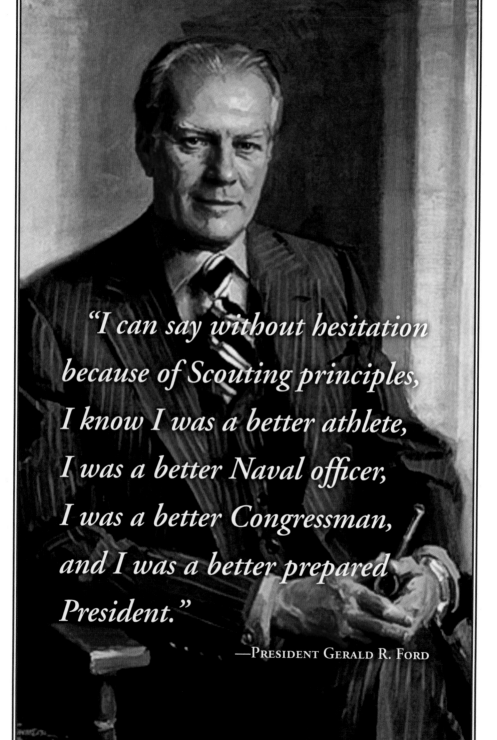

"*I can say without hesitation because of Scouting principles, I know I was a better athlete, I was a better Naval officer, I was a better Congressman, and I was a better prepared President.*"

—President Gerald R. Ford

CHAPTER THIRTEEN

GERALD R. FORD
The Eagle Scout in the White House

"To know Jerry was to know a Norman Rockwell painting come to life."

PRESIDENT GEORGE H.W. BUSH
December 30, 2006

CHIEF SCOUT CITIZEN THEODORE ROOSEVELT would have been very proud of President Gerald R. Ford. Not only was Ford a man of virtue and principle, but he also was the first president of the United States to have attained the Boy Scouts of America's (BSA) highest rank of Eagle Scout—earned in 1927.

Ford was born in July 1913 as Leslie Lynch King Jr. His mother, the former Dorothy Ayer Gardner, divorced his father who was abusive and married Gerald R. Ford Sr. when baby Leslie was just two and a half years old. His mother and stepfather changed his name to reflect their new family, whose loving upbringing would groom him for a higher calling. As a youth, young Gerald was a gifted athlete but he also was "book smart." And to compliment his budding athletic career, he threw himself into Boy Scouting.

Throughout his life of public service, Ford remained faithful to the principles and values engrained in him as a boy from the Scout Oath and Scout Law.

"There is something about Scouting that leaves an impression on you, an impression that is wholesome and is good," Ford later recalled. "And it is a stimulant for greater effort—the Scout Oath and the Scout Law—which I could almost repeat without a mistake."

Later in adulthood, the former senator, vice president, and president of the United States would comment that passing his Eagle Scout Board of Review was one of his of his life's "proudest moments."

GERALD R. FORD was elevated to the presidency in 1974 following the resignation of President Richard Nixon, becoming our 38th president of the United States. At the time, America was mired in the Watergate scandal. The break-in cover-up at the Democratic National Committee headquarters based in the Watergate Hotel by Nixon's operatives on his Committee to Re-Elect the President ended Nixon's public career and greatly embarrassed the country. But as a result, an Eagle Scout was now president.

Gerald Ford's reputation was as squeaky clean and as honorable as one would expect of a former Boy Scout—a far cry from the acts of obstruction of justice attempted by the Nixon Administration.

Ford as a First Class Scout in summer 1926 (left) and after earning the rank of Eagle Scout in 1927.

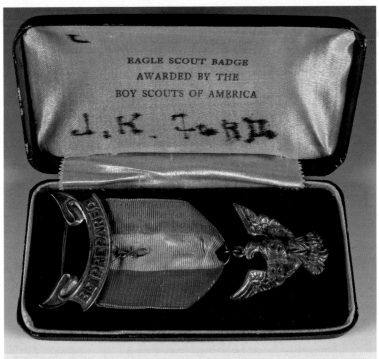

Ford's Eagle medal and presentation box. The initials "J.R." written on the box refer to him being known in his youth as Gerald R. Ford, Jr."

A team player to the end, Ford's first and most important decision was at hand, and in making it, he sacrificed his chances of being elected president on his own right.

The Eagle Scout in the White House chose to pardon Richard Nixon for his abuses of power, setting off a firestorm of criticism that would abate little during his presidency. But he did it anyway, believing it to be the "right" thing for the country at the time. He did not want to further the national trauma that undoubtedly would have resulted from a Nixon trial.

Without question, President Ford was the best person to head the country after this scandal, as he had spent a lifetime of "doing the right thing" and looking out for the betterment of all.

Years earlier, as a star player and starting center on the University of Michigan's football team in 1934, Ford took his first public stand against racism, when his African American teammate and best friend, Willis Ward, was benched because Georgia Tech refused to take the field if Ward played against them. The future president was incensed and threatened to quit the team. He only retracted his position when Ward asked him to play. Ford's courageous stand in an era marked by Jim Crow segregation laws was never forgotten by his friend.

Within the first two weeks of his elevation to the presidency, Ford invited the Congressional Black Caucus (led by Rep. Charles Rangle of New York) to meet with him at the White House—something that his predecessors had never done.

"I made a strenuous attempt to show critics that an 'open' White House meant exactly that," Ford later recalled.

Additionally, Ford appointed African American William Coleman as his secretary of transportation—the second African American man ever to serve at a cabinet level position and the first to do so in a GOP Administration.

He elevated African American Air Force four-star general Daniel "Chappie" James Jr. to the position of commander-in-chief of the North

Ford's Eagle Scout card (top), merit badge sash (right), and the Michigan service patch from the council named in his honor.

Ford as the center for the University of Michigan football team from 1932–34.

American Defense Command (NORAD/ADCOM) in September 1975 and declared women's equality in a Proclamation that year as well:

> *"In this Land of the Free, it is right, and by nature it ought to be, that all men and all women are equal before the law. Now, therefore, I, Gerald R. Ford, President of the United States of America, to remind all Americans that it is fitting and just to ratify the Equal Rights Amendment adopted by the Congress of the United States of America, in order to secure legal equality for all women and men, do hereby designate and proclaim August 26, 1975, as Women's Equality Day."*

Together, these actions provided strong evidence regarding President Ford's dedication to equality for all as well as his internalization of Scouting's values learned in his youth.

BSA WAS MOVING forward as well. In 1975, the Cub Scout Division developed a plan with the Relationships Division to expand and begin serving disabled youth.

Ford poses with a group of Cub Scouts about 1985.

Also, BSA translated basic adult leader training courses into Spanish to service the growing Hispanic membership segment.

The following year, BSA managers, through the Church Commission on Scouting, revamped the God and Country Religious Emblems Program and divided it into three new programs; the Boy Scout version (God and Church), the Cub Scout version (God and Family), and the Exploring version (God and Life).

IN OCTOBER 1974, just a few months after Ford took office, BSA's national office asked for his help in promoting the organization to the country, as Scouting was experiencing a serious decline in membership and trying to grow its ranks by appealing to urban youth. Unfortunately, the skills once stressed for life in the outdoors were not seen as relevant to inner city boys.

Ford responded generously, writing in a letter to BSA managers:

> *"My Scouting years as a Boy Scout were invaluable in helping to shape the course of my later life. I have seen firsthand evidence of the immeasurable worth of the basic values taught by Scouting programs."*

Two hundred copies of the note were requested for immediate distribution to national media outlets under the cover letter of Ford's assistant, Eliska Hasek.

The following month, BSA started publishing a monthly column written by legendary Scouting professional William "Green Bar Bill" Hillcourt titled "All Out for Scouting." Recently, Hillcourt had authored the most comprehensive biography to date on the British founder of the Scouting movement, Robert Baden-Powell.

In his new column, Hillcourt advocated to stem the loss of membership by re-emphasizing Baden-Powell's original patrol system (meaning small units of 6 to 8 boys each) and putting woodcraft and camping skills back in the program.

With the help of Hillcourt's monthly column and President Ford's letter of support, BSA staged a resurgence of sorts. Article themes like "Get Up to Standard," that encouraged patrol members to wear full uniform to all troop meetings, and "Do It the Brownsea Way," which was a reference to games like those played at the first Scout-type camp held on Brownsea Island, England, in August 1907, enticed Scouts to earn a special patch for uniform wear.

Annual Report delegation at the White House in February 1976.

Hillcourt's "All Out for Scouting" articles continued through January 1978.

IN APRIL 1975, Ford continued President Nixon's tradition by hosting the 5th Annual National Explorer Presidents Congress, where he met with those selected young leaders at the White House. He also pledged "stronger support" for the Explorer program, as well as the area of BSA High Adventure and in Scouting at-large.

Years earlier, recognizing his work as a dedicated public servant, BSA had presented Ford with the Distinguished Eagle Scout Award, reserved for top Eagle Scout lifetime achievers. But at the Explorer gathering in April 1975, national BSA managers honored him with the Silver Buffalo Award on the South Lawn of the White House that recognized his positive impact on American youth.

With the nation's Bicentennial coming up in 1976, BSA planned for festivities in the nation's capital. Among them was the presentation of the 66th *Annual Report to the Nation*. In February, Ford received BSA's delegation that consisted of fifteen specially chosen Scouts from around the nation.

"I hope that in the future there will be many presidents who will be honored, as I have been, by your presentations today," Ford told his visitors.

Later came the Eagle Scout Bicentennial Celebration on the National Mall that would be held throughout that summer. About 750 Eagle Scouts and their leaders took part in the dedication ceremony held between the Washington Monument and the Lincoln Memorial that included athletic demonstrations and Scouting skills. The program allowed anyone over the age of fifteen to participate in any of forty-three different sports exhibited from bowling to archery to jogging. Additionally, Ford "the athlete" championed the Presidential Sports Award.

Created in 1972 by President Nixon under the auspices of the President's Council on Physical Fitness and Sports, it encouraged American youth to live up to their physical potential. Scouts from across the country fought to earn it.

The President's Council had been created in 1953 by President Eisenhower in response to his concern that most European children were in better physical condition than many American children. But with Ford's endorsement, the Council's objective was amended to inform the public of the benefits of regular exercise as well as to help American business and industry establish "sound fitness programs" within their spheres of influence.

"Regular, vigorous physical activity provides a pleasant and relaxing way of filling leisure hours," said Ford. "But more than this, it enhances health, improves mental and physical performance, and even helps to prolong life."

PRESIDENT GERALD R. FORD was a devoted lifelong supporter of BSA, serving as one of its honorary vice presidents after leaving office until his death in December 2006.

And at Ford's request, his funeral procession and final services were attended by an honor guard of Eagle Scouts (see Appendix B). His local council, later renamed Gerald R. Ford Council in Grand Rapids, Michigan, fielded the calls from hundreds of Eagle Scout volunteers across the nation who wished to assemble as members of the honor guard.

In an impressive show of Scouting support for the Office of the President, hundreds of Eagle Scouts stood at attention and saluted the presidential funeral car as it passed by slowly on its procession to the Gerald R. Ford Presidential Library in Grand Rapids, Michigan—his final resting place.

To President Ford, it was a fitting final tribute.

Ford receives the Scouter of the Year Award in 1974.

I have not and will not tolerate the translation of foreign religious prejudice into domestic discrimination against American citizens.

ADDRESS, BROOKLYN, NEW YORK, OCTOBER 12, 1976

Family vacations—especially among the majestic mountains of the West—are a tradition of our family. My parents always took my brothers and myself to lakes and woods in my State of Michigan before I was big enough to go myself as a Boy Scout. There is something wonderful about the wide open spaces that are almost a necessity.

ADDRESS, YELLOWSTONE NATIONAL PARK, WYOMING, AUGUST 29, 1976

There is something about Scouting that leaves an impression on you, an impression that is wholesome and is good, and it is a stimulant for greater effort.

ADDRESS, REMARKS TO CUB SCOUTS CHARLESTON, WEST VIRGINIA
NOVEMBER 11, 1975

The great principles which Scouting encourages—self-discipline, teamwork, moral, and patriotic values—are the building blocks of character.

ADDRESS, MESSAGE TO BOY SCOUTS, 1974

I am confident that your ability to bring ideals, values, and leadership training to millions of our young people will help to bring about a new era—a time in which not only our republic will progress in peace and freedom, but a time in which the entire world shall be secure, and all its people free.

ADDRESS, HONOLULU, HAWAII, MAY 17, 1974

JIMMY

CARTER

39TH PRESIDENT OF THE UNITED STATES

1977–1981

Born: October 1, 1924 Plains, Georgia

Wife: Eleanor Rosalynn Smith (m. 1946)
Children: John William, James Earl "Chip", III, Donnel Jeffrey "Jeff,"
            Amy Lynn

Education: Georgia Southwestern College
                Georgia Institute of Technology
                United States Naval Academy (B.S.)
                Union College (M.S.)

Honors: Nobel Peace Prize (2002)

BSA Positions: Hon. President (1977–1981)
                Hon. Vice President (1981–present)
                Father of three Cub Scouts/Boy Scouts
                Troop Committee Chairman
                Cubmaster of Pack 25, Plains, Georgia Scoutmaster
                Den Mother, First Lady Rosalynn Carter
                Explorer Advisor
                Scoutmaster, Plains, Georgia (formed the Troop)

BSA Honors: Silver Buffalo (1978)

Eagle Scout Awards presented (1977–1980): 91,759

"*I am greatly impressed by the role of your fine [Scouting] program in our national life.*"

—PRESIDENT JIMMY CARTER

CHAPTER FOURTEEN

JIMMY CARTER

Volunteer-in-Chief

"As president of the United States, Jimmy Carter was deeply committed to social justice and basic human rights."

—HABITAT FOR HUMANITY INTERNATIONAL

P RESIDENT JIMMY CARTER ONCE SAID, "A strong nation, like a strong person, can afford to be gentle, firm, thoughtful, and restrained. It can afford to extend a helping hand to others. It's a weak nation, like a weak person, that must behave with bluster and boasting and rashness and other signs of insecurity."

Carter's observation is one that could well apply to the ethos of the Boy Scouts of America (BSA).

In 1977, President Carter launched a program that BSA adopted as one of its own—the President's Environmental Youth Award, which was managed by the Environmental Protection Agency (EPA).

"The whole thrust of this effort is to encourage young people to participate, to analyze how they can contribute to the quality of life around their own homes in a practical way, not just a theoretical way" Carter told an April 1978 press conference. "And to let the judgment of how successful they are be determined by those who live in the community itself."

BSA, which had embraced Project SOAR (Save Our American Resources conservation campaign) under President Richard Nixon, found Carter's program just as appealing. During the 1970s, America faced the consequences of an international energy crisis as tighter fuel supplies and ever-rising prices brought rationing and long lines to gas pumps across the country.

Carter's response to this crisis did much to stimulate the emergence of the modern day energy conservation movement. He believed the best way to reduce energy consumption was to promote the advances of conserving natural resources, develop renewable resources, and recycle.

This philosophy dovetailed with BSA's conservation history going back nearly as far as the presidency of Theodore Roosevelt. Once adopted by BSA in November 1979, more than 20,000 Cub Scouts and Boy Scouts completed requirements that included taking an active part in energy conservation and education projects to earn the certificate.

As the award developed, the EPA established ten regions that would award winners a grant of $1,000 each along with an invitation to the White House for a presentation banquet. National Boy Scout recipients were recognized for a variety of projects like "Get the Lead Out of Fishing" that removed lost lead weights from area lakes and fishing holes.

Carter receives BSA's *Annual Report* in February 1978.

For example, one award was presented to the United Nation's environmental youth program in Sweden for studying the environmental and health impact of 480 million lead weights lost in the water during fishing trips.

And the American winner of the 2007 President's Environmental Youth Awards was a Scout team from Troop 5 in Milton, Massachusetts, that collected and recycled 60 pounds of these recovered lead weights.

In December 1979, in recognition of BSA's special contribution to the welfare of the country, President Carter issued a proclamation designating December 3 through 9 as "Scout Recognition Week."

Much like the first such proclamation issued by President Woodrow Wilson in 1919 to thank BSA Scouts for their wartime service, Carter thanked Scouts for their solid efforts on behalf of energy conservation and environmental protection.

"In recent years Scouts have been particularly active in promoting energy awareness and conservation, and are continuing this important effort," he declared. "They are also planning activities designed to aid in taking an accurate census next year."

According to custom, President Carter was presented with the Silver Buffalo neck ribbon and medal in an Oval Office ceremony upon delivery of BSA's 1978 *Report to the Nation* at 10 a.m. on February 15, 1979. As one of the largest BSA delegations ever for such a ceremony, it included twenty-seven Scout delegates from Hawaii to Massachusetts, all of whom thanked the president for his continued support of the Scouting program.

LIKE THOSE IN the Scouting movement, President Carter was a proponent of ethical, faith-based, and gender equality from the very beginning of his term. As declared in his inaugural speech delivered in January 1977, Carter announced that the era of racial segregation was officially over and that racial discrimination had no place in America.

"I join in the hope that when my time as your president has ended," he declared, "people might say this about our Nation ... that we had torn down the barriers that separated those of different race and region and religion, and where there had been mistrust, built unity, with a respect for diversity."

By May 1980, Carter had done much to ease the country's racial tensions along with signing H.R. 10—the Civil Rights of Institutionalized Persons Act—to protect the rights of citizens with developmental and intellectual disabilities who live in nursing homes, correctional, and mental health facilities.

At the time, Carter was considered a "human rights president" both at home and abroad, as he championed the causes of ending discrimination throughout the world. He appointed African American human rights activist Andrew Young to be the U.S. ambassador to the United Nations in 1977, poverty rights advocate Cyrus Vance to the post of Secretary of State, and Polish American foreign policy expert, Zbigniew Brzezinski, as National Security Advisor.

According to scholar Peter J. Schrader, all were "bound" by a common desire to, among other things, attempt to eliminate human rights violations on the African continent as well as globally.

This lofty goal was formalized in the Presidential Directive (NSC-30) of February 17, 1978, declaring "it shall be a major objective of U.S. foreign policy to promote the observance of human rights throughout the world," which not only defined specific types of human rights violations but also the ones that required immediate intervention by the United States. However, many scholars believe him to have been ineffective at generating the desired results.

Scouts working on a Habitat for Humanity house in July 2001.

As an organization, BSA continued to encourage diversity education among its membership. One landmark exhibit at the 1977 National Jamboree was the Awareness Trail, where participants got the opportunity to experience life as a disabled boy would—by wearing blacked out glasses to simulate blindness or ear plugs to create the sense of deafness. Then, each participant would be put through an obstacle course based on one's basic daily activities.

The following year, BSA's national executive board modified the maximum age to earn the rank of Eagle Scout for physically or mentally disabled youth, previously being by the Scout's eighteenth birthday.

Also established in 1978 was the Whitney M. Young Jr. Service Award that recognized outstanding individuals or organizations that promoted Scouting opportunities to youth from rural, low-income, or urban backgrounds. Young, in his own right, had been a vocal American civil rights leader who worked to end discrimination in the workplace.

In 1980, BSA released two landmark program aids; *Scouting for the Emotionally Disturbed* and *A Resource Manual for Scouting Leaders of the Handicapped.* They corresponded with BSA's new partnership with the International Year of Disabled Persons set for 1981.

AFTER LEAVING THE presidency, Carter dedicated himself to humanitarian projects, the best known being Habitat for Humanity International through the Jimmy and Rosalynn Carter Work Project.

Founded in 1965 outside Americus, Georgia, by millionaires Millard and Linda Fuller, Habitat for Humanity caught the attention of the Carters because of its emphasis on helping others to help themselves. Volunteers provided funding and labor while recipients were expected to put in "sweat equity" in exchange for a free house.

The Carters started collaborating with Habitat in 1984 when the former president led a group to New York City for a week and set to work with tools given him by White House staff members when he left office in January 1981. Carter, a skilled carpenter, helped renovate a six-floor apartment building that would house nineteen families. Rosalynn Carter's experience was much different, and she recalled, "I didn't think I could use a hammer and I didn't want to use a hammer. At first it took me 15 or 20 strokes for each nail, but before the week was over I could drive one in with only four or five strokes."

The Carters have been working on Habitat for Humanity projects ever since.

Not to be left out of the fun, BSA joined forces with Habitat for Humanity in 2004 as a part of its "Good Turn for America" campaign, as a "call to national service" for the organization. Any work provided by a Scout qualified for individual or group service project hours as well as for district or council volunteer projects. Home building tasks are so varied that there are jobs suitable for all ages of Scouts, from 6-year-old Tiger Cub Scouts through 20-year-old Venturers.

"As an Eagle Scout, I learned the importance of giving back to one's community," recalled Habitat for Humanity Senior Vice-President Larry Gluth. "I am truly proud to see this tradition carried on by these young men through their efforts to help … Habitat for Humanity."

THOUGH HIS LIFE as a Cubmaster, Scoutmaster, and Troop Committeeman is not extensively documented, Carter has made reference to his days in the Scouting movement as quality time to bond with his family.

In his book *Sharing Good Times*, Carter recalls family camping trips with Rosalynn and their three sons. "I took them on occasional overnight camping trips," recalls Carter. "Designed to knit us together as closely as possible, our first was a weeklong trip around Georgia, camping out each night in a different state park, either in the mountains or along the seashore."

During the late 1950s and early 1960s, Rosalynn served as her sons' Cub Scout Den Leader, while Jimmy was the Cubmaster of Pack 25 in Plains, Georgia, eventually working his way up to Scoutmaster in a local Boy Scout troop. Jimmy's uncle, Hugh Alton Carter Sr., states in his book, *Cousin Beedie and Cousin Hot*, that his son Hugh Jr., greatly admired his cousin, Jimmy, the future president.

"All during the time Hugh Jr. was growing up, cousin Jimmy Carter was his hero," describes Hugh Carter Sr. "Jimmy was the Scoutmaster and Hugh strove to impress him. At school, [Hugh Jr] tried to emulate him."

Such has been the heavy responsibility of many a Scoutmaster across America for more than a century now.

"He was always the leader of everything he got into," writes Carter biographer Peter G. Bourne, which made his ascent to the White House not unexpected.

America did not invent human rights. In a very real sense human rights invented America.

FAREWELL ADDRESS, WASHINGTON, D.C., JANUARY 14, 1981

As a former volunteer Scout leader ... I am greatly impressed by the role of your fine program in our national life. It is a constructive initiative on the part of young Americans to explore career interests, and to become better prepared for a more satisfying and rewarding future.

AS QUOTED ON WWW.SCOUTING.ORG

REAGAN

40TH PRESIDENT OF THE UNITED STATES

1981–1989

Born: February 6, 1911, Tampico, Illinois

Died: June 5, 2004, Bel Air, Los Angeles, California

Wife: (1st) Jane Wyman (1940–1948)
             (2nd) Nancy Davis (1952–2004)

Children: Maureen, Christine, Michael, Patti, Ron

Education: Eureka College (B.A.)

BSA Positions: Hon. President (1981–1989)
                  Hon. Vice President (1989–2004)
                  Volunteer Troop Leader, Greater Los Angeles,
                     California Council, BSA
                  Volunteer Troop Leader, Golden Empire,
                     California Council, BSA

BSA Honors: Scouter of the Year (1982)
               Silver Buffalo (1982)
               Silver Buffalo, First Lady Nancy Reagan (1988)
               President Reagan send videotaped message to 11th
                  National Jamboree, Fort A.P. Hill, Virginia (1985)
                  (First Lady Nancy Reagan attends 11th BSA National
                  Jamboree in place of the President who was recuperating
                  from cancer surgery, Fort A.P. Hill, Virginia)
               Ronald Reagan District, Ventura County,
                  California Council, BSA

Eagle Scout Awards presented (1981–1988): 211,787

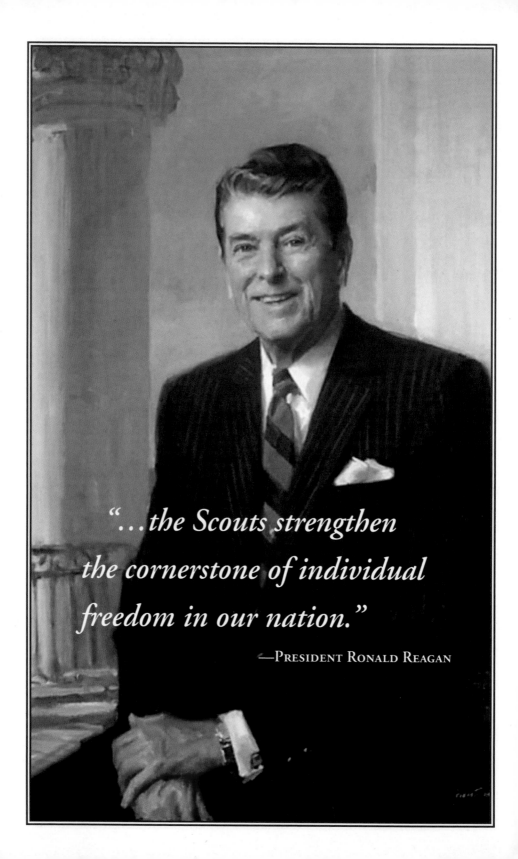

"...the Scouts strengthen the cornerstone of individual freedom in our nation."

—President Ronald Reagan

CHAPTER FIFTEEN

RONALD
REAGAN
The Ever Patriotic Boy Scout

"A man advancing in years with the sweetness and sincerity of a Scout saying the Pledge."

PRESIDENT GEORGE W. BUSH
June 7, 2004

THE BLOOMINGTON, ILLINOIS, HOLIDAY INN was abuzz on September 14, 1982. Sitting at the head table in a conference room filled with press was a young thirteen-year-old Eagle Scout named Alexander M. Holsinger. But Alex was no ordinary Eagle Scout—he was the Boy Scouts of America's (BSA) one-millionth Eagle Scout.

As *Boys' Life* magazine describes the scene, "newspaper reporters and photographers were falling all over one another" to interview and snap photos of Alex. In the audience with Alex and his parents (Illinois State University history professor Dr. M. Paul Holsinger and his wife) were eight television cameras—including one each from the CBS, NBC, and ABC networks—as well as BSA President Edward C. Joullian and Chief Scout Executive James L. Tarr.

After being introduced, Alex took the microphone.

"I love Scouting," he began. "Scouting has offered me the fun of outdoor activities, the challenge of leadership, and the chance to build self-confidence through various skills that will last me a lifetime … I plan to remain active in Scouting the rest of my life."

As reporters jotted down every word and cameras flashed, the press conference was interrupted. At 11:16 a.m., in the midst of a statement being made by Alex's proud Scoutmaster, someone entered bearing the news that President Ronald Reagan was calling from Washington, DC. Taking the phone, the remarkable conversation began.

"Alex?" asked President Reagan.

"This is Alex Holsinger," he responded.

"Well, this is Ronald Reagan [and] as honorary president of the Boy Scouts of America, it's a pleasure to join with all those gathered in Bloomington today to congratulate you on becoming the one millionth Eagle Scout in our nation's history."

Eagle Scout Alexander Holsinger speaks with Reagan in September 1982.

Reagan receives BSA's *Annual Report* in February 1981.

After five conversational exchanges, all ending with a resounding, "Sir," to the president of the United States, a stunned Alex Holsinger hung up the phone.

AS A HOLLYWOOD actor in the late 1930s and early 1940s, Ronald Reagan tended to play "heroic figures" whose "faith in American values seldom faltered despite his 'wised-up and smart-cracking exterior,'" writes biographer Stephen Vaughan. "Reagan possessed the 'heart of a Boy Scout.'"

Years later, son Michael Reagan would describe his father similarly as "an ever patriotic Boy Scout," with his Dad always running to the aid of his country in times of crisis.

And in 1975, Ronald Reagan felt his country calling.

As the presidential election of 1976 loomed, many Americans disapproved of President Gerald Ford's pardoning of his predecessor, President Richard Nixon, for crimes he might have committed during the Watergate cover-up. Knowing that the Republican Party could not support Ford's election bid, Reagan found a way to put himself on the national stage to provide an alternative to the Democratic challenger, Georgia Governor Jimmy Carter. Though Reagan did not win the Republican nomination, he was headed for the Oval Office a few years later.

WHILE PRESIDENT, RONALD REAGAN was a man of the people—a grandfatherly figure—who was sensitive to the needs of disenfranchised Americans. Decades prior, he had used his Hollywood star power to focus attention on discrimination when he aggressively denounced the Ku Klux Klan's attack of an African American man in Tennessee in 1946.

"A community that is aware of the threat to its people and security by bigoted terroristic groups will be protected from such acts," he declared on a live radio broadcast. " It is important that every citizen of Southern California be ready to assist all public officials who are attempting to check any further occurrences of this kind and to join with those civic organizations, which are laboring to bring better understanding and unity among the different elements of our society without regard to race or creed or color."

Now residing in the Oval Office, millions of others depended on him.

In 1981, making good a campaign promise, Reagan nominated Arizona State Court of Appeals Judge Sandra Day O'Connor to the U.S. Supreme Court, to replace the retiring Associate Justice Potter Stewart. She would become the first woman to serve on the Supreme Court.

Reagan receives the gift of a walking stick from BSA's *Annual Report* delegation.

In March 1983, Reagan proposed a constitutional amendment during a speech in Orlando, Florida, that allowed for prayer in the nation's public schools:

"When our Founding Fathers passed the First Amendment, they never intended to construct a wall between government and religious belief," the president argued. "The Supreme Court opens its proceedings with a religious invocation. Congress opens sessions with a prayer. I believe the schoolchildren of the United States are entitled to the same privilege. I sent the Congress a constitutional amendment to restore prayer to public schools. I am calling on the Congress to act speedily and to let our children pray."

However, it was not passed.

On November 2, 1983, President Reagan signed a bill into law that created the Martin Luther King Jr. national holiday, honoring the national civil rights leader every year on the third Monday in January.

That same year, he signed into law the Immigration Reform and Control Act that made it illegal to knowingly recruit or hire illegal immigrants without attesting to their immigration status. However, it also granted amnesty to some three million undocumented immigrants of continuous residence, who had entered the United States prior to January 1, 1982. He signed it into law standing at the base of the newly refurbished Statue of Liberty in New York Harbor.

"The legalization provisions in this act will go far to improve the lives of a class of individuals who now must hide in the shadows, without access to many of the benefits of a free and open society," Reagan announced. "Very soon many of these men and women will be able to step into the sunlight and, ultimately, if they choose, they may become Americans."

THE HANDICAPPED AWARENESS merit badge was created in 1980 (eventually to be replaced with the Disabilities Awareness merit badge in 1993), a year prior to BSA's first national conference on Scouting for the visually impaired in Washington, DC.

In 1982, the National Islamic Committee on Scouting was formed by a group of concerned Muslim citizens for the purpose of promoting Scouting among Muslim youth, helping Muslim institutions provide Scouting opportunities, and "promoting Islamic values in Scouting through program helps and the religious emblems program."

Reagan greets a Cub Scout during the delivery of BSA's *Annual Report*.

And in February 1988, BSA's national executive board voted to remove gender restrictions for all of Scouting leadership positions – thus allowing women to become Scoutmasters for the first time.

ALSO DURING REAGAN'S presidency, BSA celebrated its 75th anniversary in 1985. The largest BSA event that year was the 11th National Jamboree at Fort A.P. Hill in Caroline County, Virginia. The high point of such a jamboree always had been a visit by the president during the closing ceremonies. But Reagan was recuperating from cancer surgery, so First Lady Nancy Reagan attended in his place.

At the closing arena show, one participant recalled that the First Lady's arrival was tremendously exciting. "When we looked overhead, we saw Marine One, the presidential helicopter, flying above, and then it circled," recalled Assistant Scoutmaster and Texas Eagle Scout Bobby Higginbotham. "Then she landed on a runway behind the amphitheater." For security reasons, a large black curtain was drawn behind the stage and concealed her motorcade as she was seated in one of three back Chevrolet Suburbans with smoked windows and filled with Secret Service agents.

"We saw the First Lady's escort drive behind the black curtain where she emerged from one of those Suburbans. We didn't know which one," said Higginbotham. "And when she arrived on stage, the place erupted in applause. It was a great show!"

The First Lady's address to the Scouts expanded on her trademark "Just Say No to Drugs" campaign that was sweeping the nation. By 1987, Chief Scout Executive Ben Love was urging young readers of *Boys' Life* to "get your friends involved. It's often because of a friend's influence that a person first tries drugs—but that influence can work both ways: You can influence your friends to *just say no.*"

The Reagans always were willing to entertain a BSA delegation or audience. The previous February 1985, Scouts and National BSA officials delivered the *Annual Report to the Nation* to the White House, where the president joked that he was "pleased" to celebrate something older than himself. He then thanked the many Scouting volunteers who had made it all possible.

"Without the thousands of adult leaders, corporate sponsors, and other caring Americans," he advised, "It would not be possible for young Americans to capture the Scouting spirit and the special joys of camping, fellowship, service, and love of country. So, thanks to all of you for what you're doing for our young people and for America's future."

The year closed with Reagan issuing a Presidential *Proclamation* to mark BSA's 75th anniversary, praising its contributions to the country over the past three quarters of a century.

A FEW YEARS prior, BSA had recognized Reagan's service to the movement as both the nation's chief executive and as a dedicated Scouting volunteer back in California. In 1982, upon delivery of the 72nd *Annual Report*, Chief Scout Executive Tarr presented the president with his citation and the Silver Buffalo Award.

In 1988, in keeping with this tradition, during the delivery of the 78th *Annual Report*, Tarr presented First Lady Nancy Reagan with her own Silver Buffalo Award in recognition of her "Just Say No" crusade against drugs. It was the first time a presidential (or married) couple ever had received the honor.

In the end, President Ronald Reagan presided over the country during a period of prosperity that extended into the ranks of BSA. His passing in 2004 ended an era.

"I would like my father to be remembered as an Eagle Scout," remarked son Michael Reagan. "He is not only my father, he is my hero."

There may be no finer testimonial.

IN HIS OWN WORDS

We want a colorblind society, a society that, in the words of Dr. [Martin Luther] King [Jr.], judges people "not by the color of their skin, but by the content of their character."

RADIO ADDRESS, WASHINGTON, DC, JANUARY 18, 1986

I applaud your many efforts and programs encouraging character development and leadership among American youth. By sponsoring many useful physical, mental, and social activities designed to promote self-responsibility, the Scouts strengthen the cornerstone of individual freedom in our nation. These programs develop the youngster's confidence in his ability to deal with nature, society, and a challenging world.

AS QUOTED AT WWW.SCOUTING.ORG

All of you and thousands of your friends in nationwide organizations like the Scouts ... have made our country a better place in which to live.

ADDRESS, "CEREMONY HONORING YOUTH VOLUNTEERS,"
WASHINGTON, DC, APRIL 25, 1985

GEORGE H.W.

BUSH

41ˢᵗ PRESIDENT OF THE UNITED STATES

1989–1993

Born: June 12, 1924 Milton, Massachusetts

Wife: Barbara Pierce (m. 1945)

Children: George Walker, Pauline Robinson, John Ellis "Jeb", Neil Mallon, Marvin Pierce, Dorothy

Education: Yale University (B.A.)

BSA Positions: Hon. President (1989–1993)
Hon. Vice President (1993–present)
Father of three Cub Scouts

BSA Honors: Silver Buffalo (1990)
Attended the 12ᵗʰ BSA National Jamboree, Fort A.P. Hill, Virginia (1989)

Eagle Scout Awards presented (1989–1992): 125,986

"...*you are leading the youth of America by example.*"

—President George H.W. Bush

CHAPTER SIXTEEN

GEORGE H.W. BUSH
The Extra Mile for Scouting

"His life is a testament that public service is a noble calling [and] his humility and his decency reflect the very best of the American spirit."

PRESIDENT BARACK OBAMA

February 15, 2011

O N MARCH 28, 1989, IN THE LIBRARY at the James Madison High School in Vienna, Virginia, President George H.W. Bush answered a question on volunteerism. "During the campaign I heard a lot of people wonder and talk about what exactly you meant by the Thousand Points of Light?" asked a young lady.

The president, pleased to have an opportunity to clarify an allusion that his presidential opponents had lampooned throughout the 1988 presidential campaign, offered a more concise vision: "It's almost anything you can think of that comes under the heading of volunteerism."

From that call to action in his Inaugural Address the previous January arose a celebration of the service-oriented spirit of the country through a commendation known as the "Daily Point of Light Award."

One year later in 1990, the Point of Light Foundation was formed "to encourage and empower the spirit of service" across the country, and to administer the award. Recipients would have a commemorative plaque cemented in concrete somewhere in the nation's capital.

On October 14, 2005, Boy Scouts of America (BSA) incorporator William D. Boyce was honored with one of the first markers on the "Extra Mile Points of Light Volunteer Pathway" in Washington, DC, by the Points of Light Institute. As a member of the first class of twenty inductees, which included Red Cross founder Clara Barton, Rotary International founder Paul Harris, and Goodwill Industries founder Edgar J. Helms, Boyce's bronze seal on the pathway was sponsored by the organization he had been instrumental in founding: BSA.

"We are humbled that the Boy Scouts of America is being honored through inclusion in such a profound national monument," said BSA Strategic Initiatives Director Willie Iles. "From its very inception, Scouting has taught our nation's youth about the power of volunteerism. As the nation's leading youth service organization, we honor our [incorporator's] vision of Scouting through our daily Good Turns toward society."

Added Points of Light Institute President Robert Goodwin: "[Boyce's] legacy epitomizes the spirit of service in America and provides an inspiring example of how we all have the ability to go the extra mile for our fellow citizens."

BSA was making a difference.

Bush receives BSA's *Annual Report* delegation at the White House in February 1992.

July 4 celebrations at the George Bush Library and Museum in College Station, Texas in 2012.

As president, Bush concerned himself with improving the lives of the nation's citizens. Among the landmark pieces of legislation to come out of his administration was the Americans with Disabilities Act (ADA) of 1990 that made illegal any type of discrimination based on disability in employment, transportation, or public accommodations. Stemming from the Civil Rights Act of 1964 under President Lyndon Johnson (with the 25th anniversary of its signing being celebrated in 1989 by President Bush), this law had been a priority of Bush's since his nomination speech at the Republican National Convention in 1988, when he declared, "I am going to do whatever it takes to make sure the disabled are included in the mainstream." He added that it would make them *less* dependent on the government.

In 1990, President Bush also signed the Immigration Act into law that increased the legal limits of immigration by 40 percent, along with revising any and all grounds for exclusion and deportation, authorized new temporary protective status for members of certain countries, created new nonimmigrant admission categories, additional worker visa limits, and updated naturalization requirements. The result was that 700,000 immigrants now could enter the country legally, up from 500,000 the previous year.

ALSO, WHILE PRESIDENT, Bush had the opportunity to visit the 12th National Jamboree held at Fort A.P. Hill, Virginia, in 1989. As the highlight of the closing ceremony arena show on August 7, President Bush arrived by Marine One helicopter around 10:30 a.m to the east of the stage.

Dressed in a dark suit, tie, and a smile, and with his hand waving from side to side, he bounded down the stairs from his helicopter, and took time to shake the hand of each Marine that was serving as his guard on base. Unlike earlier presidential jamboree entrances into the arena, Bush walked up through the middle of the stage from the ground below between a column of some 800 flags spaced ten feet apart going up the stairs (and several levels) to the podium.

Arriving onstage among the throngs of cheering Scouts and leaders, the president heard a clear whistle from behind. The Secret Service agent nearest the president jumped to attention as this was not in the official script. Bush again heard the whistle from a Scout onstage in the restricted area and walked towards the lad.

Extending his arm over the barrier, the Scout handed him a patch and said in a resounding voice, "You wanna trade, sir?"

Bush speaks at BSA's National Jamboree at Fort A.P. Hill in August 1989.

Bush shakes hands with a Scout during BSA's delivery of its *Annual Report* in February 1992.

Smiling, the president cheerfully took the patch and put it into his suit pocket. As government agents were seen frantically speaking into their lapel walkie-talkies, Bush reached down inside his jacket, removed his presidential tie clip, and handed it to the amazed Scout.

After shaking hands, the deal was done and President Bush walked the rest of the way to the rostrum without incident.

"That was one of the most gracious things that I ever witnessed a president do," recalled Jamboree staff member Paul Johnston of Dallas, Texas. "Everyone backstage was talking about his kindness to one of our boys. I bet that Scout will cherish that swap forever."

ON FEBRUARY 12, 1990, in the Oval Office, President George H.W. Bush was presented with the Silver Buffalo Medal and citation by BSA's special delegation upon delivering the 80th *Annual Report to the Nation*.

And his presidential response?

"Let me say to all how deeply honored I am to receive this highest award: the Silver Buffalo," President Bush began. "I live with a Silver Fox (wife Barbara) and now she lives with a Silver Buffalo."

IN HIS OWN WORDS

The law cannot tolerate any discrimination, and my administration will not tolerate abuse of that principle.

Address, Washington, DC, June 30, 1989

A Thousand Points of Light—you could make it a million…It is the Red Cross…It is the Boy Scouts . . . It is Christian Athletes. It is almost anything you can think of that comes under the heading of voluntarism.

Remarks, James Madison High School, Vienna, Virginia,
March 28, 1989

The Boy Scouts of America has assumed a leadership role in confronting this problem [of drug abuse]. You are teaching self-protection strategies against drugs and other dangers. You have circulated these strategies in direct language in a very successful pamphlet called "Drugs: A Deadly Game." And you have done something else—you are leading the youth of America by example.

Address, Fort A.P. Hill, August 7, 1898

WILLIAM J.

CLINTON

42ᴺᴰ President of the United States

1993–2001

Born: August 19, 1946, Hope, Arkansas

Wife: Hillary Rodham (m. 1975)
Children: Chelsea

Education: Georgetown University (B.S.)
University College, Oxford England (Rhodes Scholar)
Yale Law School (J.D.)

BSA Positions: Hon. President (1993–2001)
Hon. Vice President (2001–present)
Cub Scout, Hot Springs, Arkansas, Pack 1, Ramble
Elementary School, Ouachita Area Council, BSA

BSA Honors: Silver Buffalo (1997)
Sent Video Message to 13th BSA National Jamboree,
Fort A.P. Hill, Virginia (1993)
Attended 14th BSA National Jamboree, Fort A.P. Hill,
Virginia (1997)

Eagle Scout Awards presented (1993–2000): 309,108

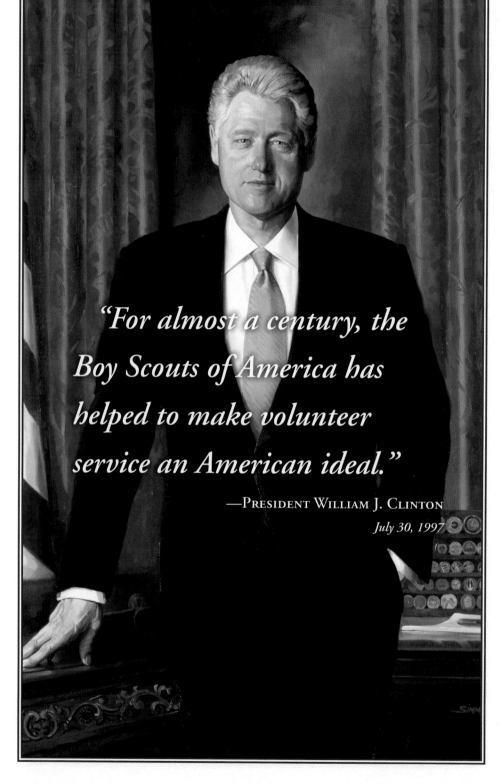

"For almost a century, the Boy Scouts of America has helped to make volunteer service an American ideal."

—President William J. Clinton

July 30, 1997

CHAPTER SEVENTEEN

WILLIAM J. CLINTON

Executive Destiny

"Bill Clinton is one of this nation's great leaders and most brilliant minds."

U.S. SENATOR BARACK H. OBAMA

ENTHUSIASTICALLY GREETED BY A MASSIVE CROWD of boys and adult volunteers cheering and waving flags, President William Jefferson "Bill" Clinton took the stage at the Boy Scouts of America's (BSA) 14th National Jamboree at Fort A.P. Hill in Virginia on the evening of July 30, 1997.

"I began as a Cub Scout in Hot Springs, Pack 1, Ramble Elementary School, Ouachita Area Council," Clinton began. "And those are the guys that are waving those flags back there. So don't boo them too hard. They're just sticking up for one of their own."

He electrified the crowd and congratulated them on their national service, which was something that he, himself, held dear. To him, holding elected office was a privilege that dated back decades.

In the days of his youth, few could have imagined the path that eventually would lead Clinton from the small American town of Hope, Arkansas, into the White House—propelled by his sparkling personality and strong work ethic. But even for the ambitious Clinton, there had to be inspiration; and that inspiration came in the presence of another United States president

Young Bill Clinton shakes the hand of President Kennedy at the White House in 1963.

by the name of John F. Kennedy. For young Bill, that brief meeting and handshake was "executive destiny."

IN 1963, HOT SPRINGS HIGH SCHOOL student Bill Clinton (one of two Arkansas Boys' State senators in the American Legion's Boys Nation) decided he wanted to be president of the United States.

Boys' State, organized in 1935 by the American Legion to teach students how to become "part of the operation of local, county, and state government," sought to counteract the socialist-inspired Young Pioneer Camps that were sprouting up during the Depression era of the 1930s, when socialist economic models were attractive to many Americans.

Boys Nation, formed eleven years later in 1946, was the national extension of Boys State where delegates were schooled on the actions of government through debate, voting on bills submitted by program delegates, learning U.S. Senate rules, and organizing a convention for the election of a national president and vice president.

Soon, the sixteen-year-old Clinton would be standing in the Rose Garden of the White House waiting to shake the hand of President John F. Kennedy.

"I decided that I wanted to be in public life as an elected official," Clinton recalled years later. "I was interested in medicine and thought I could be a fine doctor, but I knew I would never be Michael DeBakey [the inventor of the artificial heart]. But I knew I could be great in public service."

That was one of Bill Clinton's proudest moments—and the beginning of a career in public service that would lead to the White House thirty years later.

Clinton greets a Scout at BSA's National Jamboree in July 1997.

First Lady Hillary Rodham Clinton poses with Scouts during a presidential campaign stop in 1996.

WITH THAT HANDSHAKE, and Kennedy ever in mind, Clinton entered Georgetown University determined to make his vision of elected office a reality. During his sophomore year, Clinton decided to pledge a fraternity, but not just any one. He chose Alpha Phi Omega—APO—the Boy Scout-inspired national service fraternity.

APO was founded in 1925 at Lafayette College in Easton, Pennsylvania, by Frank Reed Horton under the motto, "Be a Leader, Be a Friend, Be of Service." Horton, a young naval serviceman in the First World War, witnessed younger seamen getting into trouble on leave, which bothered him greatly. Thus, he vowed to "help young people get the right start in life by holding them before a 'standard of manhood' that would withstand the test of time." Horton received an honorable discharge and launched his project.

"One evening, while attending an American Legion banquet during my sophomore year," Horton recalled, "I sat next to an inspiring man [who] was now serving as a local Scout executive." This man showed him that the structure for forming APO could be found in the Scout Oath and Law, which set standards "accepted by some of the greatest leaders the world has ever known."

Horton took the idea back to his fraternity brothers, many of whom had been Boy Scouts in their youth, and they agreed to participate. The result was APO that would provide "Leadership experience" based on "Service to others."

Georgetown University sophomore Bill Clinton pledged APO because it "ran elections and coordinated orientation activities on campus." It was a perfect fit for him because it gave him practical experience in the political process.

In 1966, he returned to Arkansas, where he worked on his first statewide political campaign for governor in backing J. Frank Holt, a former state supreme court justice and attorney general. Although Holt lost, Clinton was hooked on the process.

Rising to national prominence in 1978 as governor of Arkansas, Clinton reached the pinnacle of public life in 1992 with his election to the office of president of the United States. He was forty-six—the third youngest man to serve as president in U.S. history following John Kennedy and Theodore Roosevelt.

WHILE PRESIDENT, BILL CLINTON took equal rights among all citizens very seriously. He sought to end the era of racial profiling and instructed his Justice, Treasury, and Agriculture Departments to track the statistics of race, gender, and ethnicity of stops made by federal law enforcement. Finding some infractions, he supported "increased resources for police integrity and ethics training and to improve the diversity of local police forces."

In 1996, amidst a popular cry to end the legal requirement of Affirmative Action with regard to one's race, ethnicity, religion, or national origin in "employment, education or business," Clinton published his opinion of its importance in his book entitled, *Between Hope and History: Meeting America's Challenges for the 21ˢᵗ Century*.

"Affirmative action was intended to give everybody a fair chance, but it hasn't always worked smoothly and fairly," he argues. "Today there are those who are determined to put an end to affirmative action, as if the purposes for which it was created have been achieved. They have not. Until they are, we need to mend affirmative action, most certainly, but not end it."

It remains in place today.

Clinton shakes the hand of a Scout before his speech at BSA's National Jamboree in July 1997.

On June 9, 1998, Clinton signed into law the Transportation Equality Act for the 21st Century that protected the Disadvantaged Business Enterprise Program (it ensures that minority and women-owned businesses have a fair chance to compete for federal transportation projects) from elimination stemming from a proposed House bill.

He wished to expand the national service corps known as AmeriCorps up to one million members by the end of his term and to promote "character education" in public schools across the country.

AT THE SAME time, BSA recognized the potential impact of the rapidly growing minority populations across the country and formed ScoutReach in 1994—a program designed to aggressively recruit and promote Scouting within urban and ethnically diverse youth markets.

One result was the creation of the ¡Scouting...Vale La Pena! Service Award that recognized individuals or organizations that promoted BSA among Hispanic youth. This also could include sponsoring Scouting units or even funding Spanish-translated BSA handbooks, videos, or training materials.

Further diversification advancements included the development of Asian American Focus programs to entice Vietnamese American, Korean American, Chinese American, and Indo-Chinese American youth into the movement.

Also formulated were Rural Scouting programs and a focus on recruiting more Native American youth.

BY THE TIME of BSA's 1997 National Jamboree, Clinton was into his second term. But this was his first Jamboree to attend and it commemorated the 60th anniversary of the 1st National Jamboree held in 1937 that was hosted by President Franklin D. Roosevelt.

Walking to the site of the jamboree arena show after landing in the Marine One presidential helicopter, Clinton entered the secured backstage area at 7:40 p.m. where he was greeted by five Eagle Scouts and representatives of *Vanity Fair Magazine*. After a brief "meet and greet" with top BSA officials, President Clinton took the podium at 8:10 p.m.

"Building community and character is what Boy Scouts has always been about. So today I ask all of you to help spread the word about doing Good Turns," Clinton told the applauding legions of 36,000 Scouts and Leaders. "All of you here, each in your own way, are future leaders of this country. When you return home from the jamboree, please encourage your classmates and your friends to join you in committing to community service."

After his remarks, Chief Scout Executive Jere Ratliff joined the president on stage and presented him with the Silver Buffalo Award. Afterward, an appreciative President Bill Clinton worked the crowd across a rope line until his departure for the White House at precisely 9:00 p.m.

I have also said that affirmative action must be carefully justified and must be done the right way.

STATEMENT, WASHINGTON, DC, JUNE 13, 1995

For almost a century, the Boy Scouts of America has helped to make volunteer service an American ideal. With every act of kindness, you've strengthened our nation's commitment to community and promoted a sense of civic responsibility.

ADDRESS, 1997 NATIONAL JAMBOREE, BOWLING GREEN, VIRGINIA,
JULY 30, 1997

I think the Scouts do a world of good, and in our time they have begun to be more active in the cities, which I think is really important, to go into a lot of these places where the kids don't have a lot of family or community support.

INTERVIEW WITH JANN WENNER, *Rolling Stone Magazine*,
OCTOBER 10, 2000

GEORGE W.

BUSH

43ʳᵈ PRESIDENT OF THE UNITED STATES

2001–2009

Born: July 6, 1946 New Haven, Connecticut

Wife: Laura Lane Welch (m. 1977)
Children: Barbara Pierce, Jenna

Education: Yale University (B.A.)
             Harvard Business School (M.B.A.)

BSA Positions: Hon. President (2001–2009)
                  Hon. Vice President (2009–present)
                  Cub Scout, Buffalo Trail Council, BSA (1954)

BSA Honors: Silver Buffalo (2002)
               Sent Video Message to 15th BSA National Jamboree,
                  Fort A.P. Hill, Virginia (2001)
               Attended 16th BSA National Jamboree, Fort A.P. Hill,
                  Virginia (2005)

Eagle Scout Awards presented (2001–2008): 397,911

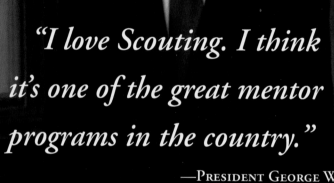

"I love Scouting. I think it's one of the great mentor programs in the country."

—President George W. Bush
March 3, 2011

CHAPTER EIGHTEEN

GEORGE W. BUSH
Rising from the Ashes

*"He is honest and straightforward,
and that is very important."*

THE DALAI LAMA
April 29, 2009

S PRESIDENT GEORGE W. BUSH WAS PREPARING to leave office in 2009, the Boy Scouts of America (BSA) unveiled its new slogan—"Where Tradition Meets Tomorrow"—in the approach to its centennial celebration to take place in 2010. The campaign would combine the older, traditional Scouting model with the new vision of modern-era Scouting in an effort to appeal to more young people of Scouting age. As the movement in America was preparing for its second century of service to youth, organizational managers felt that a healthy respect for its past would help move it forward keeping service to others squarely in view.

George Bush understood its long tradition; he had been a member of Cub Scouting in his early years. With mother (and Den Mother) Barbara Bush leading the way in Midland, Texas, young George recalled exciting trips to places like Carlsbad Caverns in New Mexico in the family car during the 1950s. As the president later would quip, "I think that's when her hair started to go white." Those lessons learned in Scouting as a boy had a lasting effect on him as a man.

And many years later, those American values would be challenged by foreign adversaries.

EARLY IN THE George W. Bush presidency, America was racked by the tragedy of a massive terrorist assault on the World Trade Center in New York, the Pentagon outside Washington, and another potential high-value governmental target. But out of the ashes of September 11, 2001, there emerged a more traditional kind of patriotism that had not been seen since the close of World War II in 1945.

Young George Bush as a Cub Scout in Midland, Texas, around 1955.

President Bush seized upon that spirit and signed legislation into law that promoted, equality, Americanism, and national heritage.

Like his predecessor, President Bush believed that racial profiling was antithetical to American values, and he put it in his homespun way.

"I can't imagine what it would be like to be singled out because of race and harassed. That's just flat wrong," he pleaded. "So we ought to do everything we can to end racial profiling."

On February 1, 2001, he announced the New Freedoms Initiative "to promote the full participation of people with disabilities in all areas of society by increasing access to assistive and universally designed technologies, expanding educational and employment opportunities, and promoting increased access into daily community life." Designed to support the Americans with Disabilities Act of 1990, Bush put his entire administration behind it.

He recognized that some schools still were not "equal in opportunity and excellence."

"Justice requires more than a place in a school," he added. "Justice requires that every school teach every child in America. The habits of racism in America have not all been broken. Laws against racial discrimination must be vigorously enforced in education and housing and hiring and public accommodations."

With regard to early actions regarding national conservation, his 2003 executive order authorized the *Preserve America* initiative. The president laid out a vision to provide "leadership in preserving America's heritage by actively advancing the protection, enhancement, and contemporary use of the historic properties owned by the federal government." It would promote "intergovernmental cooperation and partnerships for the preservation and use of historic properties."

It allowed for up to $17 million in grants to be awarded "to protect our cultural and natural heritage in all 50 states," that included 220 grants to recognize over 700 locations as Preserve America Communities.

Award recipients in 2008 created projects that restored 39 historic Texas courthouses, relocated 20,000 human remains from a 17th century African American burial ground in Manhattan, and funded a tourism initiative for the Corinth Unit of the Shiloh National Military Park in Tennessee dating to the Civil War.

Bush also pushed for conservation policies and environmental land protections that included the creation of 15 new National Wildlife Refuges and the re-emphasis of goals under the Endangered Species Act.

He authorized $1 billion to be used for "assessments and clean-ups" in 10,000 contaminated industrial sites through the Brownfield Programs that cleaned up local properties riddled with hazardous waste.

He placed under federal protection 140,000 square miles of coral reef ecosystems that supports 7,000 species of marine life in the Northern Hawaiian Islands, expanded the Monterey Bay National Marine Sanctuary by 775 square miles, and increased funding for the National Oceanic Atmospheric Administration by $770 million during his administration.

In 2008, the president hosted the White House Conference on North American Wildlife Policy to "facilitate the expansion and enhancement of hunting opportunities and the management of game species and their habitat."

Thus President Bush continued to build on the legacy of presidential conservation championed by Theodore Roosevelt in 1901 as it allowed the common citizen to participate in the rescue of the country's great natural resources.

Yet these millions of federal dollars were dwarfed by the economic strength generated by the American people through their power of mass volunteerism. BSA could offer more national help by recruiting more volunteers.

KNOWING THAT THE growing Hispanic population was attracted to the game of soccer, BSA's first Hispanic member of its Executive Board and first Hispanic recipient of the Silver Buffalo award, Jose F. Niño, developed and promoted the use of the sport to attract those youth. The result was the creation of the Soccer and Scouting program launched in the summer of 2004 in partnership with the National Soccer Coaches Association of America. Now, a healthy dose of their favorite pastime would be sandwiched between two halves of a Scout meeting. Rank patches would be worn on the left uniform sleeves of their game jersey. That program attracted over 100,000 Hispanic youths to BSA.

In 2005, BSA conducted major research on the major ethnic cultures living in the United States in preparation for the development of its 2006 —2010 Strategic Plan. BSA found that African American boys were most influenced by musicians and that selected ones should be approached to become spokesmen for the program. Hispanic boys wanted a program based upon activities and sports (making Soccer and Scouting a positive influence), while Asian American lads likely would join if Scouting was promoted by their teachers or other successful members of their ethnic community.

Bush hugs Cub Scout Bryson Hicks during the delivery of BSA's *Annual Report* in February 2007. In May 2008, Silver Buffalo recipient Tico Perez (far left) became the first person of Hispanic origin to serve as BSA's National Scout Commissioner.

BSA now was making well-planned, concerted efforts to take the Scouting program out to the kids of all ethnicities rather than trying to attract those kids into the program.

IN HIS 2002 State of the Union address to Congress, President Bush called upon the nation to rally and to rebuild itself after the September terrorist attacks that had happened just a few months prior.

"My call tonight is for every American to commit at least two years—4,000 hours over the rest of your lifetime—to the service of your neighbors and your Nation," he said. From that call to action came the President's Volunteer Service Award.

Awarded at bronze, silver, and gold levels; the President's Call to Service Award for lifetime achievement can be earned by kids, young adults, and family units based on their cumulative service hours spent working within the community.

To date, over 1.5 million individuals have earned the various levels of the award with 28,000 certifying organizations having been registered to attest to

Bush poses with Scouts at BSA's National Jamboree at Fort A.P. Hill in July 2005.

the service performed. Not surprisingly, one of those certifying organizations is BSA's own national society of honor campers—the Order of the Arrow.

During the summer of 2008, the Order of the Arrow joined forces with the U.S. Forest Service to perform much-needed maintenance work in selected national parks across the country. This became known as the *Arrow-Corps5* project for "5 parks, 5 weeks, and 5 thousand Arrowmen" with the amassed Scouts giving 280,000 service hours that resulted in $5.6 million worth of improvements in estimated labor and project costs.

But BSA's spirit of service has gone much further over the recent decades. Performed annually since 1988, its National Good Turn has been the mass collection of canned goods for local food banks. It is known as "Scouting for Food."

HOSTED BY EVERY BSA council at the request of the current Chief Scout Executive, the Scouting for Food National Good Turn service project typically takes place over one or two weekends. On the first Saturday, Scouts canvass their neighborhoods and place food collection bags on the doors of their neighbors. The following week, Scouts and their leaders pick up the filled bags and deliver them to pre-selected local food banks for distribution to needy families.

In its inaugural drive in 1988, over 60 million cans of food were collected by nearly 4.2 million Cub and Boy Scouts in service to the less fortunate in their communities. Since then, more than a billion cans have been collected and donated in this way.

In 2009, one of the families that gave canned goods to the Scouting for Food campaign organized by the Circle Ten Council of Dallas, Texas, were new residents George and Laura Bush.

ON THE MORNING of February 21, 2009, a small contingent of Cub Scouts from Pack 19 in Circle Ten Council's North Trail District made their way to the security barricade in the Dallas neighborhood of the former president that was manned by a small army of Secret Service agents. Since prior arrangements had been made, Wolf Cub Den Leader Nancy Burke led her young Scouts across the barricade and into the collection area for their Scouting for Food canvass.

"You had to do a bit of coordinating with the Secret Service and with President Bush's scheduler," Burke said later in a TV interview.

Bush shakes the hand of Cub Scout Chandler Burke of Pack 19 in Dallas' Circle Ten Council in February 2009 during the annual Scouting for Food drive.

Bush poses with BSA's *Annual Report* delegation in March 2005 at the White House.

But knowing the uniqueness of the opportunity, she did so, even to the extent of holding a drawing for the Scout who would have the honor of ringing the president's door bell to collect the food bags.

Opening the door in his presidential bomber-style jacket, Bush greeted the lads with a hearty "Come on down!" and motioned the rest of the Scouts to join him on the lawn.

Albeit shocked, the lads slowly approached the nation's former chief executive, who either had been their state's governor or president during the entirety of their short lives, and joined him for a photo session that was captured by a former *Dallas Morning News* staff photographer, Carolyn Herter Stalder, now an adult leader in Pack 19.

After signing autographs and handing over several bags of food (one of which included a container of Bush's Baked Beans), the former president and first lady said "goodbye" and returned inside. Neighbors reported that the former First Family "is just trying to fit in, so they helped the Scouts help thousands, because that's what good neighbors do."

And the Bushes have donated canned food every year since.

YEARS EARLIER DURING the delivery of the 92nd *Annual Report to the Nation* in 2002, BSA presented the Silver Buffalo Award to President George W. Bush in recognition for his being an "advocate for youth" in addition to his duties as Honorary President of the Boy Scouts of America.

IN HIS OWN WORDS

As a Nation, and as individuals, we must be vigilant in responding to discrimination wherever we find it.

PROCLAMATION 7664, APRIL 15, 2003

The goodness of a person and of the society he or she lives in often comes down to very simple things and words found in the Scout Law. Every society depends on trust and loyalty, on courtesy and kindness, on bravery and reverence. These are the values of Scouting, and these are the values of Americans.

ADDRESS, FORT A.P. HILL, VA, JULY 30, 2001

Every day, Scouts are showing that the greatest strength of America lies in the hearts and souls of our citizens. Through your Good Turn for America initiative, Scouts have given more than 1.4 million hours of volunteer service this year alone . . . On behalf of a grateful Nation, I thank the Boy Scouts for serving on the front line of America's armies of compassion.

ADDRESS, FORT A.P. HILL, VA, JULY 31, 2005

——— BARACK H. ———

OBAMA

44TH PRESIDENT OF THE UNITED STATES

——— 2009–PRESENT ———

Born: August 4, 1961 Honolulu, Hawaii

Wife: Michelle LaVaughn Robinson (m. 1992)
Children: Malia, Sasha

Honors: Nobel Peace Prize (2009)

Education: Occidental College
     Columbia University (B.A.)
     Harvard Law School (J.D.)

BSA Positions: Hon. President (2009–present)
       Cub Scout, Jakarta, Indonesia (1970–1971)

BSA Honors: Silver Buffalo (2012)
        Sent Video Message to 17th BSA National Jamboree,
        Fort A.P. Hill, Virginia, (2010)

Eagle Scout Awards presented (2009–2013): 274,253

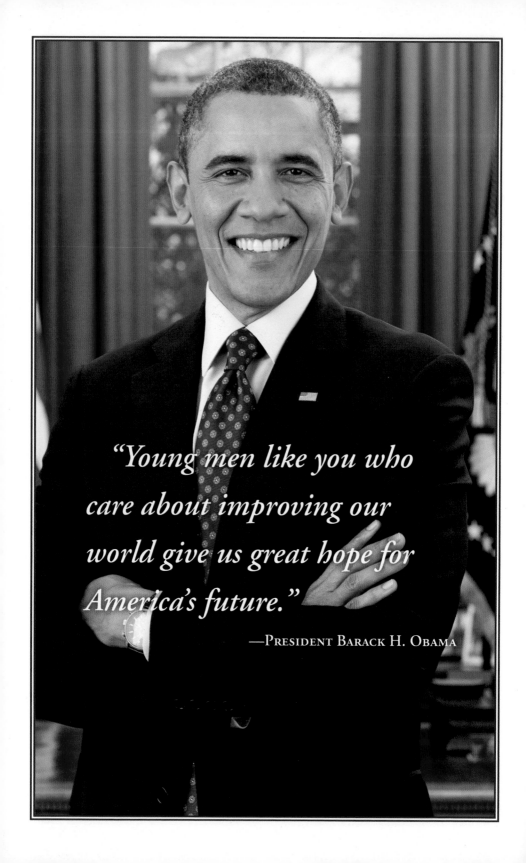

CHAPTER NINETEEN

BARACK H. OBAMA

Scouting's Centennial President

"Senator Obama has been a great inspiration for millions of people around the country."

PRESIDENT WILLIAM J. CLINTON

FROM THE "BULLY PULPIT" OF THE OVAL OFFICE, the nation's chief executive always has communicated his appreciation for the Boy Scouts of America (BSA) and their legacy.

Barack H. Obama is no different.

Spending some of his young life in Indonesia—home to the greatest number of Scouts in the world at over 15 million—his mother believed it important for him to be a member of the Cub Scouts, known as the Siaga. While a resident of Jakarta, Obama—then known as "Barry"—he was recalled by a former classmate as being a "good kid" who partook in the program at the Besuki Elementary school from 1970–1971.

"We learned, at that time, how to use rope for building camp tents, [and] climbing," recalled his former Scout friend. "But Barry Obama never got the chance to camp outside the city ... he went back to Hawaii in 1972."

ELECTED TO THE U.S. presidency in 2008, the nation's first African American chief executive presided as BSA's Honorary President during the organization's centennial year celebrations in 2010.

"Our Nation's future depends on how well we educate the next generation of leaders," he wrote in a message delivered to BSA's 100th anniversary gala held in a Washington, DC, hotel during the record-setting February 2010 blizzard. "By building a strong foundation of service, character, and active learning, we can open doors of opportunity for our children and secure a brighter future for our country."

But to obtain that brighter future in a rapidly changing, technology-driven world of computers, mobile devices, video games and Internet social media, the nation's youth must learn that self-worth is gained through hard work in school rooms in their communities, and the "school rooms of nature."

Obama greets a BSA delegate during the delivery of the *Annual Report* in March 2011.

"THEODORE ROOSEVELT WAS one of my favorite presidents, one of our greatest presidents and certainly one of our greatest conservation presidents … [whose conservation] legacy is an extraordinary achievement," President Obama declared at the April 16, 2010, signing ceremony of his America's Great Outdoors initiative.

In recognizing the importance of Roosevelt's vision of outdoor preservation, Obama introduced his own objective: re-introduce Americans to our nation's natural wonders.

"Americans are blessed with a vast natural heritage," Obama wrote. "[We] take pride in these places, and share a responsibility to preserve them for our children and grandchildren. Today, however, we are losing touch with too many of these places and proud traditions that have helped make [America] special … We will work to connect these outdoor spaces to each other, and to reconnect Americans to them."

Through February 2013, the America's Great Outdoors initiative had designated over two million additional acres of wilderness, three more national parks, and more than 1,000 miles of "wild and scenic rivers" as federally protected.

As there is a wide "patchwork of groups" ranging from government entities to nongovernmental organizations to ordinary citizens—with an interest in such resources, the Obama Administration held many "listening sessions" with thousands of Americans to determine how best to use protected lands.

From those discussions, the concept of a Conservation Service Corps (CSC) came to light as a way for the country to unify under the banner of land preservation. This was not unlike BSA's *ArrowCorps5* work for the National Park Service through its Order of the Arrow society of honor campers during the George W. Bush Administration. Either way, volunteer service performed by the country's youth would ensure its success.

In BSA's 2010 *Annual Report to the Nation*, it noted that Scouting volunteers donated an average of 20 hours a month to community service projects, which totaled over 273 million hours. This volunteerism equaled about $5 billion given to the nation over the year.

And of these millions of service hours, 56,000 Eagle Scout projects accounted for $210 million "in service to schools, churches, and communities across the nation."

And as BSA delegates proudly pointed out to the president, "The Boy Scouts of America is where young people can learn what those values mean, commit them to memory, and—more important—put them into practice."

Additionally, with a similar premise is First Lady Michelle Obama's "Let's Move" campaign against childhood obesity. BSA supports and promotes an active lifestyle of healthy living through sports, recreation, and strenuous achievement at the nation's numerous camps and National High Adventure Bases, at which over a million Scouts participated during its centennial year.

Obama poses with a Scout during the delivery of BSA's *Annual Report* in March 2009.

DURING THE SUMMER of 2012 at the Philmont Scout Ranch in Cimarron, New Mexico, BSA held its first national Spanish Woodbadge advanced adult leader training course that was taught in both the English and Spanish languages. Under the watchful eye of Course Director Jose F. Niño, the sessions instructed Hispanic Scout leaders as well as persons wanting to expand the Scouting program into their local Hispanic communities. Being a product of BSA's new All Market Strategy designed to aggressively promote Scouting within all ethnic communities and diversely populated areas, it was deemed a success and a second course has been planned for the future. But this event pales in comparison to the dramatic new membership policy voted on at the 2013 National Annual Meeting in Grapevine, Texas.

At that gathering, BSA managers and selected council representatives affirmed a new policy allowing homosexual youths to join as members – a decision that caused ripple effects across Scouting and the nation. As a caveat, sexual orientation was not to be discussed or promoted within the organization's ranks. Not surprisingly, some approved, others did not.

A YEAR EARLIER AT BSA's 2011 National Annual Meeting held in San Diego, California, the organization introduced a new partnership with the White House aimed at encouraging members to "engage, educate, and empower youth to adopt a healthy lifestyle that includes regular physical activity and good nutrition." Working in tandem with the President's Council on Fitness, Sports and Nutrition (PCFSN) and the First Lady's "Let's Move" campaign, Scouts and leaders worked to earn the President's Active Lifestyle Awards through the President's Challenge initiative.

The President's Challenge is the premier program offered by the government's Council on Fitness. It is administered by the Amateur Athletic Union, which "helps people of all ages and abilities increase their physical activity and improve their fitness through research-based information, easy-to-use tools, and friendly motivation." Founded in the 1960s, with an initial program consisting only of youth fitness testing, the Council on Fitness expanded to include adult fitness tests and the President's Active Lifestyle Award (PALA).

PALA is designed for participation by children from the age of six through adulthood. It encourages activity at least 60 minutes a day, five days a week for eight weeks for youths under 18 years of age, and for 30 minutes a day for adults. Alternative challenges are 13,000 steps a day for boys, 11,000 steps for girls, and 8,500 steps a day for adults. Successful participants receive an official patch.

ON FEBRUARY 16, 2011, nine youth members of BSA passed through security checkpoints at the White House.

Fresh from meetings with Speaker of the House John Boehner, Defense Secretary and Distinguished Eagle Scout Robert Gates, CIA Director Leon Panetta, and Chairman of the Joint Chiefs of Staff Admiral Mike Mullen, the delegation made its way down the long corridors to the Oval Office anteroom.

Soon the two large doors opened and a smiling president greeted the Scouts.

"President Obama had such a magnificent personality," recalled Order of the Arrow National Chief Jonathan Hillis. "He really just drew us in."

National Venturing President Jennifer Lowe of Utah agreed.

"I was so nervous," she said. "I kept reminding myself that this was real. We're in the Oval Office with the president!"

Obama opened the conversation by asking each Scout his or her name and shaking everyone's hand.

"We introduced ourselves," recalled Lowe, "and he asked about the Venturing program."

Led to the famed presidential desk made from timbers of the *H.M.S. Resolute* (a British Royal Navy vessel caught in the ice of the Arctic Circle

Obama receives BSA's *Annual Report* in November 2010 from National Sea Scout Boatswain M. Robert Marks.

in 1854, abandoned, and salvaged by an American whaling ship in 1855). Some of its timbers were made into a desk and given to President Rutherford B. Hayes in 1880 by a grateful Queen Victoria.

Lowe, assigned to present BSA's *Annual Report* to the president, gently opened the case, held it briefly for White House photographer Pete Souza to capture, then turned it over to a cheerfully smiling and receptive President Obama.

"It was really significant," said Lowe, "because it was the one hundredth year report."

After a few more photographs, the delegation was led out of the Oval Office. However, its members still were coming to the realization that Scouting had taken them to meet the president of the United States.

"That was a pretty unforgettable experience," recalled Hillis. "I'll be telling my grandkids about [it] one day."

National Venturing President Jennifer Lowe presents Obama with BSA's Centennial *Annual Report* in March 2011.

IN HIS OWN WORDS

For we know that our patchwork heritage is a strength, not a weakness. We are a nation of Christians and Muslims, Jews and Hindus, and non-believers. We are shaped by every language and culture, drawn from every end of this Earth; and because we have tasted the bitter swill of civil war and segregation, and emerged from that dark chapter stronger and more united, we cannot help but believe that the old hatreds shall someday pass; that the lines of tribe shall soon dissolve; that as the world grows smaller, our common humanity shall reveal itself; and that America must play its role in ushering in a new era of peace.

INAUGURAL ADDRESS, WASHINGTON, DC, JAN. 20. 2009

We congratulate you on earning the rank of Eagle Scout. Your hard work, dedication, and sense of service have earned you this recognition as one of our Nation's bright young leaders.

We hope you continue to draw upon the values you learned as a Scout to benefit your community and your country. Young men like you who care about improving our world give us great hope for America's future.

PRESIDENTIAL LETTER OF CONGRATULATIONS TO EAGLE SCOUTS

from the OVAL OFFICE

THEODORE **ROOSEVELT**

I EARNESTLY BELIEVE IN
THE BOY SCOUT MOVEMENT

FEBRUARY 10, 1911

Mr. [Executive Secretary] James E. West

My dear Sir:

I earnestly believe in the Boy Scout Movement because I see the national possibility of this movement among boys. There are several things which we should see in the lives of our American boys. They should grow up strong and alert, able to stand the strain of an honest day's hard work, and of an honest attempt to help forward the material and moral progress of our nation.

American boyhood should be resourceful and inventive so that the American man of the future may be ever ready to help in the hour of the nation's need. American boys should always show good manners, and the desire to help all who are in trouble or difficulty and indeed to help the weak at all times. Courtesy is as much the mark of a gentleman as truthfulness and courage, and every American boy should be a gentleman, fearless in defending his own rights and the rights of the weak, and scrupulous to inflict no wrong on others. The boy who is to grow into the right kind of man should scorn lying as he scorns cowardice, and he should remember that [one] is always considerate of and courteous towards others. In this nation of ours, the ideal of everyone should be to help in the work of all.

Therefore let each boy try to render service to others, and try to do well in every task that comes to his hands, big or little. The boys of America should understand our institutions and their history; they should know of the lives of the great men that have blazed the trail for our national greatness, and of the mighty deeds that they wrought; they should feel a high pride of country and a real spirit of patriotism, which will make them emulate these careers of gallant and efficient service and of willingness to make sacrifices for the sake of a lofty ideal.

American boys should grow up understanding the life of the community about them, and appreciating the privileges and the duties of citizenship, so that they may face the great questions of national life with the ability and resolute purpose to help in solving them aright. Each boy should make up his mind that . . . he will do his part in serving the nation as a whole.

I believe heartily in the work your Association is doing for the community about them, and appreciating the privileges and the duties of citizenship, so that they may face the great questions of national life with the ability and resolute purpose to help patriotism, true citizenship, true Americanism. I wish all success to a movement fraught with such good purposes.

Faithfully Yours,

APPEAL TO THE BOYS OF AMERICA

OCTOBER 7, 1913

Through *Boys' Life* I wish to send this message, not only to the Boy Scouts, but to all the boys of America. The prime lesson that the Boy Scout movement is teaching is the lesson that manliness in its most vigorous form can be and ought to be accompanied by unselfish consideration for the rights and interests of others.

Indeed I can go a little further. I wish that I could make the especial appeal to the American boy to remember that unless he thinks of others he cannot fit himself to do the best work in any great emergency.

The names in our history to which we now look back with pride are the names of men who have rendered great service. This service may have been rendered at the same time that they themselves gained glory or reputation. But neither the glory nor the reputation would have been gained save as an incident to the service.

In our history there is now practically no mention of any great financier, of any great business man, who merely made money for himself. If at some crisis in the nation's history that financier rendered a great national service, or if he identified himself in useful fashion with some great movement for good, whether in art or philanthropy or otherwise, then his name remains. But even under these conditions it remains as of secondary value. America's contribution to world history has been made by the statesmen and soldiers whose devotion to the country equaled their efficiency, by men of science, men of art, men of letters, by sane and honest reformers, who did great work and treated that work as in itself a great reward,

The two greatest men in our history are Washington and Lincoln. They possessed great ability, great intellect, and especially great sanity of mind; but it was the fact that they each possessed the highest character, a character both very strong and very unselfish, which gave them their preeminence over their fellows.

There have been very able and very unscrupulous statesmen in our history. But not one of them has ever come within even measurable distance of the achievements of Washington and Lincoln, or of the reputation of Washington and Lincoln; and this precisely because they were unscrupulous, because they lacked character.

Let me illustrate what I mean by an example from my own experience.

When fifteen years ago I was helping to raise the regiment of Rough Riders, I did my best to get both officers and enlisted men those men, and those men only, who I believed would make formidable fighters in a battle, rugged men in a campaign, and men of indomitable purpose to see the war through. I would not take any man who was not strong, hardy, brave, able to live in the open, able to handle both horse and rifle.

But even if the man had all those qualities, if he were quarrelsome or egotistical, or bent only on his own selfish advancement, and if I knew that this was the case, I would not take him. If he cared only for himself I was sure that he would be apt to be a bad instead of a good element in the regiment. These were some men from the plains whom I refused, although I knew that they were formidable fighting men, because I also knew that they were quarrelsome bullies and would wish to exalt themselves at the expense of their comrades; and I did not wish any man with me unless he was prepared to put the honor of the regiment and the army and the flag first of all. If a man of the wrong type got into the regiment and I found that, though brave, he was thinking only of his own advancement and shirked doing work that might help others, or intrigued against them, or failed to support them, I got rid of him or discriminated against him or else took the first chance to punish him as roughly as I could. The best work could be done only by the m a n who, in addition to possessing formidable fighting qualities, had the desire to help others and the willingness to sink his own advantage i n the common advantage.

What was trine on a very small scale in my regiment is true on a very big scale of American citizenship as a whole. The boy is not worth anything if he is not efficient. I have no use for mollycoddles, I have no use for timid boys, for the "sissy" type of boy. I went to see a boy able to hold his own and ashamed to flinch. But as one element of this ability to hold his own, I wish to see him contemptuously indifferent to the mean or brutal boy who calls him "sissy" or a mollycoddle because he is clean and decent and considerate to others. If a boy is not fearless and energetic, he is a poor creature; but he is an even poorer creature if he is a bully of smaller boys or girls, if he is guilty of cruel mischief, and if in his own home, and especially is his relations with his own mother and sisters, he is selfish and unfeeling.

I believe in play with all my heart; but I believe in work even more. While boy or man plays, I want to see him play hard; and when he works I don't want to see him play at all.

BOY SCOUTS, YOU'VE MADE THE TEAM

September 2, 1917

Excerpts of an address by Col. Theodore Roosevelt to the Encampment of Boy Scouts at Mineola, Long Island, tender the auspices of the Nassau County Council, of which Col. Roosevelt is Honorary Scout Commissioner, Sunday afternoon, September 2nd, 1917. It was Mr. Roosevelt's expressed intention that in speaking to this audience he should be understood as addressing all Boy Scouts throughout the United States, and all the friends of the organization. Every Scout will be thrilled by these ringing words from the most virile American alive.

FELLOW BOY SCOUTS: Of course, I have a right to say "Fellow Boy Scouts," for I sit here as one of your Scoutmasters. I am not only proud of Nassau County for what you boys have done in organizing this body here in this country as you have, but I congratulate with all my heart the American people on the Boy Scout movement; and I want you boys to feel this. Boys of your age ordinarily cannot feel as yet that they have done much for the country as citizens, but you boys - the Boy Scouts - are different. Because of the leadership given by your organization you are already doing your part. You are on the team now - Uncle Sam's Team. You are doing your bit. And I tell you, it is worthwhile. I do not know a man or a boy worth his salt who has not got the desire to be a part of the team that counts, and to do his share in making it count. That is what every red-blooded American has got to feel, or he isn't worth being called an American. It is what you boys are doing.

We have got 258,000 Boy Scouts, and about 75,000 [Scoutmasters] who are in the movement as leaders, and I won't be content until instead of 258,000 we have 2,580,000.

And now, boys, nothing could have pleased me more than what President Earle said in introducing me, when he spoke of a sentence I had used, and said it ought to be the motto on which the Boy Scouts act. It ought to be the motto on which all of us here act, and also on which every grown-up American acts: "NEVER BE NEUTRAL BETWEEN RIGHT AND WRONG."

One of the lessons that it is most important to teach the average American—the men you boys are to be—is to teach him that when he is neutral between right and wrong, he is helping the wrong. If you are not with the right, then you are against the right. And you boys have got to cultivate not only the habit of being decent yourselves, but of helping to make other people decent. Therefore, you have got to be good, decent and efficient. I have got mighty little use for the type of good man or good boy of whom all you can say is that he is harmless.

Boy Scouts, I want you to count in the game of life. I believe in this movement with all my heart. The democracy of our Government must be based fundamentally on the kind of spirit you show—the service you give. No man is entitled to a privilege if he does not perform a duty. You can't, any of you, enjoy the privileges of a Boy Scout if you stay out and don't do any of the work.

On the whole, the Scoutmasters and similar officers represent a very high type—an unusually high type—of leadership in the community. We have a right to expect the very best men in the community to come forward to do that work, and I wish to emphasize with all my power that it is an unpatriotic thing to let the Boy Scout movement be hampered in any way by the fact that the Scoutmasters and leaders of the boys have shown their patriotism by going into the army, and I urge you who stay at home, show that you know what patriotism is by coming in and taking their places.

And now I appeal to all good Americans who wish to help the America of the future to help it in some tangible way by taking the places of the Scoutmasters or other officials of the Boy Scouts of America who have gone to the front, and who have made all of us their debtors by going to fight the battle for American manhood and civilization.

Many of the Scoutmasters and leaders of this organization have shown their patriotism by going to war, and now let every good American show his patriotism by encouraging and supporting the Boy Scouts of America in every way within his power.

Good luck to you.

WOODROW WILSON

ADDRESS TO NATIONAL COUNCIL

FEBRUARY 11, 1915

Gentlemen:

I am sincerely glad to have the pleasure of this visit from you, and to have an opportunity to express my very sincere interest not only in the organization of the Boy Scouts but in the objects that that organization has. From all that I know of [the Boy Scouts of America], and from all that I have been able to observe personally, it is an admirable organization, devoted to the objects that I myself thoroughly believe in.

There is only one rule in the world, and it applies to all professions, and that is that you are expected to "make good." No excuses are allowed in this school of life, and the only way to make good is to keep faith. That is the reason I like the idea of the Boy Scouts – because of their secure notion of being responsible to society. They are responsible to the people who live around them—to help maintain the standards of order and fidelity upon which the community depends.

You are recruits in the ranks that we all stand in, and that is to serve the country in some way that will tell, and that has nothing particular to do with our own personal benefit. The man who devotes himself exclusively to the development of his own character will succeed in nothing except to make of himself a prig. But if he devotes himself to helping other people his character will not only take care of itself but it will grow to a very noble stature.

I congratulate you for belonging to it and hope you will honor it in every way by your conduct and allegiance.

LETTER TO CHIEF SCOUT EXECUTIVE
JAMES E. WEST

JUNE 4, 1915

I am very much interested by what you say of the special edition of *Boys' Life* you are planning to get out, and as honorary president of the Boy Scouts of America, I cannot let this opportunity pass to send my warmest greetings and best wishes.

It is fine to have the boys of the country organized for the purposes the Boy Scouts represent, and whenever I see a group of them, I am proud of their manliness and feel cheered by the knowledge of what their organization represents.

This is just to bid you Godspeed.

LETTER TO BSA PRESIDENT
COLIN H. LIVINGSTONE

MARCH 14, 1918

Will you again muster the full strength of the Boy Scouts of America for co-operation with the Treasury Department in securing subscriptions for the Third Liberty Loan? As in the two previous campaigns it is desired to have the Boy Scouts of America serve as "gleeners" in a house-to-house canvass after the "reapers," gleaning during the days set aside for your special campaign.

The patriotic and effective service of the Boy Scouts in your definitely planned program of war work activities is a splendid testimonial to the organized boyhood in helping our country win the war.

It is my earnest wish that every troop of Boy Scouts and every Scout and Scout official take part in your war service activities and especially in these Liberty Loan campaigns. But only is this of practical service to our country in these critical times, but it is of great educational value to the boys in preparing them for the responsibilities of citizenship.

LETTER TO THE BOY SCOUTS OF AMERICA

NOVEMBER 4, 1920

It gives me pleasure to tell you of my deep appreciation of the intelligent and conscientious manner in which you, as a member of the Boy Scouts of America, have secured subscriptions for Thrift and War Savings Stamps.

You have exercised courage, courtesy, thought and untiring effort, and in so doing have set an example for all boys – an example that will surely aid in the growth of valuable qualities of heart and mind. I thank you in the name of the whole country, and I wish to convey to your parents, your community and your Boy Scout organization my appreciation of the training that has developed in you such a fine spirit of wholesome and loyal citizenship.

Cordially and sincerely yours,

A PROCLAMATION BY THE PRESIDENT OF THE UNITED STATES OF AMERICA

MAY 1, 1919
(ISSUED DURING THE PEACE CONFERENCE AT PARIS)

The Boy Scouts of America have rendered notable service to the Nation during the world war. They have done effective work in the Liberty Loan and War Savings campaigns, in discovering and reporting upon the black walnut supply in cooperating with the Red Cross and other war work agencies, in acting as despatch bearers for the Committee on Public Information, and in other important fields. The Boy Scouts have not only demonstrated their worth to the Nation, but have also materially contributed to a deeper appreciation by the American people of the higher conception of patriotism and good citizenship.

The Boy Scout movement should not only be preserved, but strengthened. It deserves the support of all public-spirited citizens. The available means for the Boy Scout movement have thus far sufficed for the organization and training of only a small proportion of the boys of the country. There are approximately 10,000,000 boys in the United States between the ages of twelve and twenty-one. Of these only 375,000 are enrolled as members of the Boy Scouts of America.

America cannot acquit herself commensurately with her power and influence in the great period now facing her and the world unless the boys of America are given better opportunities than heretofore to prepare themselves for the responsibilities of citizenship.

Every nation depends for its future upon the proper training and development of its youth. The American boy must have the best training and discipline our great democracy can provide if America is to maintain her ideals, her standards and her influence in the world.

The plan, therefore, for a Boy Scout week during which a universal appeal will be made to all Americans to supply the means to put the Boy Scouts of America in a position to carry forward effectively and continuously the splendid work they are doing for the youth of America, should have the unreserved support of the Nation.

Therefore, I, Woodrow Wilson, President of the United States of America do hereby recommend that the period beginning Sunday June 8th to Flag Day, June 14th, be observed as Boy Scout Week through the United States for the purpose of strengthening the work of the Boy Scouts of America.

I earnestly recommend that, in every community, a Citizens' Committee, under the leadership of a National Citizens' Committee, be organized to cooperate in carrying out a program for a definite recognition of the effective services rendered by the Boy Scouts of America: for a survey of the facts relating to the boyhood of each community, in order that with the cooperation of churches, schools and other organizations definitely engaged in work for boys, adequate provision may be made for extending the Boy Scout program to a larger proportion of American boyhood.

The Boy Scout movement offers unusual opportunity for volunteer service. It needs men to act as committeemen and as leaders of groups of boys. I hope that all who can will enlist for such personal service, enroll as associate members and give all possible financial assistance to this worthy organization of American boyhood. Anything that is done to increase the effectiveness of the Boy Scouts of America will be a genuine contribution to the welfare of the Nation.

In Witness Whereof, I have hereunto set my hand and caused the seal of the United States to be affixed.

Done this first day of May in the year of our Lord one thousand nine hundred and nineteen and of the independence of the United States of America the one hundred and forty-third.

GREETINGS FROM SENATOR HARDING TO CHIEF SCOUT EXECUTIVE JAMES E. WEST

OCTOBER 1920

It is particularly a pleasure to comply with your request for a word of greeting to the army of Boy Scouts of America.

It is also gratifying to have you remind me that under your practice the President of the United States automatically becomes Honorary President of the Boy Scouts of America.

To occupy that post would certainly be to any real American one of the satisfactions incident to the office of Chief Executive.

Probably the Great War [First World War] had brought on all to realize more acutely than ever before that the Boy Scouts of today are the boys who, almost without question, would be the National Army, if there were necessity for us again to raise a great force to protect our country and our institutions.

The parents of this country, at least, have been able to realize how short a step it is from the age at which boys constitute your splendid organization to that at which they become eligible for service in the armed forces of the Nation. The determination to draft men for the Army and Navy from the age of eighteen years up reminded us how very short a time may be elapsed between the boy's doffing of the Boy Scouts uniform and his donning of the military or naval uniform of his country.

The war taught us that the young soldier is the most easily trained and physically fit man in the service, as a rule. I fully believe that the great work of your organization in inculcating principles of self-reliance and capacity to take care of one's self, was one of the important contributions to making our army the great and magnificently effective organization that we know it was. We all hope most devoutly that the time will never come when we need again to summon our young manhood to the duties and sacrifices of the battlefield; but if such a time shall come, we are bound to realize that your organization will have contributed very greatly toward preparing our young men for the service that will be required of them.

Not only did the Boy Scout organization contribute very much to developing the spirit of the soldier, of discipline, of willing subordination and competent command, but it did much more. The activities of the Scouts reached to a very wide range in the national interest and from the beginning of the war. They helped to sell Liberty Bonds, their participation in the Loan drives having resulted in the sale of over two hundred seventy-eight million dollars of bonds. In addition to that, they sold over forty-two million dollars of War Savings stamps. More than four million buyers were numbered among those who bought bonds or stamps from the Boy Scouts. The Treasury Department medal for service in the various Liberty Loan drives was awarded to nearly seventy thousand numbers of your organization.

The Boy Scouts rendered service in connection the Red Cross, the United War Work Committee and many other organizations auxiliary to the work of the government whose value could not be estimated.

The fine spirit of responsibility of responsibility and patriotism displayed by the boys was an inspiration to all of their elders. They conducted thousands of war gardens and war farms in all parts of the country, thereby adding notably to the food supply, which was so absolutely necessary to provide the needs of ourselves and our allies.

I could wish that it might be possible for us to know how many thousands of the soldiers who served during the War had previously been members of your organization, and to know how their record of service compared with that of other young men who had not had the sort of previous training that your organization gives to its members.

I have heard testimony from many officers that the training given by the Boy Scouts had gone far towards laying the foundation of character and understanding upon which it was possible, most quickly, to build a good and effective soldier.

Because I had thus referred to the service of the Boy Scouts during the war, I would not have it understood that I am disposed too greatly to emphasize that service, as if the organization was one chiefly useful as a sort of training school preliminary to possible military service. On the contrary,

I feel that your organization is one that has the very greatest usefulness in time of peace; usefulness not only to its members, but to the community at large. Its ideals are those that make for the best kind of manhood, the most illuminating type of citizenship. I have been informed that since the war ended there has been some relaxation of interest, and a reduction of your membership. To me, this is a matter of the utmost regret. I would like to see this splendid organization go on increasing its numbers and the scope of its useful activities. I hope the parents as well as the boys will agree with this view and give every encouragement to the development and support of the work.

We cannot begin too early to inculcate in our young citizenship the fullest appreciation of the usefulness of such a service and training as you provide. The interdependence of all elements, groups and occupations in modern society is so absolute that we need very much to encourage useful organizations and cooperation that shall make for proper discipline and devotion to the interest of the whole community.

This ideal of unselfish service, I take to be rather the finest thing about the Boy Scout organization. What better model could have been prescribed for the boys of today, who will be the men of tomorrow, than that of the Boy Scouts: "On my honor I will do my best: (1) To do my duty to God and my country and to obey the Scout Law; (2) To help other people at all times; (3) To keep myself physically strong, mentally awake, and morally straight."

In that pledge, it seems to me, is presented and excellent epitome of all that is necessary in the building of the best character and the noblest idealism.

To the officers and members of your organization, I expend all good wishes, and the assurance that I will always be ready to cooperate for your prosperity and advancement in every possible way.

Sincerely and cordially yours,

12TH ANNIVERSARY GREETINGS

MARCH 1922

To the Boy Scouts of America:

Sincere congratulations to the Boy Scouts of America on their Twelfth Anniversary, February eighth.

The anniversary of any organization whose ideal is peace and friendship, quite strikingly coincides with the birth of a new hope for world peace and friendship at the recent conference of the nations here in Washington. The responsibilities disclosed by that conference must be met by the men who come after us and I look with growing confidence to that steadily increasing number of boys who effectively trained to "do their duty to God and their country" and to "help other people at all times," as are the Boy Scouts of America.

THE HARDING AWARD LETTER

1923

I am pleased to learn that your Council has met the specified conditions and is entitled to the award of the Anniversary Round-Up Streamer, which I take great pleasure in presenting, with additional streamers for qualified troops. Please extend to each member of the Local Council, and others associated with you in the work, my hearty congratulations and good wishes. I desire especially to convey appreciation to the Scoutmasters and to the boys and troops which have earned the troop award.

It is most stimulating to realize that through the Boy Scouts of America over 130,000 men are now enrolled for definite volunteer service, and that at present there are over 440,000 boy members of this splendid organization. Certainly it can be truly said that the men who are in any way supporting this movement, and especially those who are serving as active leaders, are helping in a most practical fashion to produce for the Nation its greatest need—men of character, trained for citizenship.

I am keenly anxious to do all in my power to extend the influence of the Scout Program, because America must avail itself of every resource for producing that type of American Citizenship which will not be content with acceptance of the privileges of citizenship without active participation in meeting the responsibilities of citizenship. In the Boy Scout movement, you not only place emphasis upon service, but you have worked out your program in such a way that boys actually "learn by doing," and in a natural manner acquire that attitude of mind which brings to them a consciousness that they must be citizens of that participating kind, and not mere onlookers.

I do most sincerely hope that you will continue your efforts to recruit increased leadership and greater resources, in order that more boys of Scout age may have the advantages of this movement, which has earned for itself appraisement as one of the greatest assets our Nation has today.

SERVICE: THE GREATEST THING IN LIFE
REMARKS AT THE BALLPARK, BUTTE, MONTANA

JUNE 29, 1923

Scouts:

I do not know of anything on our western journey that has afforded me greater pleasure than this ceremony. The greatest thing in life is to be of service, and the superlative degree of service is rendering help in the hour of need. I know how a great trial appeals to the latent manhood of every one of us. I know that somewhere inherent in this nature of ours is strength to respond to a call at the moment of urgent need. I rejoice to look upon you as fine examples of young American manhood who have met great responsibility and performed distinguished service. It is a fine index to the part which you will play in the life before you. I am proud of you as commander-in-chief of the Boy Scout organization; I am proud of you as president of the Republic, because you are a fine example and inspiration to all your fellows throughout the length and breadth of the land.

Note: Thereupon President Harding, with appropriate remarks to each, pinned the medals on the coats of the Scout Executive and Boy Scouts. After this ceremony the President spoke as follows:

Ladies and Gentlemen:

I quite despair of making myself heard at so great a distance from this splendid audience, but I cannot let the occasion pass without giving some expression of my appreciation to you for the cordiality, the heartiness and the generosity of your very fine greeting today. I am glad you came out to participate in the little ceremony which we have just concluded. It has been a great pleasure to bestow these medals, which bear the tribute of your city and of the great Boy Scout organization, to those boys who have been of signal service to their fellows. It is a great thing to emphasize the world's appreciation of service, and I am glad that I happened to be in the city of Butte at the opportune moment to present to these boys this testimonial and expression of appreciation.

I have a very great regard for the Boy Scouts and the Girl Scouts and all the youth manhood and young womanhood of America. They constitute our greatest and richest possession, and I have come to the conclusion that we see the finest examples of each in the wonderful West.

It is too warm to keep you standing, and it is too difficult to be heard without the modern amplifying appliances. I know that the people on the stand do not hear my voice at all; so I will ask those who are immediately in front of me to convey to them for me an expression of the gratitude we feel for the courtesy and kindness you have shown us while visiting your great city. It is a joy to come here. We shall go away with the most agreeable memories and I know that you will feel we are a little closer to you. It is a pleasure to know you and it is a pleasure to work with you in making ours the best government on earth under which to live.

Good-bye.

CALVIN COOLIDGE

ACCEPTANCE OF THE HONORARY PRESIDENCY

August 16, 1923

You may be assured of my readiness to accept the honor of the Presidency of the Boy Scouts of America, as other Presidents have done from the organization of the Scouts. I esteem this post as one of the incidental duties of a President, and likewise one of the most agreeable among them. I have always been deeply interested in the work of the Scouts, which I regard as an ideal mode of citizenship development and character construction. Both my sons are Scouts, and my observation of the benefits they have derived from their affiliation has strengthened my conviction of the organization's usefulness. I shall be glad to render any proper service I can to the organization at any time.

TELEPHONE REMARKS TO A GROUP OF BOY SCOUTS: "WHAT IT MEANS TO BE A BOY SCOUT"

July 25, 1924

There was no Boy Scout organization in my boyhood, but every boy who has the privilege of growing up on a farm learns instinctively the three fundamentals of Scouthood.

The first is a reverence for nature. Boys should never lose their love of the fields and the streams, the mountains and the plains, the open places and the forests. That love will be a priceless possession as your years lengthen out. There is an instructive myth about the giant Antaeus. Whenever in a contest he was thrown down, he drew fresh strength from his mother, the earth, and so was thought invincible. But Hercules lifted him away from the earth and so destroyed him. There is new life in the soil for every man. There is healing in the trees for tired minds and for our overburdened spirits, there is strength in the hills, if only we will lift up our eyes. Remember that nature is your great restorer.

The second is a reverence for law. I remember the town meetings of my boyhood, when the citizens of our little town met to levy taxes on themselves, and to choose from their own number those who should be their officers. There is something in every town meeting, in every election, that approaches very near to the sublime. I am thrilled at the thought of my audience tonight, for I never address boys without thinking, among them may be a boy who will sit in this White House. Somewhere there are boys who will be presidents of our railroads, presidents of colleges, of banks, owners of splendid farms and useful industries, members of Congress, representatives of our people in foreign lands. That is the heritage of the American boy.

It was an act of magnificent courage when our ancestors set up a nation wherein any boy may aspire to anything. That great achievement was not wrought without blood and sacrifice. Make firm your resolution to carry on nobly what has been so nobly begun. Let this nation, under your influence, be a finer nation. Resolve that the sacrifices by which your great opportunities have been purchased will be matched by a sacrifice, on your part, that will give your children even a better chance.

The third is a reverence for God. It is hard to see how a great man can be an atheist. Without the sustaining influence of faith in a divine power we could have little faith in ourselves. We need to feel that behind us is intelligence and love. Doubters do not achieve; skeptics do not contribute; cynics do not create. Faith is the great motive power, and no man realizes his full possibilities unless he has the deep conviction that life is eternally important, and that his work, well done, is a part of an unending plan.

These are not only some of the fundamentals of the teachings of the Boy Scouts, they are the fundamentals of our American institutions. If you will take them with you, if you will be living examples of them abroad, you will make a great contribution toward a better understanding of our country, and receive in return a better understanding of other countries; for you will find in foreign lands, to a very large extent, exactly what you carry there yourselves. I trust that you can show to your foreign associates in the great Scout movement that you have a deep reverence for the truth and are determined to live by it; that you wish to protect and cherish your own country and contribute to the well being, right thinking and true living of the whole world.

CHRISTMAS GREETING

DECEMBER 17, 1925

As you are representatives of [an organization] of the boys and girls of America who live in or are interested in the open country, with which I come into an official relation, I want to extend to all of you a Christmas greeting. It seems a very short time ago that I was a boy and in the midst of farm life, myself helping to do the chores at the barn, working in the corn and potato fields, getting in the hay, and in the springtime doing what most of you have never had an opportunity to see—making maple sugar.

I did not have any chance to profit by joining a Scout organization… That chance ought to be a great help to the boys and girls of the present day. It brings them into association with each other in a way where they learn to think not only of themselves, but of other people. It teaches them to be unselfish. It trains them to obedience and gives them self-control. A very wise man gave us this motto – "Do the duty that lies nearest you." It seems to me that this is the plan of [your organization]. We need never feel that we shall not be called on to do great things in the future, if we do small things well at present. It is the boys and girls who work hard at home that are sure to make the best record when they go away from home. It is the boys and girls who stand well up towards the head of the class at school that will be called on to hold the important places in political and business life when they go out into the world.

There is a time for play as well as a time for work. But even in play it is possible to cultivate the art of well-doing. Games are useful to train the eye, the hand and the muscles, and bring the body more completely under the control of the mind. When this is done, instead of being a waste of time play becomes a means of education.

It is in all these ways that boys and girls are learning to be men and women, to be respectful to their parents, to be patriotic to their country, and to be reverent to God. It is because of the great chance that American boys and girls have in all these directions that to them, more than to the youth of any other country, there should be a Merry Christmas.

PRESIDENT COOLIDGE ON THE SCOUT OATH AND SCOUT LAW

May 1, 1926

The more I have studied this movement, its inception, purposes, organization, and principles, the more I have been impressed. Not only is it based on the fundamental rules of right thinking and acting but it seems to embrace in its code almost every virtue needed in the personal and social life of mankind. It is a wonderful instrument for good. It is an inspiration to you whose duty and privilege it is to widen its horizon and extend its influence. If every boy in the United States between the ages of 12 and 17 could be placed under the wholesome influences of the Scout program and should live up to the Scout Oath and rules, we would hear fewer pessimistic words as to the future of our Nation.

The boy on becoming a Scout binds himself on his honor to do his best, as the Oath reads:

"1. To do my duty to God and country, and to obey the Scout Law.
2. To help other people at all times.
3. To keep myself physically strong, mentally awake, and morally straight."

The 12 articles in these Scout Laws are not prohibitions, but obligations; affirmative rules of conduct. Members must promise to be trustworthy, loyal, helpful, friendly, courteous, kind, obedient, cheerful, thrifty, brave, clean, and reverent. How comprehensive this list! What a formula for developing moral and spiritual character! What an opportunity or splendid service in working to strengthen their observance by all Scouts and to extend their influence to all boys eligible for membership! It would be a perfect world if everyone exemplified these virtues in daily life.

Acting under these principles, remarkable progress has been made. Since 1910, 3,000,000 boys in the United States have been Scouts - one out of every seven eligible. Who can estimate the physical, mental, and spiritual force that would have been added to our national life during this period if the other six also had been Scouts?

HERBERT HOOVER

MESSAGE TO THE WORLD SCOUT JAMBOREE

AUGUST 7, 1929

I hope you will express on my behalf the appreciation the whole of America has for this magnificent contribution to the development of our youth. The assembling of fifty thousand young men and boys from seventy different races and nationalities, in good fellowship without competition, and the self-discipline which makes this possible are in themselves without precedent, and constitute, I trust, an augury for development of common ideas and friendship amongst nations.

As Honorary President of the Boy Scouts of America, I think I may speak on behalf of the millions of boys in the United States who have received benefits from Scouting, and I send my hearty congratulations to the assembly.

ADDRESS COMMEMORATING THE TWENTIETH ANNIVERSARY OF THE BOY SCOUTS OF AMERICA

MARCH 10, 1930

Mr. Chairman, officers of the Boy Scouts, and your guests:

We meet this evening under the cloud of deep sadness. Since many of you started your journey to Washington, the most beloved of Americans has passed into the Great Beyond. And in determining not to cancel this occasion your committee has acted in the spirit of William Howard Taft. A lifelong open heart and a devotion to boys, the first honorary president of the Boy Scouts, would, had he known of it, insisted that your work should go forward.

This occasion commemorates the 20th anniversary of the Boy Scouts, and it is indeed in keeping with the true tribute to his great spirit whose name graced your first anniversary.

Together with his sister, the boy is the most precious possession of the American home. I sometimes think that one of the sad things of life is that they will grow up. Literature and lore have established our boys in a varied relationship to life: as a growing animal of superlative promise, to be fed and watered and kept warm; as a periodic nuisance; as a joy forever; as the incarnation of destruction; as the father of the man; as the child of iniquity; as the problem of our times and, above all, as the hope of our Nation.

And the Boy Scout movement has opened for him the portals to adventure and constructive joy by reviving the lore of the frontier and the campfire, by establishing contacts with the birds and sometimes with the bees, by matching his patience to the deliberative character of fish, by efficient operation of swimming holes, by peeps into a thousand mysteries of the streams, and the trees and the stars. And, it is more than this. By the promotion of sense of sportsmanship, it builds character. Contest and competition with zeal but without unfair advantage and without bitterness, with restraint that remarks nothing of others which cannot be at once forgiven, with the willingness to subordinate one's self into teamwork for the common aim—that is sportsmanship.

There cannot be Boy Scouts without organization and leaders. And by leaders I include particularly those devoted men who as troop leaders become the inspiration and the friend of boys and upon whom rests the responsibility of actually administering constructive joy.

And through its organization our boys learn of discipline, they learn unity of effort, cooperation, and the democracy of play and work, and they learn the duties and satisfactions of service. All of these are the foundations of life, the basis of liberty and happiness, and the safeguards against destructive joy in the grownup life hereafter.

The priceless treasure of boyhood is his endless enthusiasm, his store of high idealism and his fragrant hope. His is the plastic period when indelible impressions must be made if we are to continue a successful democracy. We assure ourselves that the cure of illiteracy and the fundamentals of education are to be had in the three R's—readin' and 'ritin' and 'rithmetic. To this we must add one more R and that is responsibility—responsibility to the community—if we are not to have illiteracy in government, we must do this. The conviction that every person in the Republic owes a service to the Republic; that the Republic rests solely upon the willingness of everyone born into it to bear his part of the duties and obligations of citizenship is as important as the ability to read and write—for that is the only patriotism in peace.

It is true that our teachers are guiding our children in the first steps of democracy, but I know of no agency that can be more powerful--and that is more powerful—in the support of this purpose than the Boy Scouts. If we look over the Republic today, we find many failures in citizenship—we find many betrayals by those who have been selected to leadership. I cannot conceive that these failures would take place if every citizen who went to the polls was a good "Scout," that every official who was elected had ever been a real Boy Scout.

I give you a powerful statistic. There are about 1 million Boy Scouts in the United States. There is the raw material for 10 million more.

MESSAGE ON THE TWENTY-FIRST ANNIVERSARY OF THE BOY SCOUTS OF AMERICA.

JANUARY 23, 1931

BOYHOOD is the period of development. By the time he comes of age a boy has acquired, in body, brains, and character, the tools he must use in life. His work and play, his love of camping and knowledge of nature, his courage, his sportsmanship, his desire to serve his fellow men, have become a part of him, of what he will always be.

Scouting, too, has come of age. Through twenty-one years it has summoned Youth to the great adventure of lofty living. As the twenty-first year marks Youth's formal passage to legal maturity, so the coming of the twenty-first year of the Boy Scout movement in America marks its entry into an era of more mature service. I hope it may continue through years of increasing usefulness to release that deep love of humanity, that eagerness to make life fuller and sturdier. That is the very core of democracy itself.

ADDRESS BEFORE THE
U.S. JUNIOR CHAMBER OF COMMERCE

CHICAGO, ILLINOIS, JUNE 16, 1950

A Scoutmaster was calling the roll of his troop as to what good deed each had performed during the week. All passed except for four. The Scoutmaster told the four to go at once and come back in the afternoon, each with a good deed report. When they returned, the first replied that he had helped a lady across the street. The second, third, and fourth made the same reply. The suspicious Scoutmaster inquired if this was all about the same lady. The first boy replied, "Yes sir. She was on the wrong side of the road and it took all four of us to get her over."

FRANKLIN D. ROOSEVELT

LETTER TO BSA PRESIDENT WALTER W. HEAD

OCTOBER 7, 1933

My dear Mr. Head:

You are thoroughly familiar with my personal enthusiasm for the Boy Scouts of America based upon my actual experience as President of the Boy Scout Foundation of Greater New York during the past twelve years. It naturally follows, therefore, that I am most happy in the development of the Mortimer L. Schiff Scout Reservation. This memorial will ever be a reminder of the generosity of his mother, as well as of Mr. Schiff's own contributions, not only financial, but in unusually intelligent and devoted volunteer service to the Boy Scouts of America over a period of twenty-three years.

Scouting, like all worthwhile educational movements, is dependent in the last analysis upon the degree of understanding and skill of its leaders. The fact that this well equipped Reservation is now available for training purposes will in my opinion mean a greater advance in the cause of Scouting in the years to come, notwithstanding its marvelous record of the past.

As I had occasion to say incident to my recent visit to the Ten Mile River Boy Scout Camps, the fact that men who had Scout training and who enlisted in the Civilian Conservation Corps naturally became the leaders in many of these camps, is splendid testimony as to what Scouting is doing for the country. I hope it will be generously supported by our people in all parts of the country.

The Mortimer L. Schiff Scout Reservation through its training facilities will greatly add to the ability of the Boy Scout Movement in making a greater contribution to the life of America.

Very sincerely yours

MESSAGE TO THE BOY SCOUTS OF AMERICA ON THEIR TWENTY-FIFTH ANNIVERSARY

FEBRUARY 8, 1935

President Head, Members of the Boy Scouts:

The year 1935 marks the Twenty-fifth Birthday celebration of the Boy Scouts of America. During these years the value of our organization in building character and in training for citizenship has made itself a vital factor in the life of America. That is why not only the Boy Scouts of today, but the millions of men and boys who have graduated through Scouting, will be joined by millions of other Americans in the proper marking and celebration of our anniversary.

As I review the record of these twenty-five years of Scouting in America, I am impressed with the extent of the volunteer service we have rendered. We as a Nation are proud of the fact that in addition to our splendid system of education and of other services made available through funds secured by taxation, there are in each community so many well-organized and efficiently administered agencies which supplement the work of Government and make available additional opportunities which strengthen the best objectives of the home, the church and the school.

Every Scout seeks to do a good turn daily; every troop seeks to accomplish some community benefit; and occasionally, as last year, Scouts everywhere unite to do a good turn nationally. A year ago, as your Honorary President, I started the national Scout effort to collect household furnishings and clothing and supplies for those in need; and the results were truly amazing. Hundreds of thousands of families were helped by the Boy Scouts.

The program for this year, embracing as it does over one million boys, lasts throughout the year. In May there will be a gathering of the Leaders of Scouting at the Twenty-fifth Annual Meeting of the National Council.

But the outstanding event will be America's first National Jamboree, to be held here in the City of Washington from August 21st to August 30th. I hope to attend it in person. Since I extended the invitation a year ago, definite plans have crystallized. With the cooperation of various officials here in Washington a fine camp site has been made available and will be all ready to receive thirty thousand boys when the meeting starts. I am glad to know that the selection of these boys is being made on the basis of merit and, furthermore, that in many cases these boys will come to Washington at the expense of the troop and not merely because the boy's economic situation in life is such as to make it possible for his parents to send him.

Thirty thousand Scouts brought together under such conditions will mean the most thoroughly representative group of American boys ever mobilized for a purpose of this character.

We hope, too, that other countries will send at least small delegations to meet with us on this occasion. Because Scouting is now in active operation in almost every civilized Nation of the world, this will give us a splendid opportunity to enlarge our basis of mutual respect, of understanding and of friendship among the people of the world, regardless of race or creed.

In a moment Dr. West is going to lead the Scouts in thousands of halls and other meeting places in every State in the Union in repeating the Scout Oath and Law. I hope that the people who are listening to my voice will give careful heed to this Scout Oath. It is the basis of good citizenship; it is the basis of good government; it is the basis of orderly progress for our country in the years to come.

INVITATION TO THE BOY SCOUT JAMBOREE IN WASHINGTON

FEBRUARY 8, 1937

Fellow Scouts:

Today we are celebrating our twenty-seventh anniversary. From one end of the country to the other we are taking stock of what has been accomplished during all these years and paying a deeply felt and well deserved tribute to the ideals of Scouting.

I like to think on such occasions as this that there are many thousands of men—some young, some entering middle age-who, though not actively participating in our celebrations, have, nevertheless, found it to be true that "once a Boy Scout, always a Boy Scout." The ideals of Scouting are not simply ideals for boys. They are ideals for men. For the ideal of service to others can never be outgrown, however often it may be lost sight of by some.

Tonight I am especially happy to renew my invitation for the Boy Scouts to hold a Jamboree here in the nation's Capital in the early summer. We were all of us greatly disappointed because the Jamboree to which I had invited the Boy Scouts in 1935 had to be cancelled. But now we are going ahead with plans which I am confident will result in a demonstration on the part of boyhood the like of which has never been seen before in this country. I am glad that this is going to be an encampment because it is fitting that a movement such as ours should hold its first great national demonstration in the out-of-doors.

Yes, we are planning to have a city of tents rise here in the Capital actually within the shadow of the Washington Monument. On a site only a short distance from the room from which I am speaking to you today twenty-five thousand boys will live together under canvas from June thirtieth to July ninth. It stirs my imagination and I am sure that it gives all of you a genuine thrill.

Our country was developed by pioneers who camped along the trails which they blazed all the way from the Atlantic Ocean to the slopes of the Pacific. To the American people for generations camping was a way of living—it is in our very blood. I believe that this Jamboree is going to be a great success because I believe in the effectiveness of trained boyhood. Incidentally, I am gratified to know that there was a greater increase in Boy Scout membership in 1936 than in any previous year. And, as showing that true Scouts always rise to every emergency, I am glad to say that I have received gratifying reports of the practical aid they are extending in cooperating with flood relief workers in the Ohio and Mississippi valleys.

Our Jamboree, besides being an event long to be remembered by the boys who participate, will afford a practical demonstration of the principle of self-reliance which Scout work is developing in all of you. There will be gathered together a thoroughly representative group mobilized from all parts of the country. Other countries will send delegates to meet with us. Scouting is now organized in almost every civilized nation in the world. The Camp here in Washington will afford an opportunity for us to extend our horizon and enlarge our friendships, on the basis of the ideals expressed in the Scout Oath and Law.

I extend to you all my greetings and my good wishes for the year ahead. And now our Chief Scout Executive, Dr. James E. West, will lead us in re-dedicating ourselves to the Scout Oath.

RADIO GREETING TO THE BOY SCOUTS OF AMERICA

FEBRUARY 7, 1938

Fellow Scouts:

I am happy to receive this report from Mr. Head on the accomplishments of our organization. On this twenty-eighth birthday of the Boy Scouts of America we should be especially thankful for a youth movement which seeks merely to preserve such simple fundamentals as physical strength, mental alertness and moral straightness—a movement to support the ideals of peace.

I congratulate our leaders and especially our Scoutmasters who have made an outstanding record possible. We have increased in numbers and I am confident on the basis of what I, myself, have observed that we also are improving in the quality of Scouting. Last summer I had the opportunity to visit with thousands of you, from all parts of the country, in your great Jamboree camp here in Washington. I am really sorry that every citizen of the country did not see, as I did, the great national encampment of Scouts here along the Potomac River. I have seen no more cheering sight from the standpoint of the national future.

The theme chosen for our Boy Scout Week Observance-"Building a Stronger Generation"—is thoroughly worthwhile. I have always believed that Scout training does help to build health for boys and young men. It encourages them to get out into the open, to develop good health habits. It helps to make them hardy and vigorous. Of course, we all recognize that "Building a Stronger Generation" involves more than good health. It involves strong character, initiative, resourcefulness and ideals of service— qualities that you practice in your Scouting experiences.

But it involves, also, learning all about other people—your neighbors and their problems, the people who live in the other end of town and their problems, the people who live in the next town and their problems, those who live in the next State and their problems—in other words, the problems of every part of the United States. When you have accomplished that you will realize, also, that there are problems outside the United States which affect you and your family and friends. Thus, the ideals of Scouting include not only character and service but also knowledge. They will be as real and vital to you in your manhood as they are to you today in your boyhood.

I extend to you my best wishes for the year to come. Boy Scouts today—you will be the citizens tomorrow, with a nation's keeping in your charge. I believe that you will be worthy of the trust.

RADIO ADDRESS FOR THE THIRTY-FIRST ANNIVERSARY OF THE BOY SCOUTS OF AMERICA

February 8, 1941

Fellow Scouts:

The record of your achievements during the past year is something of which we can all be proud. I am most favorably impressed with the scope and the magnitude of the emergency service training program that is now being developed by the Boy Scouts of America.

The Boy Scouts of today are approaching manhood at a grave hour in the world's history. Recent events have threatened the security of free men everywhere; and the democratic way of life is being challenged in many parts of the world. The United States must be strong if our free way of life is to be maintained and for our national policy we, as a Nation, have adopted the motto of the Boy Scout organization—BE PREPARED.

In many ways the Boy Scouts have sought to emulate the deeds of the early American pioneers who subdued the wilderness and established on a new-found continent a better human society. But it is not primarily for mere physical feats that the Boy Scout movement has won the high praise and the esteem of the American people. It is rather because the Boy Scouts have dedicated themselves to the development of those qualities of character, those qualities of citizenship, upon which the future of our democracy rests.

In this grave hour national defense dominates the heart and mind and soul of America. The Government must take the major responsibility, since it alone represents all of the people acting in concert. But the Government cannot and should not preempt those fields of private endeavor that have become an indispensable part of life in America.

You who are members of the Boy Scouts have a great opportunity in your organization to do your part in this great task. In your Scout troops you have the opportunity to develop the type of leadership, the group co-operation, which is so greatly needed in a democracy such as ours. You have opportunities in. your Scouting program to develop those physical and mental qualities upon which the survival of a self-governing community depends.

The Boy Scouts have made and will continue to make an important contribution to the welfare of America's young manhood. The Boy Scouts have always responded generously when called into action in the service of their communities and their fellow citizens. And so the Nation is confident that the Boy Scouts stand ready to contribute to the national welfare in these critical hours. It follows, therefore, that I am proud of what you have done, I am proud of what you are doing—and I am proud of what I know you will do in days to come in playing your part in our American defense.

GREETING TO THE BOY SCOUTS

FEBRUARY 7, 1943

Fellow Scouts and Scouters:

Today, with the Nation at war, we observe the thirty-third birthday of the Boy Scouts of America. The job of winning the war and assuring a decent and lasting peace is the concern of every American.

I heartily approve the slogan adopted for the Boy Scouts for 1943—to "Toughen Up, Buckle Down, Carry on to Victory." I am informed that to date more than 327 of those who have been decorated for heroism by our country have been identified as having had Scout training.

The leaders of our armed forces in training camps and on the battle fronts have emphasized the value of Scout training in developing knowledge and skill, as well as courage, self-reliance, resourcefulness, and initiative which are proving to be so essential in our determination to win the war.

I have always been a staunch believer in Scouting, and now, in time of war, as your honorary president, I urge everyone connected with Scouting, boys and men, to see to it that Scouting is maintained at its full strength and effectiveness as a practical contribution to the war effort.

Certainly those who help to make boys physically strong, mentally awake, and morally straight in these times deserve the appreciation of all who are leaders in America. I am confident that full cooperation will be accorded leaders of the Boy Scouts of America, who are dealing with a most important aspect of our manpower problem.

So I bring greetings on this the thirty-third birthday to all the members of the Boy Scouts of America and say:

"Reach out and make it possible for every boy who wants to be a Cub or a Scout to have a meeting place and the necessary leadership as a service to your country. Carry on! Make your slogan for 1943—'Toughen Up, Buckle Down, Carry on to Victory'-a definite and vital part of all of your activities."

ANNUAL MESSAGE TO THE
BOY SCOUTS OF AMERICA

January 2, 1945

To the Boy Scouts of America:

Your theme for your thirty-fifth anniversary gives me great satisfaction. For many years the Boy Scout Movement has been a real force among the democratic countries in helping to promote better understanding among nations and international good will.

At the time of our National Jamboree in 1937 I was happy to note the many Scouts from across the seas who came to camp with the Boy Scouts of America and learn more of our way of life. At the world Scout Jamborees Scouts from the freedom loving nations live together, found common interests and ideals, and formed friendships of lasting value to themselves and others.

How the Boy Scouts of America comes forward with a positive program for emphasizing the world brotherhood of Scouting. It is the youth of the world who must share and maintain the peace now being purchased so dearly on he battle field fronts. I am convinced that Boy Scouts and Cubs, as well as senior groups, through their mutual understanding, mutual appreciation and mutual respect will be among the leaders in the promoting of comradeship among the democratic peoples of the earth.

Friendship is a basis of our Scout ideals and a part of our Scout Law. Let us live by it and strengthen it.

God bless you all.

HARRY S. TRUMAN

ANNUAL MESSAGE TO THE
BOY SCOUTS OF AMERICA

FEBRUARY 7, 1946

To the Boy Scouts of America:

In a world that has suffered so grievously from the most awful war in history, your theme for the year, "Scouts of the World—Building Together" is timely, refreshing and appropriate.

Evidence of your determination to help your fellow Scouts in other lands less fortunate than ours is worthy indeed of the Boy Scouts of America. Your record for wartime services accomplished is enviable. Analyze it and you will find that planning, enthusiasm and, above all, cooperation helped you win through in your various campaigns.

Now that hostilities have ceased you Scouts and your brother Scouts overseas help the world maintain a secure peace by fostering good-will, understanding, and respect through continued cooperation.

Good Scouts, good Scoutmasters and good Scouting! There is a real contribution to the new world now in the making.

Keep on "Building Together: in this, the thirty-sixth year of the Scout Movement in America, and all the years to come!"

ANNUAL MESSAGE TO THE BOY SCOUTS OF AMERICA

FEBRUARY 7, 1947

To the Boy Scouts of America:

Tomorrow we celebrate the thirty-seventh anniversary of the forming of the Boy Scout Movement in the United States. Scouting is stronger than ever before in our country and gaining renewed strength abroad.

Those of you who will go to France in August to attend the Sixth World Jamboree will camp with brother Scouts from many countries. I am confident you will make the most of this opportunity to further cement our bonds of friendship. What better ambassadors of peace could we send abroad than you Scouts who will make this journey.

Your theme for the year, "Scouts of the World—Building for Tomorrow" has real meaning. Congratulations to all of you on the progress of your activities to relieve suffering in war-torn countries. Helping Scouts in stricken lands to help themselves is commendable.

Scouting's growth in our country is an inspiration. Increased numbers enable us to render greater service at home and abroad. The Movement enriches the lives of all it touches. The daily Good Turn, respect for the customs, convictions and traditions of others is indeed the true spirit of Scouting.

May god bless you and prosper your work.

ANNUAL MESSAGE TO THE BOY SCOUTS OF AMERICA

JANUARY 27, 1948

To the Boy Scouts of America:

Through your inspiring ne program of action, you and your leaders have voluntarily accepted responsibilities which will strengthen the home, the community, our Nation and the world. This is another milestone in Scouting's performance, in which 14,500,000 members have participated over 38 years.

It gives me great pleasure to congratulate you on your fine record of achievement and to wish you progressive fulfillment of the movement's ideals of character building, citizenship training and service to others.

ANNUAL MESSAGE TO THE BOY SCOUTS OF AMERICA

JANUARY 24, 1949

To the Boy Scouts of America:

Your crusade to "Strengthen the Arm of Liberty" which starts on February 8, the thirty-ninth anniversary of Scouting in America, is further evidence of the patriotism that motivates our great movement.

Scouting's constant growth and record of service to the United States gives me confidence that you will attain your objectives of providing a richer experience for more boys. Since 1910, records of membership show that Scouting has influenced the lives of more than 15 million members. It is my hope that many of these Scouts of yesterday, men of high character, will return to the Movement as leaders of the Scouts of today.

Scouting provides fun and adventures in the outdoors and emphasizes the fact that the American way of life is worthy of everything put into it. The Scout Oath and Law, a recognized code of honor, gives boys stability in their daily lives.

On the occasion of Boy Scout Week, I extend greetings to our Scouts and leaders. As your Honorary President, I challenge you to achieve maximum results as you go forward with your crusade to "Strengthen the Arm of Liberty."

ANNUAL MESSAGE TO THE
BOY SCOUTS OF AMERICA

JANUARY 25, 1950

To the Boy Scouts of America:

I welcome this opportunity on the occasion of our fortieth anniversary, to extend, as your Honorary President, my cordial greetings to all of you—Scouts and leaders alike.

Our active membership of 2,500,000 reveals a great growth during the past year and must be gratifying news to every American interested in the character building and citizenship training program of the Boy Scouts of America.

With major activities such as you have arranged for this year you should attain another peak in growth. Your "Crusade to Strengthen Liberty," your program to erect models of the Statue of Liberty in various sections of the country, and your second National Jamboree to be held at Valley Forge, PA, June 30 to July 6 next are further evidences of Scouting's vitality and why it enjoys such widespread national respect.

I am keenly interested in the success of the jamboree because its 40,000 participants will dramatize to the world the full meaning of our liberty. Your great encampment will remind us that Washington and his Continental Army stood steadfast in spite of the privations they endured during the bitter winter of 1777–1778 at Valley Forge. It will challenge us to uphold the ideals and principles which these patriots gave us and the strengthen liberty by seeing that each new generation of Americans is kept aware of our great heritage.

ADDRESS AT VALLEY FORGE AT
THE BOY SCOUTS JAMBOREE

JUNE 30, 1950

As Honorary President of the Boy Scouts of America, I am proud to open this Scout Jamboree. I understand that there are nearly 50,000 Scouts in this encampment. I am glad to see such evidence of the Strength of the

Scout movement. And I think it most appropriate in times like these that you have chosen to hold your Jamboree at this historic shrine of Valley Forge.

When George Washington brought his army to this spot in December 1777, the cause of independence appeared to be lost. His army at that time numbered only 11,000 men—less than one-fourth the number of Scouts attending this Jamboree. Washington's men were without adequate food. They were in rags. Some had no shoes. They had to build their own shelter against the bitter weather. The enemy occupied the capital city of Philadelphia. Few men believed that George Washington's tiny force could survive. Victory seemed out of the question.

Just suppose that George Washington had had about 15 miles of that 35 miles of hot dogs you have here. Think what that would have meant to him and his army at that time. You ought to appreciate how well fed you are, how well taken care of you are in this great Nation of ours. There are thousands and thousands of people in this world who are right on the verge of starvation, and who are starving to death. You should be thankful for the privileges which you have under this great Government of yours.

But the men of Washington's army stuck it out. They stuck it out because they had a fierce belief in the cause of freedom for which they were fighting. And because of that belief, they won.

I know that we still have, in this country, that same unconquerable belief in freedom.

Many of you know, I am sure, that men from other countries came over here, during our Revolutionary War, to fight with us for freedom. Lafayette was a Frenchman; Von Steuben, a German; Pulaski, a Pole, and many others were here with our army at Valley Forge.

Today, even more than in Washington's time, men in other countries share our belief in freedom and our willingness to make sacrifices for it. These men are just as eager as we are to achieve peace in the world based on freedom and justice. If we are to succeed in our common struggle for peace, we must know and work with these freedom-loving people of other countries. We need to understand their problems and they need to understand ours, so that all of us can work together effectively.

I am very glad that the Boy Scouts are doing so much to further this understanding among the people from different countries. You are to be congratulated on sending so many food and clothing packages overseas and on your support of the United Nations Appeal for Children and the World Friendship Fund.

At this encampment there are Scouts from every State in the Union, from Alaska, Hawaii, Puerto Rico, and from the Philippines and many other foreign countries. This is a practical demonstration of how to achieve world understanding. When you work and live together, and exchange ideas around the campfire, you get to know what the other fellow is like. That is the first step toward settling world problems in a spirit of give and take, instead of fighting about them.

The Scout movement is good training for this kind of international work. Scouting is based on the ideal of human brotherhood. Scouts know that the men of other lands are very like ourselves. They have the same desire to work for human advancement.

We are deeply and sincerely interested in the well-being of the youth of the world-not only American youth, but the young people of all countries. We are working, and we will continue to work, for a world in which young people are not regimented and exploited, but instead are given the opportunity to develop their capacities and contribute to a better future.

The United States, together with the other free nations, is striving to build a world in which men will live as good neighbors and work for the good of all. Our program for peace is not directed against the people of any land. It is designed to bring to all people the benefits of justice and freedom.

I hope that you young men in the Boy Scout movement, in this country and other countries, will take home from this Jamboree a clearer understanding of the meaning of human brotherhood. I hope that you will work for freedom and peace with the same burning faith that inspired the men of George Washington's army here at Valley Forge.

We cannot succeed in building a peaceful world unless we all work as hard as we know how. I am confident that you will all do your very best.

ANNUAL MESSAGE TO THE BOY SCOUTS OF AMERICA

February 6, 1951

To the Boy Scouts of America:

In sending you warm greetings and hearty congratulations on the occasion of Boy Scout Week, February 6 to 12—your forty-first anniversary—I speak for all patriotic citizens who believe Scouting is a bulwark against the evils of our times.

Scouting's determination to give to every boy the chance to absorb the benefits of the movement's program for physical, mental, moral and spiritual development promises well for our Nation. In the days ahead we will need, as never before, men of higher character, resolute purpose and unflinching courage to meet successfully the problems of a challenging future.

Your enrollment of 17,500,000 members since 1910 and your present active membership of 2,750,000 as disclosed in official records is a great achievement. It speaks eloquently for our democratic way of helping boys through devoted volunteer leadership.

Your determination to continue with your campaign to "Strengthen the Arm of Liberty" is most reassuring and merits sustained public approval. One and all, you have earned the confidence of our people and I salute you for your patriotic and selfless service.

ANNUAL MESSAGE TO THE BOY SCOUTS OF AMERICA

JANUARY 28, 1952

To the Boy Scouts of America:

I learn with great satisfaction that the national observance of Boy Scout Week will engage the attention of all Scouts and their friends during the days from February 6 to 12.

Since Scouting was founded in 1910, its record has been outstanding. You have gained in membership each year. You have created a desire on the part of Scouts to do their duty to God and country. Your growth in Scout camping, both winter and summer, is most encouraging, as it strengthens body and mind and the spirit of comradeship. Your daily "good turn" has a beneficial impact on the entire on the entire nation.

The record reveals that there are now 2,900,000 Scouts and leaders, and that since 1910, you have served 19,000,000 boys and men. I doubt if anyone can measure the strength in character, the capacity for leadership and acceptance off individual responsibility that results from Scout training.

I heartily endorse the three-year program, known as "Forward on Liberty's Team," which you launch this week. I know it will provide the benefits of Scouting to a greater number of boys. This program should have the unqualified support of our citizens because it will help initiate boys into our democratic way of life.

Your nonpartisan national "good turn," urging all citizens to do their duty by registering and voting during the elections this year is of major importance. It should have the support of all political parties and civic organizations. Certainly, it has my hearty endorsement. Your enterprise is commendable.

You have a great cause and a fine program. May God continue to bless your unselfish and useful work. It is richly rewarding to the country.

GENERAL EISENHOWER PROUD
OF SCOUT RECORD

DECEMBER 1945

I accept this medal from all the Boy Scouts of America and I shall cherish it. I need not tell you that I am proud of the record the Boy Scouts of America achieved during the war. Frankly, I knew they would come through in meeting the quota they themselves set in the Waste Paper Salvage Campaign. Doubling it was more than the most optimistic of us anticipated and it proves that you can depend on the Boy Scouts.

The Boy Scouts Movement merits the unstinted support of every American who wants to make his country and his world a better place in which to live. Its emphasis on community service and tolerance and world friendship promotes a speedier attainment of the enduring peace among men for which we all strive.

By developing among its members both a spirit of sturdiness, self-reliance and a realization of the need for cooperative effort in every major enterprise, the Movement is a prime force in preparing tomorrow's men for their duty to themselves, their country and their world.

Here in the United States, the Boy Scouts of America has accomplished much in its thirty-six years of service. But today, more than ever before, we need expansion of its membership and influence.

BOY SCOUT JAMBOREE
VALLEY FORGE, PENNSYLVANIA

JULY 4, 1950

"I pledge allegiance to the flag of the United States of America and to the Republic for which it stands, one nation, indivisible, with liberty and justice for all."

Boy Scouts, friends. Simple are the words in the pledge of allegiance to the flag, but within it is the core of the American code—molded in the fire of revolution, hammered on the anvil of battle, tested and proved through seventeen decades of arduous yet glorious trial. I hope that, as you Scouts repeated its phrases of dedication, you were joined by your parents, sisters, brothers, and friends throughout the breadth and length of this land. The times demand that every American be proud to proclaim his loyalty.

Here in Valley Forge, on July Fourth, both day and place join with our voices to fortify us in the allegiance that we declare. We celebrate the anniversary of our Independence Declaration on the spot where the resolution of our nation's founders met and surmounted its sorest trial.

The ideas set forth in that Declaration shattered political shackles as old as humanity.

Through the mounting years, since they were written, they have heartened others across the world in defiance of tyranny. They still inspire men to labor and to sacrifice; even to risk the grim tragedy of war in order that human freedom may not be torn from peoples, by themselves, too weak to resist ruthless attack.

For us in Valley Forge, where every field and hill and stream reminds us of George Washington, how can we doubt eventual success, if we meet these issues firmly?

In our affections and admiration, each of us has his own particular reasons for placing the Father of our Country above all other citizens. Some of us may think of him principally as a battle leader, especially in his moment of triumph at Yorktown. We see him crossing the icy Delaware to initiate a march whose daring thrills us; it stands in military annals as an example of what courage and boldness can do. We respect the wise and firm hand he kept upon the helm of State as he guided the Republic through her first eight years. We hear the words of his farewell to his army, of his Newburgh address. We salute the statesmanship of his final farewell to public life. Yet most of us at the Boy Scout encampment would likely agree that the crowning glory of his whole career was Valley Forge.

To this spot Washington led his defeated and retreating army—to the cold hardships of a bitter winter. Discouragement was his daily ration. He seemed deserted by the Continental Congress and abandoned to bear burdens that were almost unbearable. He lost, from starvation and freezing, during that winter, more than 3,000 out of his tiny army. When we consider how he, single handed, kept his forces together during those long days and months, hearing the pitiful cries of the suffering and witnessing the despair in the eyes of the dying, we gain some faint understanding of the greatness of spirit of George Washington. In doing so, we turn to our own problems of today with increased confidence. Here at Valley Forge, every relic, every monument assures us that even hunger, pain, nakedness and indescribable hardship cannot wholly dishearten those whose spirit is steeped in faith and in loyalty to a lofty purpose.

This place is an eternal witness to the worth—and to the cost—of the liberty we possess. Men here proved that they valued it above comfort or safety, as they paid for it in pain and blood and life. We pray that no obligation to our country may ever again demand such a price; but any who dodges the least duty of citizenship nullifies, that much, the heroism of Valley Forge. They shall lose freedom who think it may be preserved without sweat and sacrifice.

But we do not depend upon Valley Forge alone for inspiration. With us every day of our lives, is the flag that stands for more than victory in war or richness in peace. The American flag represents what the multitudes of humanity have yearned for through the ages—friendship among men, liberty for men, justice toward men. America, under God, is a way of life ruled by the eternal truths of human brotherhood, human dignity, human rights. Whatever our frailty, our defects of deed or mind, our errors or our prejudices of the past, no one of us can fail to grow stronger in loyalty, stouter in the performance of duty, richer in good will when he humbly stands before the symbol of free America.

Among ourselves, we do not speak openly and frankly, as often as we should, of patriotism—love of country. It is not that we fear the jeering of the smart-aleck; possibly we forget that men grow in stature only as they daily rededicate themselves to a noble faith. More likely, we thoughtlessly assume our blessings of liberty to be indestructible.

True patriotism places the public good above individual advantage. It is not tainted by false pride in might, in size, in overwhelming power; it never seeks to compel others to a blind obedience to our wishes. It is among the greatest of human virtues. Fortunate are we whose devotion is to a country that seeks the good of all its citizens, without distinction, that firmly champions the cause of human rights, and offers the hand of friendship to every other nation whose purpose is peace and justice.

May none of us be backward in seeking ways to perform our duty to the Nation. Let us not be discouraged if some seem to be slackers, who deride our earnestness and selfishly profit out of our sacrifices. Every society, every crowd has its weaklings, its cowards, its self-centered individuals. We must not be influenced by their actions—if we are to escape the shame that is theirs. You Boy Scouts of this Jamboree, and your comrades in the nation, are growing up in a time of peril, crisis, tension. Few among you can remember a day free from war, rumor of war, fear of war! That you may not, in your young manhood, be sacrificed to war is indeed the primary purpose of our foreign policy today. And you shall not be, if the pledge of allegiance stands always before the world as the guiding light of our national life. You can help make it so. Leadership is measured by example and action and earnestness of spirit—not by years of age.

The glory of this nation is that it was conceived in courage, born in sacrifice and reached its maturity in the unselfish devotion and labor of patriots. So long as time endures, America will need these qualities of her citizens. And so long as these qualities do endure, so long will this country stand free, strong and pre-eminent among the nations. The future is bright when America with one voice, with a stout heart and with utter sincerity, says: "I pledge allegiance to the flag of the United States of America and to the Republic for which it stands, one nation, indivisible, with liberty and justice for all."

PRESIDENT EISENHOWER ON THE SCOUT OATH

"The 44th National Council Meeting of the Boy Scouts of America," May 29, 1954, Washington, DC

One of my great heroes of American history is Robert E. Lee, and he said something once, I think, which all of us could remember. He said, "We cannot do more than our duty. We would not wish to do less." So, frankly, when we have said or expressed that first phrase of the Scout Oath, we have said about all that is ennobling in human purpose.

But it goes on: To be considerate of others, and to obey the law—to be an integral part of society, that means.

To do my part of the job, to be considerate of others, and to obey the law; and finally, as it goes on, you know—To be physically strong and mentally awake. Was there ever a time when the United States needed to be economically and materially stronger, and when we needed to be more vigilant and mentally awake, and morally straight?

This Government, represented in its Legislature and its Executive departments and its Judiciary, has but one great purpose in its relationships with all other nations: to be morally straight—honest—known as a people and a government of integrity, to be wise enough to determine what methods and procedures will best advance the happiness, the spiritual and intellectual and material welfare of all nations. And, of course, to carry that out, to be physically strong, not to waste our strength where it will do no good, or in chasing visions, but to be strong to carry out these great and noble purposes.

It seems to me, then, that you people in working with Scouts, in the sense of this very noble Scout Oath, are doing a very, very great job of providing an America of just a very few short years from now that will be better and stronger in its position in the world, and among ourselves.

MESSAGE TO THE BOY SCOUTS OF AMERICA

JANUARY 27, 1956

To the Boy Scouts of America:

On the occasion of the 1956 observance of Boy Scout Week I extend warm greetings and congratulations to you and your leaders.

I am, of course, delighted that the number of Cub, Boy Scouts, Explorers and adult leaders now totals more than four million. This growth gives heartening assurance that in the years to come our Nation will continue to have citizens prepared in body, mind, and character to serve it and to further its strength and progress.

In preparation for citizenship—for the exercise of its rights and the discharge of its obligations—spiritual training plays a major part. I therefore congratulate you on the fact that your organization will round out its first half century with the four year program, "Onward for God and my Country"—a program which will strengthen your knowledge or our heritage and your capacity to contribute to the welfare of your fellow man and the Republic.

As you begin work under this program I wish all of you the greatest possible success.

50TH ANNIVERSARY MESSAGE TO THE BOY SCOUTS OF AMERICA

FEBRUARY 12, 1960

My fellow citizens:

I have long been interested and active in the Boy Scouts of America, both as a member of its National Executive Board, and more recently as its Honorary President. In that capacity, I have the special privilege of calling upon our Nation to join in honoring the 50th anniversary of this great youth movement.

For half a century the men who have led this virile movement have been making a great and wise investment in time and energy voluntarily given. The dividend they have reaped has been a rich one. Today the Scouting movement counts a membership of 5 million boys and men and women, too. Over 30 million boys have been members since its founding here in Washington just 50 years ago.

In thousands of churches, schools, meeting halls of all kinds, Scouts and their leaders are rededicating themselves to the Scout Oath. These 32 words might well serve as an appropriate guide for good citizenship at any age level:

"On my honor I will do my best to do my duty to God and my country and to obey the Scout Law; to help other people at all times; to keep myself physically strong, mentally awake and morally straight."

The active and abiding interest of the adult citizens of this Nation is important to the furtherance of this great movement. I ask that you join with the Boy Scouts as they celebrate this anniversary by giving them that active support by your helping your son—or another's—to become a Scout; by volunteering as an adult leader; by making available the resources needed.

Thank you very much.

REMARKS AT A DINNER COMMEMORATING THE 50TH ANNIVERSARY OF THE BOY SCOUTS OF AMERICA

JUNE 1, 1960

Mr. Chairman and distinguished guests:

I am here this evening to join all those, who by coming to this dinner, wanted to pay their tribute to the Boy Scouts of America and to their leaders, both their local leaders and national leaders, their instructors, and all those supporters that have made it possible to carry this movement forward through these 50 years so successfully.

Twenty-five years ago, I learned through a personal experience something about Boy Scout training that I have never forgotten. My family and I had gone into Mexico to visit on a large ranch. My son was then shortly past 12 years, and at that time there was a solo march required of the boys to make the next grade—probably First Class Scout—14 miles he had to march.

Now it happened that the gate of the ranch was exactly seven miles away from the house, so John decided that this would be his march, he would get this credit point while he was down in Mexico. So he announced his intention.

Well, there was nothing said, except that his mother and his doting grandmother both decided that there would have to be a car go along, and there would have to be orange juice, Coca Colas, and water, and everything that you would take along to make sure that he got through, to follow him through this wild country of cacti and greasewood and all the rest of it.

Well now, we had a "storm." This boy had decided that he was going to do something and he was going to have nobody going along in a boat escorting him as we did his swimming trick. He was going alone. And this got to be rather a hot argument.

And so, exercising what every man always thinks is his prerogative, I made the decision and said, "Go right ahead, John, that will be all right-go ahead."

Well, he started out because he had his dad's authority. But I was still in the house. And the very tough looks, to say nothing of the talk about a hard-hearted parent and an old soldier that didn't know better than to do this to his son. I heard all the exaggerations about the occasional coyote that was found out on the ranch, and some of these old horn cows that were as gentle as a Hereford always is, but looks very large and big to the ladies—and about the rattlesnakes and all the other dangers. And finally I had to surrender.

But I wasn't going to get in John's way. So I took the station wagon and I wound around through the desert, staying away from that trail, but always making sure that I could come back and report that nothing was wrong.

Well, he made the trip back—there and back. Came in in fine shape. And I found this: the tremendous pride that boy had in making sure—getting the self-confidence that he could do a thing by himself, that some of his doting parents did not think he could do.

And moreover, it occurred to me that possibly we are doing a little bit too much of the paternalistic care about our young, and we don't give them an opportunity to develop independence. And when I saw the pride that boy exhibited—not saying a word, but you could see his chest come up a little bit—and he combed his hair that evening. He was a different boy, and he has been a different boy ever since, in my opinion.

And I think even the ladies of the household learned that they do have to allow the young birdling to spread its wings once in a while and try them out. Boy Scouts have done this for the boy. Scout leaders and the Boy Scout executives and even the Explorers helping the younger ones—they have done this for years. In doing so they have made America a different country than it probably could have been.

Because of this lesson that I learned in this little homely incident, I have followed what is happening to these Boy Scouts. Whenever it is possible for me to stop along the road and to see a group of Cubs or Brownies and Girl Scouts or Boy Scouts, I try to get a word—two or three words—two minutes—to see what they are thinking about, what their morale is. And it is always at the top.

They get this morale, why? Because they are trained or they are taught that they can render a service. I might say that after I finally lose the loving care of the Secret Service, that should I be standing one day on the corner of a busy street and a Boy Scout sees this rather elderly looking fellow looking a little doubtful, if he offers to take me across the street, he can do it. Because the way these boys and their counterparts among the girls are growing up is to believe there is an honor and a satisfaction in doing a service for others. To my mind, that is the great thing about Scouting. It doesn't make any difference whether they wrap up their bedrolls just right, or pitch their tent exactly right, or whether they do their cookout and burn the eggs and the bacon not fit to eat. As long as they have that feeling and that development—if they get the same feeling that we did when we read in our Bibles the Parable of the Good Samaritan and then as time comes along, if they individually and collectively begin to think of their nation in part as a "good Samaritan," doing the decent thing in this world, then I will tell you: Scouting is indeed doing something for all of us that is not only necessary but I would say vital to our vigor as a nation based upon a religious concept, but is ready to take on its own shoulders its duty with respect to itself, with respect to those that are less fortunate. Only in this way, in my opinion, is America going to be able to lead the way to that goal that mankind has sought so long, and so far so futilely, a peace with honor and with justice.

Thank you very much.

ANNUAL MESSAGE TO THE
BOY SCOUTS OF AMERICA

FEBRUARY 7, 1961

I am delighted to send a message of greeting to the Boy Scouts of America as they mark their fifty-first anniversary.

As the Boy Scouts enter their second fifty years, more than five million boys and men are actively engaged in this outstanding volunteer organization.

Well over thirty million have taken an active part in the work of the Scouting movement since its foundation. America owes much to the character and leadership qualities of the Boy Scouts.

With every good wish,
Sincerely yours

ANNUAL MESSAGE TO THE
BOY SCOUTS OF AMERICA

FEBRUARY 1963

To the Boy Scouts of America:

I am very pleased to extend to each one of the Boy Scouts of America and the thousands of leaders who are helping them into responsible young men my warmest personal greetings.

Through your activities as Boy Scouts, you are preparing for lives of good citizenship and are learning to appreciate the great values and tradition which have always made Americans proud of our heritage of freedom and justice for all.

To each one of you, my very best wishes for continuing accomplishments.

STATEMENT FOR BOY SCOUT TAPE RECORDING

Undated, JFK Presidential Library

It is my privilege to extend my personal greetings to each of the 25,000 Cub Scouts, Boy Scouts and Explorers taking part in the great Scouting Exposition at the New York Coliseum. I am also pleased to talk briefly with those of you who have come to witness the work of the boys and to lend your support to Scouting.

When I was a boy, I was a Boy Scout, and enjoyed the fun and adventure of Scouting's outdoor program, just as a million of other American boys have done over the years. As your President, I am increasingly aware of the value of Scout training in the preparation of our boys for their future responsibilities as the leaders of our nation and of the free world.

It is a matter of satisfaction to me that all of my cabinet and official family were Scouts as boys with the exception of two who later served in Scouting as Scouters.

Your Exposition slogan 'Be Prepared—America!' expresses most clearly the need for training our boys in preparation for their citizenship responsibilities, and for civic leadership. I salute the Boy Scouts of America for the service it is rendering the nation, and the part that it is playing in fostering understanding and friendship among youth everywhere—at home and abroad.

THE PRESIDENT'S REMARKS TO A REPRESENTATIVE FAMILY SELECTED BY THE BOY SCOUTS OF AMERICA IN CONJUNCTION WITH BOY SCOUT WEEK

FEBRUARY 8, 1962, WASHINGTON, DC

I want to congratulate the Boy Scouts of America on this anniversary, to congratulate the Fair Family who have been chosen the Scouting Family of the Year ... I think we have a great American family and I think they have typified what Scouting means to this country—more than 5 million people, young boys who are active in it and girls. I strongly believe in Scouting. I believe it to be a source of strength to us. I greatly appreciate all the adults who give leadership. I would recommend it to the sons and daughters of every American family. I am particularly glad this year that they are putting special emphasis on fitness—physical fitness—as an important ingredient to our national strength. So I congratulate you all and tell you that I am grateful to you and the millions of families that you represent today.

LYNDON B. JOHNSON

MESSAGE TO THE BOY SCOUTS OF AMERICA

Christmas 1963

I am pleased to extend warm Christmas greeting to the Boy Scout of America and their leaders.

Our Nation's future is continuously taking form in the hearts and minds of its young people. What America will be like tomorrow will be determined to a large extent by how young Americans shape their lives today, by the good deeds they perform or fail to perform, by the direction they pursue in work and play.

This is a time for renewed application of our national heritage, for rededication to our national purpose. It is a time to consider anew the true meaning of goodwill, of brotherhood, or our triumphs and our tragedies.

I wish each of you a good Christmas and a New Year filled with the deep satisfaction of personal achievement.

REMARKS AT THE BOY SCOUT JAMBOREE IN VALLEY FORGE

July 23, 1964

[BSA President Thomas J.] Watson, Scout leaders, members of the Boy Scouts of America: The America that you will build and live to see will be far different from the America of today.

In 50 years there will be 400 million Americans instead of 190 million Americans. Man will have reached into outer space and probed the inner secrets of human life. And some of you will take those journeys. New inventions will have changed the way in which you live, just as the automobile and the airplane and the television have brought changes to my life. Fast planes and satellites will make neighbors of distant lands.

You will see wonders and participate in achievements of which we older Americans can only dream.

This is an exciting challenge. I envy you the great adventures which await you.

But it was an American President, Woodrow Wilson, who said, "A nation which does not remember what it was yesterday does not know what it is today nor what it is trying to do." If you are to do great things, you must remember also what America has been.

For this country of ours is not just a collection of factories and banks. It is not simply 190 million people, or crowded cities, or broad highways.

This country of ours is a community built on an idea. Its history is the history of an idea. And its future will be bright only so long as you are faithful to that idea.

It all began right here where we are standing tonight. In 1777, in Valley Forge, a few thousand men suffered and starved through the freezing cold of the harsh winter. They did not have, as you have, regular meals, a decent place to sleep, protection from harm.

But they did have an idea, an idea and a dream. That idea gave them the strength to survive the winter, and when their ordeal was over, George Washington led them forth to liberate and to create the United States of America.

Throughout our history, most Americans have shared the common purpose which gave strength to the soldiers at Valley Forge. Most Americans share those purposes tonight. The American idea is, first of all, the belief in freedom and the rights of man.

Government was to be chosen and directed by the people. And every individual citizen was to have the right to speak his views, to worship as he wanted, and to be safe from the arbitrary acts of Government. Even if a single man stood alone against the entire Nation, that single man was to be protected in his beliefs and in his right to voice those beliefs.

This dedication to freedom was founded on the great moral truth that all men were created equal. This was a recognition that all men were equal in the eyes of God. Being equal, the poorest and the most oppressed among us had the same right as all others to share in Government, to enjoy liberty, to pursue happiness as far as his abilities would take him.

It will be up to you to carry this idea forward. For it is not yet a reality for all in this land. If Government was to be chosen by the people, it must exist to serve the needs of the people. This, too, is part of the American idea.

As a result, in America we have a Government which exists to protect the freedom and enlarge the opportunities of every citizen. That Government is not to be feared or to be attacked. It is to be helped as long as it serves the country well, and it is to be changed when it neglects its duty.

I know that to many of you the Government in Washington must often seem far away, must often seem very difficult to understand.

But your Government is made up of people, people like those you know in your own hometowns, people who are chosen by your parents and your neighbors and sent to Washington to serve your towns and your States.

Government is an Irish boy from Boston who grew up to become President of the United States.

Government is the son of a German immigrant from Pekin, Ill., who became a leader of the American Senate.

Government is a rancher from Montana, a banker from New York, an automobile maker from Detroit.

Yes, Government is the son of a tenant farmer from Texas who is speaking to you tonight.

And I am sure that here tonight within the sound of my voice are others who will grow up to work for this country in the councils of Government.

The American idea is also the belief in expanding opportunity and in progress. This was not to be a country where a few were rich and most were deprived. It was to be a country where every citizen had the chance, through his own work and skill, to provide for his family and to enrich his life. And that is the kind of country that we have built.

In the early days a man needed only an axe and a gun to build a new life in the open spaces of the West. Today it takes knowledge and skill. Today they must have that in order to have a chance to find a job, in order to take a rewarding place in the life of our country.

But because we have been faithful to this idea, more men have greater opportunity in America than in any other country in the history of civilization.

These ideas are as old as your country, but they are not old-fashioned ideas. They are as alive and as vital as America itself.

I have no doubt that if you remain true to them, you will remember these days of scouting as only the beginning of a lifetime of useful service to America.

The qualities you will require for this task are those contained in your Boy Scout Oath. Its pledge has meaning not only for you but has great meaning for all of our citizens.

What that pledge really means is the theme of this jamboree. It means "This Is My Country," and "I must prepare myself to serve it well."

Be faithful to it. And your life and the life of your country will be the richer for it.

It is wonderful to come here and be with you this evening, and to look into your smiling, optimistic faces. It will give me strength that I need in the lonely hours that I spend in attempting to lead this great Nation.

It is wonderful that you could be here in this peaceful atmosphere of one of the great States in our Union and at such an historic site.

You have much to be thankful for. Yes, we have much to preserve and much to protect.

I am grateful that your great leader, Mr. Tom Watson Jr., asked me to come here to be with you tonight, and I want to thank you from the bottom of my heart for receiving me so warmly.

God bless you all.

55TH ANNIVERSARY MESSAGE

JANUARY 15, 1965

As the Boy Scouts of America prepare to observe their fifty-fifth anniversary, I am delighted to extend to each of you my warmest congratulations and good wishes.

I welcome this opportunity to express my pride and deep sense of gratitude for the outstanding example and enviable reputation for human understanding and fair play, which have throughout the productive life of your organization been hallmarks of Scouting everywhere. Your conduct, both individually and in your group activities, has been worthy of admiration by all the young citizens of our land.

Today, as we face the challenges of an increasingly complex and frequently disturbing world, America needs an alert, responsible, and energetic youth to provide her with a vital resource in a hopefully happier and fuller future for all. As I applaud your past, I also urge you to rededicate yourselves on this anniversary to the ideals of the Scout Oath, and to reaffirm your obligations to your God and to your country. In so doing, you will contribute to the strengthening of America's heritage and thereby to the realization of our common goals in the Great Society.

REMARKS ON THE 55TH ANNIVERSARY OF THE BOY SCOUTS OF AMERICA

FEBRUARY 8, 1965

[BSA Presiden Thomas J.] Watson and Members of the Scouts:

I want to welcome you here this morning. It is a particular privilege to have you come and visit this house.

Yesterday, sometime Sunday afternoon, someone around here suggested that this meeting should be postponed—on the grounds that we might not have much time this morning.

I vetoed that suggestion in a hurry. I said we might delay it but we wouldn't postpone it, because whatever comes to this house for decision and action, our first concern always is for the young men and young women of America. For every American President the number one priority and the number one interest has been, and I think always will be, the young people of our land.

I am very glad this morning that we can be together on this 55th anniversary of the beginning of the Boy Scouts of America.

Over nearly the full span of this century, Scouting has served our Nation well and served it faithfully. Today there are more than 5-1/2 million members, from 4 million homes, that are dedicated to the goals of helping each boy to become a man of character, a responsible citizen, with a strong and vigorous body, physically strong, mentally awake, and morally straight.

I congratulate all of you Scouts and adult leaders alike. I am especially pleased by your plans for a breakthrough in 1965—to extend Scouting to all neighborhoods: rich and poor, educated or not, for all boys of all races and all religions.

Your new program will mean much for Scouting, but it is going to mean a lot more for your country—the beloved America that is ours.

You, and all your contemporaries, are members of a challenging generation. You shall be challenged as none before us to keep the flame of freedom burning, to keep the hope of peace from being extinguished. But you will be challenged even more to find for yourselves—and to help others find with you—a new meaning for life on this earth. If the life you know has many comforts—as I hope it will—your life will also have many trials and tests. I believe and I hope that you will be ready for them.

Over the years of this century, men abroad—and some at home—have made great mistakes in miscalculating the character and the strength and the fortitude of the young people of America.

I hope that none today, anywhere, will repeat that miscalculation about our youth or about our Nation.

We love peace. We shall do all that we can in honor to preserve it—for ourselves and for all mankind. But we love liberty more and we shall take up any challenge, we shall answer any threat, we shall pay any price to make certain that freedom shall not perish from this earth. I know that this is the spirit in your hearts.

Last night I read the winning essays in your Nathan Hale contest. I was impressed by the papers—but there was one I especially liked.

I don't know Cub Scout Jim Karkheck of Durham, NY—but he is a young American and I would love to meet him. He wrote on "Why I Love America," and this is his paper, in full.

"I have three turtles. They have a beautiful terrarium with rather low sides. They have everything they could want except one thing—freedom. Every chance they have, they climb out.

"People in many countries in this world lack the same thing. Not in America.

"In America we have freedom of speech, freedom to go wherever we please, freedom of the press, freedom to worship God as we wish, freedom to choose people to govern us.

"A boy like myself can grow up to be whatever he dreams of being. That is why I love America."

So, my young friends, the Boy Scouts, I can only add one thing this morning. I hope all we are doing now—at home and throughout the world—all the things we are doing I hope will some day make it possible for all young men and young women to grow up and, as Jim said, be whatever they dream of being.

I want to thank you for coming here and I want to wish you well in the years ahead.

I will take great pride in watching your development as we go down the road together.

Thank you.

ANNUAL MESSAGE TO THE BOY SCOUTS OF AMERICA

FEBRUARY 1965

To the Boy Scouts of America and Their Leaders:

The story of Scouting reflects America's vitality of spirit and generosity of heart. It represents fifty-six years of service to progress and achievement. And its hero, the Boy Scout, continues to be a living symbol of our aspirations and hopes for a better world.

Over 40 million Americans have found Scouting to be a rewarding experience. And its many salutary programs have often been the springboard to their success.

The role of the volunteer leader, so indispensable in our time, has had in Scouting a ready testing ground. It has served to develop in our youth the qualities of mind and character which in years ahead will enable them effectively to guide the Ship of State.

In observing Boy Scout Week, you rededicate yourselves to the high principles of the Scout Oath and Law. And you renew your determination to secure for every American boy the opportunity of Scouting membership.

I salute your desire to share in the building of the Great Society, and I especially applaud your efforts to "Keep America Beautiful."

Honor, integrity, and devotion to your country have made you responsible citizens. And they have made the story of Scouting a genuinely American story.

ANNUAL MESSAGE TO THE BOY SCOUTS OF AMERICA

FEBRUARY 1966

To the Boy Scouts of America and Their Leaders:

Every society has vested its hope for tomorrow in the caliber of its youth. For youngsters without purpose of inspiration will grow into a generation without leadership or concern.

Young men must be trained well in the duties and opportunities of citizenship. They must develop strength of character and an intense loyalty to the institutions of freedom. They must be physically fit and morally keen.

The Boy Scouts of America adopt these qualities as goals. Boy Scout Week calls our attention to the wholesome influence of Scouting on the lives of millions of Americans—and thus on our progress as a nation. It also is an occasion for commending the volunteers and sponsors who sustain the Boy Scout Movement.

And in this special year, I want to join in welcoming Scouts of other lands to the United States. I trust that the 1967 World Jamboree will quicken among boys of many nations the desire for understanding and passion for peace upon which rests the future of all men.

ANNUAL MESSAGE TO THE
BOY SCOUTS OF AMERICA

FEBRUARY 1967

To the Boy Scouts of America and Their Leaders:

I am delighted to salute the nation's Scouts and future leaders during the traditional observance of Boy Scout Week.

For fifty-eight years, you have shown the world the truest meaning of honor, integrity, loyalty, and patriotism. And you have done it through example, not preaching; by deeds, not words.

You have kept pace with the times, but you have not lost faith in our time-honored traditions.

Since 1910, you have played an indispensible part in the lives of both your members and the nation you serve.

Your helping hands have stopped at no barriers. You have reached out to boys in low income areas, and given those in remote rural America a chance to participate in the fullness of our land.

Out nation is greater for your role in its history. And generations of its men are physically and morally stronger for their part in your great and growing movement.

RICHARD M. NIXON

REMARKS OF VICE PRESIDENT NIXON

Sioux City, IA, September 17, 1960

Out at the airport today greeting us were a number of very interesting groups but one that particularly impressed me were 300 Boy Scouts in uniform, standing at attention—not in the goose-step rigid attention that you see in a totalitarian country like the Soviet Union in a pioneer camp for youth—but standing in the way Boy Scout groups usually stand, with the freedom of movement and expression that we expect from an organization of that type. The thing that ran through my mind I'm sure was what would run through your mind—that the most important question and the most important responsibility for the next President of the United States is to see that those boys and thousands like them are always in uniforms of peace and never have to be in uniforms of war.

REMARKS ON RECEIVING THE BOY SCOUTS' *ANNUAL REPORT* TO THE NATION

February 5, 1970

I particularly appreciate this *Report to the Nation* to the Honorary President of the Boy Scouts and the emphasis that the report has made on the work that Scouts will do in the field of the environment.

Our young people have an enormous interest in the environment and Scouts have had from the time of their foundation because they know of the natural beauty of this country, and they want to preserve it—preserve it for their children and for all the generations to come.

I think that if the 5 million Scouts, as an individual example, can give leadership to the whole Nation with regard to doing everything individually that he can do to leave every place he goes a little bit cleaner, a little bit better for the people who follow him, that this will help us enormously on this attack on the problems of the environment, because this is a struggle that must be waged and won on many fronts.

You can't just say government is going to do it or industry is going to do it. Every individual has to enlist if we are going to make the environment of this country what we want it to be and what I want all the Scouts in the future to find in the years ahead. So thank you very much.

PRESIDENT NIXON TO J. HOWARD KAUTZ, SCOUT EXECUTIVE, NATIONAL CAPITAL AREA COUNCIL, BSA

JANUARY 15, 1971

The volunteer spirit that fills the ranks of the Boy Scouts of America gives encouragement to a nation that recognizes and applauds the significant contributions of your fine service organization.

As a resident of the Nation's Capital, I find it especially heartening that the Area Council of the Boy Scouts has chosen as their theme, "America's Manpower Begins with Boypower." I particularly commend your positive approach and your determination to be "for" instead of "against." At a time when the viability of our most sacred national institutions is being questioned, you and your colleagues throughout the country show what constructive self-appraisal can do in setting new goals that work for the benefit of our whole society.

The success of your "Commitment for Tomorrow Campaign is essential to the future of the Scouting program in our city. And since Scouting offers such a unique opportunity for young Americans to fully develop their potential for public accomplishment and to become effective leaders in their communities, your efforts are even more vital for the future well-being of our nation.

I am proud of your stimulating role in an organization that reflects the highest tradition of the American way of life. May you further expand this role and, with it, your successful character building programs. And may you continue to encourage more youngsters to an early and active participation in the work of civic progress.

REMARKS TO DELEGATES ATTENDING THE NATIONAL EXPLORER PRESIDENTS' CONGRESS

JUNE 2, 1971

I want to express my appreciation to … all of the Explorers that are here.

I realize that isn't the usual thing you may sometimes hear these days. I know that for people in the younger generation, you naturally think, as you should think, of all the problems we confront in the world today, the problems America has abroad, the problems America has at home, and you wonder whether this is really a good time to be young, whether this is a good time to be an explorer, an explorer with a capital "E" or a small "e"; whether this is a good time to be an American, to live in this country.

Well, I just want to tell you that I have a great deal of faith in not only this country but in you. And one of the reasons I have faith in this country is because of my faith in you and in your generation.

Let me put it in this context: At the present time, I think that your generation, the generation from 14 to 21, has the best chance of any generation in this century to enjoy what we have not had in this century in America—full generation of peace.

That may seem far away, but we are ending the American involvement in the war in Vietnam in a way that will contribute to a lasting peace, and you are going to be the beneficiaries of that.

More than that, we find very significant new developments in the field of foreign policy. You have been hearing about them; you have been reading about them. The kind of a world that you will grow up in, that you will take positions in, in your professions and your lives, can be a very different world.

Oh, it isn't going to be a world without challenges; it isn't going to be a world without dangers. But it could be a world of peace, and it could be—and I trust that this may be the case—a world where explorers, capital "E" or small "e," can go any place in the world.

What we are trying to do through our new initiatives in foreign policy is not only to bring peace to America and to the world but to open up the world, to open up the world so that your generation can not only know America and Europe and South America and Africa, but you can know Asia and the great legion of people who now live in Mainland China.

I believe this is going to come. And I believe for that reason, the world here is going to be a more exciting one, a more interesting one, a more peaceful one for all of you.

Now, having painted that prospect for the future, let me just say one word with regard to what we need and what we know and what I am sure we will get from you:

You are going to be required, as a younger generation, to help America maintain this strong national defense that is needed so that we can play a peaceful role. Some of you are going to be required, in addition to that, to make a contribution to America's economic strength. As a matter of fact, all of you, in one way or another, are going to contribute to that, and all of you—and this I consider more important than either of the first two, either our military or economic strength—all of you are going to be needed to contribute to the character of this country.

In a few minutes you are going to take a tour of this house. For 180 years, Presidents of the United States have lived in this house. It isn't really called officially the White House; it is the President's House. John Adams first lived there, and all the Presidents since have lived in the White House.

As you look at that house, and as you go through it, you will think of the history, of the great trials this country has gone through, of the men who lived there, the challenges this Nation faced, and how we got where we are.

What you will be reminded of is that when America was very young, as you were very young, America was weak economically, it was also weak militarily; but it was the hope of the world because we had a moral and a spiritual strength and an idealism that caught the imagination of the world.

America stood for something, stood for something among peoples far away that were never to know this land. That was true 180 years ago. I can tell you that it is still true today; that there are millions of people in the 70 countries I have visited all over this world who look at America as the hope of the world, despite all of our problems, despite the ones that we hear and see night after night on television, read about in the newspapers.

It is your challenge not only to help keep America strong, and not only to help keep it prosperous, but to keep the character of this Nation, its idealism: to make it a nation where there is true opportunity for every American; to make it a nation where character really does count; to make it a nation, too, where, in spite of all of the temptations to turn to those particular activities that would weaken our national strength, you maintain those great traditions that you have learned in Scouting and that you are continuing in your role in this great organization, the Explorers.

I would simply conclude with this final thought: Sometimes, I know, you may get the impression from what you may hear or see on television or read in the newspapers, or perhaps what you hear in the classrooms, that this is rather a bad time to be alive. You tend to be a bit pessimistic about it.

Here we are: We have a war. We have problems of strife within the country, and wouldn't it have been better to live at another time or maybe in another nation?

Don't you believe it. If I had my life to live over again, and if I had at this time to pick a nation, of all the nations in the world, in which I wanted to live, and a time in which to live, I would pick the United States of America.

This is a great country, and you can be proud of the fact that your country will play and is playing a role for real peace in the world. We don't threaten any other country's peace or freedom. You can be proud of the fact that the challenge you face is that what America does—not just our military and economic strength, but more, the strength of our character—will determine whether the billions of people on this earth are going to enjoy peace, and more of them are going to have an opportunity for freedom in the years ahead.

I simply want to say to you: Don't lose faith in your country. I know that you love it; otherwise, you would not be in this great organization. Keep your faith in America. There are things wrong with it, but in changing what is wrong, let's not destroy what is right. What we want to do is to build America, to build it up rather than tear it down; to stand up for America, to stand up for it when it is under attack; to correct those things that are wrong; and to make it the good and great country that we know it is.

So with that, let me say I hope you enjoy every minute of your stay in Washington. I am glad that the rain that was predicted this afternoon did not come, and I hope that all of you enjoy your tour through the White House.

Incidentally, you will find a lot of things lying around. Usually I say to guests, "You can pick up anything that isn't nailed down." As far as you are concerned, I know that you will enjoy this visit, and as you go through those rooms, think of the history of the country, think of the heritage which is yours, and I hope all of you will come out with just a little more pride in being an American and having the opportunity to lead America.

REMARKS ON RECEIVING THE BOY SCOUTS' *ANNUAL REPORT* TO THE NATION

FEBRUARY 22, 1973

I want to express my appreciation to all of the delegation here, the outstanding representatives of Scouting in the United States, and I am glad you have finally recognized the importance of having some girls in Scouting, too.

Also, I want you to know that your projects are of very, very great interest to me personally and to all in the United States, I can assure you, including those who cover us in the press, because they have heard us often discuss the problem of drug abuse. They heard the speech, for example, last week of the problems of the environment. They, of course, are enormously interested in physical fitness. Our young people generally, and Scouts throughout this country, 6 million of them, and all of those who support them, are working toward those goals individually and voluntarily.

We, as a government, can do a great deal, but unless the people of the country cooperate, we can accomplish nothing.

I think there is no other organization-certainly there is none larger in the United States--which enlists more volunteers for these great goals than this one here.

The other thing I would like to say, which I am sure all of you will appreciate, and particularly your mothers and fathers: This is the fifth time I have received this group, because, as you know, the President is the honorary president of the Boy Scouts of America. But this is the first time as

President I have been able to receive you at a time when I could say to you, you no longer are confronted with the draft. You can have a choice now as to whether you want to enter the armed services. I hope some of you may, because it is a very honorable and important profession.

And also, it is the first time that I can meet with you, and I can say that the United States is at peace with all nations in the world. My greatest hope for you, in addition to progress on all of these fronts, which are so important at home, is that you and your brothers and your sons may grow up in a world of peace. Thank you very much.

GERALD R. FORD

PRESIDENTIAL LETTERS OF CONGRATULATIONS TO EAGLE SCOUTS

1974–1977

Congratulations on achieving the rank of Eagle Scout. I hope you will continue in life the high goals you set or yourself in earning this distinctive honor.

It is with great interest that I learn you recently attained the rank of Eagle Scout. Please accept my sincere congratulations.

Having been an Eagle Scout myself, I can well understand the sense of pride and accomplishment that comes with earning the Boy Scout's highest honor.

Best wishes in the years ahead. Always remember the lessons from your Scouting days—they will serve you well.

With kindest personal regards.

EAGLE SCOUT CONGRATULATIONS LETTER TO BRIAN G. KATHENES

NOVEMBER 1, 1982

Thinking back on my Scouting years, I find it difficult to extract any one incident that helped to shape my career. I firmly believe it was the total Scouting experience that helped me on the road that eventually led to the Presidency.

There is not organization anywhere in the world, which stands for greater qualities of leadership than Scouting does. In my own life, I know that if I've had any success at all, a good deal of the credit must be given to some of the lessons I learned as I was advancing up the path to Eagle Scout.

Wearing the Scouting insignia tells the world that you are someone special, and, for the rest of your life, many people will expect more from you than just ordinary performance in anything you decide to undertake. It creates a commitment to the pursuit of excellence, which can be attained by incorporating the Scouting ideals in your daily life.

Warmest, best wishes,

REMARKS BY VICE PRESIDENT GERALD R. FORD AT A BOY SCOUT CONFERENCE IN HONOLULU, HAWAII

MAY 17, 1974

It is good to be with you today. I'm still a Scouter in spirit, although it has been many years since I've been in a Scout uniform.

One of the proudest moments of my life came in the Court of Honor when I was awarded the Eagle Badge. I still have that badge. It is a treasured possession.

I envy you Scouters in your work with young people. I served for some time as a Scout Advisor in Grand Rapids after World War II, but I regretfully left that work when I was elected to Congress.

I have great admiration and respect for those who continue to give of their time and energy to the Scouting program. Some of my happiest memories go back to the days when I was a Scout in Troop 15 of the Trinity M.E. Church in Grand Rapids.

Those memories involve the hikes, the camping, the outdoor life which I believe are a major factor in the continued success of Scouting. Those outdoor activities are of greater and greater importance to our nation as it becomes more and more a nation of cities and metropolitan areas, rather than of farms and small towns.

The concrete of the streets and highways and the bricks and steel of buildings wall us away from that close contact with the earth and sky which can help us realize what is important in life and what is not.

We all need the sense of renewal that close contact with Nature brings.

One of the most intense students of Nature, Henry David Thoreau, realized that some of the most basic truths can be found outdoors. In his book, Walden, Thoreau says: "I went to the woods, because I wished to live deliberately, to front only the essential facts of life, and see if I could not learn what life had to teach…"

That to me emphasizes the importance of Scouting. It does get us out into the woods. It does give us a chance to look at the essential facts of life, and to learn from them lessons that can help each of us meet the challenges of life.

So I am greatly heartened by the fact that scouting continues to emphasize the out-of-doors life—and, in fact, expands it far beyond the simple camping trips of my youth to include the "high adventure" experiences. I hope your Scouting leaders continue to emphasize the out-of-doors in your program.

It didn't occur to me at the time I was hiking, camping, cooking, canoeing, and taking part in the other outdoor Scouting activities that I was learning some things which would play an important part in my life.

One of the most important lessons was self-discipline. You and I know that you don't camp for the night successfully unless you have a schedule of things to do before you crawl into the sleeping bag. And you have to follow that schedule. If you don't, you're liable to be facing some unpleasant consequences, like having your tent blow down because it wasn't staked properly.

I think that principle of setting a schedule as to what you want to achieve and how you want to go about achieving it has helped me as much as any single thing I learned in Scouting. I feel, therefore, that your work in showing the Scouts how to properly set themselves tasks and then to follow through on those tasks is of great importance. The more citizens we have who practice self-discipline, the better off our country will be.

We have all heard the doom-criers who weep these days about our country's future. They claim the nation is falling apart. They see nothing but trouble ahead for all of us. Well, to me, your very presence here is proof positive that those doom-criers are wrong. They are 180 degrees off course.

In fact, here you are playing a major role in helping build the leaders who will bring new strength and purpose to our people. I believe that

Scouting provides the best leadership training program for young people anywhere in the world.

I mentioned earlier the self-discipline which Scouting helps develop. There are other important leadership qualities which Scouting builds. The entire program is a daily demonstration of the usefulness and power which comes from teamwork. It shows what a team can do, if coordinated and properly motivated.

In my 25 years in political life, I have found that teamwork really helps get things done in government. Those who best understand the power of a group of people working together for a common goal are those who become the leaders of our nation.

The more you can do to bring to the boys and young men with whom you work the idea of teamwork, the better leaders you will develop. Another most important part of the Scouting program in building leadership—and this I offer from my heart as well as from my experience—lies in the moral values if offers the individual. These are values without which leadership is difficult. Many think it fashionable those days to look down upon Scouting values as kid stuff—all right for boys, perhaps, but hopelessly out-of-date for adults in a cynical world. What a mistaken idea!

In my travels around the country—and I've been in more than half the states of our nation in the past 5 months—I have found a deep hunger for those basic values which the Scouting program teaches. You know them.

The Scout Law: A Scout is Trustworthy. A Scout is Loyal. A Scout is Helpful. A Scout is Friendly. A Scout is Courteous. A Scout if Kind. A Scout is Obedient. A Scout is Cheerful. A Scout is Thrifty. A Scout is Brave. A Scout is Clean. A Scout is Reverent.

Those points of the Law, with the Scout Oath or Promise to help other people, to keep himself physically strong, mentally awake and morally straight, and to do his duty to God and his country, from basic values on which to build one's life.

They are basic values on which to build a nation.

They are basic values on which to build a world.

The more people we have who do a good turn for another each day, the less suspicion and distrust we will see. The more people we have who believe in truth and honesty, the fewer problems we will have in government.

The more people we have who respect our nation, its laws and its flag, the less we will hear about our country falling apart. The three great principles which Scouting provided—self-discipline, teamwork, and moral and patriotic values—are the basic building blocks of leadership. I applaud Scouting for continuing to emphasize them.

I am greatly heartened by the success in the BOYPOWER '76 program, which is reaching so well toward its goals for the bicentennial year. The effort to bring the Scouting program into the inner cities and poverty areas of our country is of immense importance and can play a major part in helping alleviate some of the problems which those areas pose for our country.

I encourage your efforts, too, in directing the Scouting program toward another area of concern to our nation—conservation.

The more our young people can learn about the energy and environmental difficulties we must overcome, the better equipped they will be to help us overcome those possibilities. The road to solution of our energy problems is not a short one. But in charting our course down that road, clear knowledge of the problems and of the directions in which we must go to meet them are of great value.

All in all, it seems to me that as we near the Bicentennial year which is the goal of the BOYPOWER '76 program, Scouting is stronger and more important to the nation than ever before. In fact, I find that Scouting and the Bicentennial have a strong bond between them—youth.

It is well for all of us to remember just how young was much of the leadership which created out nation nearly two centuries ago. Nathan Hale, an officer in the Continental Army, was just twenty-one years of age when he said before he died: "I regret that I have but one life to lose for my country."

Thomas Jefferson, elected to the legislature of Virginia at twenty-five, was exactly thirty-three years old when he wrote the Declaration of Independence.

Jonathon Dayton, one of the signers of the Constitution, was twenty-six. James Madison, a legislator from his mid-twenties, was thirty-five when he drafted the plan that became the basis for a remarkable document, our Constitution.

Alexander Hamilton became the first Secretary of the Treasury in his early thirties. He was a member of General Washington's Staff during the Revolution at the age of twenty-four.

As you continue to work toward your goals for the Bicentennial, I hope you will keep in mind the fact that very young people played a very important part in winning our freedom and bringing into being this great Republic.

I am confident that today, two centuries later, the youth of this nation will play at least as important a part—if not more important—in moving this Republic and its people into a better world.

I am confident that your ability to bring ideals, values, and leadership training to millions of our young people will help to bring about a new era—a time in which not only out Republic will progress in peace and freedom, but a time in which the entire world shall be secure, and all its people free.

Thank you.

STATEMENT TO THE BOY SCOUTS OF AMERICA

OCTOBER 30, 1974

My early years as a Boy Scouts were invaluable in helping to shape the course of my later life. Throughout my public service and extensive travels around the country, I have seen firsthand evidence of the immeasurable worth of the basic values taught by Scouting programs. The Scout Path to help other people, to keep physically strong, mentally awake and morally straight and to do one's duty to God and to our country provides a solid base on which to build both individual and national strength.

The three principles which Scouting encourages—self-discipline, teamwork and moral and patriotic values—are the building blocks of character. By working for these principles, those who belong to and support the Boy Scouts of America add greatly to the vitality of our society and to the future well-being of its people.

REMARKS AT THE BOY SCOUTS' ANNUAL AWARDS DINNER

DECEMBER 2, 1974

I think they say once a Scout always a Scout, and I can tell you from my own experience that is true. After all these years I still love the outdoors. I still know how to cook for myself, at least at breakfast. And as anyone who saw those pictures of me in Japan will know, on occasion I still go around in short pants. [Laughter]

I am particularly grateful for your invitation to be here tonight for a very personal reason. It has recently been said that I am too much of a Boy

Scout in the way I have conducted myself as President, and so I reviewed the Boy Scout laws and Boy Scout Oath.

They say that a Scout is trustworthy, loyal, helpful, friendly, courteous, kind, obedient, cheerful, thrifty, brave, clean, and reverent. That is not bad for somebody who knew it 46 years ago.

And the Boy Scout Oath is, "On my honor, I will do my best to do my duty to God and my country, and to obey the Scout Law, to help other people at all times, to keep myself physically strong, mentally awake and morally straight."

Well, if these are not the goals of the people of the United States, what they want their President to live up to, then I must draw this conclusion: Either you have the wrong man or I have the wrong country, and I don't believe either is so.

I happen to believe that the ideals and the aspirations of all Americans and all Boy Scouts are one and the same, and I will continue to use those ideals as a guide and as a compass in all of my official duties. I think our goal ought to be, or should be, more Boy Scouts in government, not less.

Coming here this evening, after an interesting press conference, to receive this coveted award takes me back a good many years to one of the proudest moments of my youth: the day I was awarded the Eagle Scout badge, more than 46 years ago.

I remember the pride I felt then in the court of honor and the pledge that I made to myself never to dishonor that badge. As Betty knows, I still have that badge, by the way. It is a very treasured possession, and over the years it has been, I think, a good reminder to me. It is a reminder of some of the basic, good things about our country and a reminder of some of the simple but vital values that can make life productive and very rewarding.

A very great American, Dwight D. Eisenhower, once said that his faith in our young people was as unbounded as his faith in America. I share that faith. I believe that the youth and America go hand-in-hand. For it is America's youthful spirit, strength, its idealism that are the keys to our country's greatness—even today as we approach our 200th anniversary as a nation, we are still a very young country, a young people compared to most other nations on this Earth.

And that is where Scouting comes in. The teamwork, the self-discipline, and just as important, the sense of adventure that grow out of the Scouting experience are the very things we need today to build a better America.

So often, the deepest, the most profound emotions and ideas are expressed in very simple words. Today, when some people are casting about for new values, new answers, and new outlooks on life, the key to many of our problems lies in the basic values of the Scout Law—in trust, in loyalty, courtesy, thrift, bravery, reverence.

In most Americans, he once said, there is a spark of idealism which can be fanned into a flame. Scouting is one of these things that keeps that spark of idealism alive, that plants it in the hearts of young Americans while preparing them for manhood and for citizenship.

That is why, as an old Scout who still tries to live by the Scout Law and the Scout Oath, with no apologies, I am proud and honored to accept this award tonight.

Thank you very much.

ANNUAL MESSAGE TO BOY SCOUTS OF AMERICA

FEBRUARY 4, 1975

As an Eagle Scout and now as Honorary President of the Boy Scouts of America, I am proud to congratulate Scouting's fifty-seven million past and present members who are this year observing the Movement's sixty-five years of distinguished service to our nation.

Your theme for 1975, "Be Prepared for Life: Be Safe, Be Fit," is particularly appropriate and reflects the main thrust of all your programs to build better citizens for the future. It is most fitting that your Bicentennial program places such a major emphasis on Neighborhood and community activity.

I warmly commend your plans to redouble your efforts in the area of conservation through the continuation of your successful Project SOAR, and I salute your initiatives to conserve the energy we need to become self-sufficient.

Your endeavors continue to reflect a sensitivity and awareness of today's needs. They are well tailored to the times in which we live. And it can truly be said that, through them, you fulfill Scouting's obligation of duty to country.

REMARKS AT CUB SCOUT INDUCTION CEREMONIES IN CHARLESTON

November 11, 1975

Mr. Walls, Governor Moore, all of you wonderful Cub Scouts, Boy Scouts, Scouters, et cetera:

It is just great to be here. This is the kind of gathering I love to come and say just a word or two.

For a good share of my life, beginning a good many years ago, I spent a tremendous amount of time, starting as a Tenderfoot and going on through there, on through to a troop commissioner and a counsel—whatever they call them—and I was darned proud of my association with Scouting from the beginning to the end. And I am proud of all Scouting today and you should be, too.

I don't think there was a prouder moment in my life than when I was privileged to become an Eagle Scout. And I still have the merit badge sash, and I still have that Eagle badge. It means a great deal to me today, as it did then.

There is something about scouting that leaves an impression on you, an impression that is wholesome and is good, and it is a stimulant for greater effort—the Scout Oaths and the Scout Law—and I could almost repeat them without a mistake.

But I can say to you, you will enjoy yourself, you will do better, you will be happier, you will just make a greater contribution to your country, to your State, to your city, to your family, to yourself, if you live by the Scout Oath and the Scout Law. They are good for you today, and they will be good for you tomorrow, and they will be good for you a long time from now.

So, enjoy what you are doing, but make a big effort to do the best today as a scout. If you do, you will do a better job for your country in the years ahead.

Good luck. God bless you. Thank you very much.

REMARKS UPON RECEIVING THE BOY SCOUTS OF AMERICA'S *ANNUAL REPORT* TO THE NATION

FEBRUARY 24, 1976

I have many fond personal memories of Scouting going back a good many years, not only as a scout—they didn't have Cub Scouts in those days—but also as a participant in the senior activities of Scouting.

I think the fact that 60 million young men have participated over a period of 66 years, is indicative of the strength that Scouting has contributed to a better America. I just hope that Scouting goes on forever, because it is a great contributor to all of what we stand for in this country.

I hope that in the future there will be many presidents who will be honored, as have been, by your presentations today. This has been a fine opportunity, not only to meet you but all of these outstanding young men and women who are here in the Oval Office on this occasion.

Good luck.

JIMMY CARTER

BY THE PRESIDENT OF THE UNITED STATES OF AMERICA, A PROCLAMATION

DECEMBER 7, 1979

Scouting teaches boys and girls self-reliance, physical fitness and good citizenship. It fosters character development and nurtures a love and understanding of nature and of other people.

Scouting has a long and proud tradition of service and leadership training. Many of our Nation's most accomplished men and women in every field of endeavor are former Scouts, and cite Scouting as one of their most important early experiences.

Through the years Scouts have broadened their activities to meet the changing needs of young Americans and help them prepare for useful and rewarding lives.

In recent years Scouts have been particularly active in promoting energy awareness and conservation, and are continuing this important effort. They are also planning activities designed to aid in taking an accurate census next year.

By House Joint Resolution 448, the Congress has designated the week of December 3 through December 9, 1979 as "Scouting Recognition Week."

Now, Therefore, I, Jimmy Carter, President of the United States of America, call upon all Americans to recognize the contributions of Scouting and to support Scouting programs in their communities.

In Witness Whereof, I have hereunto set my hand this seventh day of December, in the year of our Lord nineteen hundred seventy-nine, and of the Independence of the United States of America the two hundred and fourth.

ADDRESS TO THE NATION ON THE EVE OF THE PRESIDENTIAL ELECTION

NOVEMBER 5, 1984

For me, a vivid recollection [was a] whistle-stop train tour through Ohio in that historic ear that once carried Franklin Roosevelt, Harry Truman, and Dwight Eisenhower across America. America had a smile in her heart that day. At each stop and through each community, whether gathered on their sidewalks, back lawns, or the plowed fields of their farms, again and again it was the young people I remembered—Cub Scouts in blue shirts and bright yellow kerchiefs, high school bands, college crowds. There's more than the freshness of youth on those faces I've seen; there is the future and hope of all America.

REMARKS BY TELEPHONE TO EAGLE SCOUT AWARD RECIPIENT ALEXANDER M. HOLSINGER

SEPTEMBER 14, 1982

Well, this is Ronald Reagan. And, Alex, I'm kind of familiar with the place where you are right now. I played football a few times there in Bloomington against Illinois Wesleyan a long time ago. But now as honorary president of the Boy Scouts of America, it's a pleasure to join with all those gathered in Bloomington today to congratulate you on becoming the 1 millionth Eagle Scout in our nation's history.

Well, listen, this accomplishment not only represents a major achievement in your own life, but it also demonstrates the important contribution that

Scouting continues to provide to so many young people. You, I know, must be very proud. And, indeed, you should be very proud of this outstanding honor, as I'm sure your parents and your friends are.

Mr. Holsinger: Yes, we are, sir.

The President: Well, your hard work and high ideals have carried you on a successful journey through the ranks of Scouting. And along the way, I know you've learned many valuable lessons and have built a framework on which to constructively lead the rest of your life.

You've joined an elite group of Scouts, too, because some of them are close associates of mine—former President Gerald Ford; Secretary of Health and Human Services in this administration, Richard Schweiker; Secretary of Housing and Urban Development Samuel Pierce; and our good friend, Jim Brady. Your accomplishments in Scouting are, indeed, something to be very proud of. And I join you in extending my congratulations and best wishes for many more prospective years to come.

Mr. Holsinger: Thank you, sir.

The President: Well, it's been a pleasure to be able to participate even from long distance in what's going on. So please give my best to your family and friends. And again, to you, congratulations.

REMARKS AT A WHITE HOUSE LUNCHEON COMMEMORATING THE 75TH ANNIVERSARY OF THE BOY SCOUTS OF AMERICA

FEBRUARY 8, 1985

Good afternoon and welcome. And forgive me for interrupting our lunch.

I'm delighted to be able to help celebrate the 75th anniversary of the Boy Scouts of America. I'm delighted to celebrate anything that's older than I am— [laughter] but 75 years of unparalleled service to the youth and the families and the communities of our nation.

As you might imagine, in my job there's some things I must do and some I want to do and a few special things that I just can't wait to do. And this celebration is one of those special moments.

On Inauguration Day I spoke of the American sound—those symbols of our democracy and echoes of our past that give us purpose and guide us forward. And I said that sound—our heritage, our song—is hopeful, big-hearted, idealistic, daring, decent, and fair. And you know, come to think of it, I could have added trustworthy, loyal, helpful, friendly, courteous, kind, and the rest of the Scout Law, because the Boy Scouts of America and the values that you hold close are an important part of the American sound and have been for 75 proud years.

And it was in the early days of Scouting that the life of a young New Yorker was changed forever. Manhattan's Lower East Side was a very tough neighborhood, and far too many young men were drawn into the turmoil and the violence there and never recovered.

But this particular youngster from the Lower East Side found the Boy Scouts. He was challenged to learn positive values—leadership, camping, fitness. Aaron took up the challenge and gained in moral strength, confidence, and ambition. He became a successful attorney. And his son became the second Eagle Scout in the family.

But Aaron never forgot his roots and, in 1943, left the practice of law to give more of his time to Boy Scout fund-raising.

And his son? Well, during our first term, Ken Duberstein served here in the White House as my Assistant for Legislative Affairs. So, I'm very pleased that they're both here today.

You know, America sure turns out winners. And much of the credit belongs to organizations like the Boy Scouts. And so it's not surprising that yesterday's Scouts have helped to shape our today—in business, government, the media, science, medicine, education, show business, and—well, the list goes on and on.

Former Scouts have walked on the Moon, become President, and won the Heisman Trophy. Today they serve as Cabinet Secretaries, as my Press Secretary, and in the Congress. In fact, about two-thirds of the Members of the Congress have been in the Boy Scouts. I can't help but think, two thirds of them Boy Scouts—[laughter]—how nice it would have been if the Boy Scouts had a merit badge for a balanced budget amendment. [Laughter]

But you can be certain that today's Scouts will help shape America. And when they do, I'll bet there'll be Scouts like the ones who are with us today, like Randy Reed of nearby Vienna, Virginia. Two days ago Randy received the Boy Scouts' highest and rarest award—the Honor Medal for Lifesaving with Crossed Palms for extraordinary heroism.

And he's not alone. I've just been sitting beside a young man here, Freddie Hill, who also is wearing that medal very proudly. But Randy, also, at the extreme risk of his own life, rescued a young man who had slipped, who had struck his head and fell unconscious, wedged between rocks in 14 feet of murky water. With great bravery and skill, Randy did everything his Scout training would tell him to do and more. And, Randy, congratulations and God bless you.

Let me ask: Freddie, how many others in here are wearing that medal also? Which Scouts? Look at you, too. Freddie is wearing the medal.

Thank you. Well, it's easy to understand why the Boy Scout badge, the American eagle superimposed on the north sign of the mariners compass, means "Follow me, I know the way." The Boy Scouts of America do know the way, the way to set high standards and how to live by them, and the way to build character, train in citizenship, and foster fitness of mind and body.

And here's one last thought: Without the thousands of adult leaders, corporate sponsors, and other caring Americans, it would not be possible for young Americans to capture the Scouting spirit and the special joys of camping, fellowship, service, and love of country.

So, thank all of you for what you're doing for our young people and for America's future. We're in good hands. So, God bless you all, and God bless the Boy Scouts of America.

PROCLAMATION 5421 - SEVENTY-FIFTH ANNIVERSARY OF THE BOY SCOUTS OF AMERICA

DECEMBER 15, 1985

By the President of the United States of America, A Proclamation

The Boy Scouts of America, our Nation's largest organization for young people, has served our youth since 1910. Thanks to dedicated adult volunteers, more than 70 million young people have learned Scouting's lessons of patriotism, courage, and self-reliance over the past 75 years, and millions more have benefited from the service, inspiration, and leadership of the Boy Scouts.

Former Scouts have gone on to become leaders in all fields, including business, education, and government. The values they learned through Scouting have given them the confidence to make ethical choices and to realize their full potential as active and responsible citizens.

America's young people have always been treasured as our most precious resource. Since Scouting has had a strong positive influence on young people, it has played a vital role in shaping America's future. The Boy Scouts have clearly shown that it is possible to innovate while remaining faithful to their original principles. I am confident that they will continue to play an important role in American society for many years to come, molding our youth with programs that build confidence and competence, and instilling in them principles that can guide them through their lives.

The Congress of the United States, by House Joint Resolution 159, has designated the year 1985 as the "75th Anniversary of the Boy Scouts of America" and has authorized and requested the President to issue a proclamation to commemorate this event.

Now, Therefore, I, Ronald Reagan, President of the United States of America, do hereby proclaim the year 1985 as the Seventy-fifth Anniversary of the Boy Scouts of America.

In Witness Whereof, I have hereunto set my hand this fifteenth day of December, in the year of our Lord nineteen hundred and eighty-five, and of the Independence of the United States of America the two

REMARKS TO REPRESENTATIVES OF
THE BOY SCOUTS OF AMERICA

February 13, 1989

First, I want to thank you for having me now be the honorary president of the Boy Scouts. And I want to thank you for that annual report. But even more, I want to thank you for the good turns—as you call them—the good turns that you do, as your own motto says. Boy Scouts are helping…the homeless and disabled and the elderly and, in short, the most vulnerable in our society. And to those that have been left behind, you guys are saying, "Hey, we're going to help you catch up." And to those who have given up on themselves, you say as Scouts and Scouters, "We've not given up on you." And you made a difference, helping to combat drug abuse, child abuse, hunger, illiteracy—working with the homeless, unemployment.

You believe in America's greatest treasure—its ability to care. And for nearly a century now, the Boy Scouts have cared about our children. And you've helped them, enriched them, and helped our children enrich mankind. And so, I want to come by and say: Keep up the good work! I think if we do this enough and if I make the point how strongly I feel about what you do, I think the country will understand very clearly what I mean when I talk about One Thousand Points of Light, because I think of the Scouts, and I think of what you all do to help others. And it's clear, bright light, bright and shining, and you're an inspiration to all of us. And I'm grateful that you came here, and I'm proud to have my gold [lifetime membership] card here that I promise I'll keep right there in that desk in the Oval Office to remind me of the good work that the Scouts do for everybody.

Thank you very much.

REMARKS AT THE BOY SCOUT NATIONAL
JAMBOREE IN BOWLING GREEN, VIRGINIA

AUGUST 7, 1989

Your Scout Law commands you to be trustworthy, loyal, helpful, friendly, courteous, kind, obedient, cheerful, thrifty, brave, clean, and reverent—What a mouthful! And that might sound like a lot to remember, but it isn't. For at the core of that code is something simple: a desire to serve with honor, a sincere feeling for one's fellow man and for one's country. Serving is not a lifelong chore to be carried out. As Chief Scout Citizen Teddy Roosevelt put it: "The full performance of duty is not only right in itself but also the source of the profoundest satisfaction that can come in life." In short, to serve and to serve well is the highest fulfillment we can know. Bill Swisher, who gave so much time and commitment to this Jamboree—he certainly knows this. Around the country, Americans like you are serving others in a thousand ways, providing a Thousand Points of Light and doing a good turn daily.

I know that Boy Scouts have always helped out through times of disaster, from fires to flash floods. The Boy Scouts were there when Franklin Delano Roosevelt appealed for help during the Great Depression, gathering almost two million articles of clothing, household furnishings, and food for the needy. And the Boy Scouts were a strong helping hand at home when older brothers fought a war in Europe. And today the Boy Scouts have taken on a new struggle: to defeat what you call the five unacceptables: illiteracy, unemployment, child abuse, drug abuse, and hunger. In fact, fighting hunger alone, Scouts, Cub Scouts, and Explorers rounded up—now get this—65 million cans of food for local food banks, the largest collection of food ever undertaken in the history of the United States of America.

And your focus, then, is right on target. Today we can be grateful as a nation that no depression or no war looms ahead of us. The Boy Scouts of America has assumed a leadership role in confronting this problem. You are teaching self-protection strategies against drugs and other dangers, and you've circulated these strategies in direct language in a very successful pamphlet called "Drugs: A Deadly Game." And you've done something else: You are leading the youth by example. For years, the Boy Scouts of America has led our nation in taking the antidrug message to every community. By actively engaging in the lives of others, you are demonstrating a central theme, a central idea of this administration: that from now on in America, any definition of a successful life must include serving others.

And there are other, more positive challenges facing your generation. When the first Boy Scouts chapter was formed, Americans had just tamed the farthest reaches of the West. There were only a few remote places in the world, unseen by man. And since then, the world has become smaller, and so has the room for our imagination and daring—a narrowed space for the restless spirit of freedom that is so much a part of our national priority and of our national identity. But you and I know that there's a new frontier, a frontier without limits—space.

And once again, the Boy Scouts has played a leadership role in preparing a generation for space exploration. It's no coincidence that half of all astronauts were once Scouts: Admiral Richard Truly, who ably heads NASA, is an Eagle Scout; Gus Grissom, an American hero who lost his life in the early space program, was a Scout; David Scott, who operated that first lunar rover, was a Scout; And Jim Lovell, another lunar explorer, whom I'm told is with us today. And I guess, Jim, if you're here, it's true what they say: Once an Eagle Scout, always an Eagle Scout. And I doubt that any of the Scouts who participated in the 1969 seventh Jamboree in Idaho will ever forget Eagle Scout—[applause]—go Boise—will ever forget Eagle Scout Neil Armstrong, who made man's first step on the Moon and later sent his greetings to the Jamboree from deep space. The first spacefarers were unique, the lucky few. But your generation will have a broader, greater opportunity to live in space, to travel, to establish an outpost on the Moon, and explore the mysteries of Mars. And this is the challenge of the next century—your century, your challenge.

You are privileged to be the generation that will witness the first large movement of men and women into space. And as this happens, I know that the Boy Scouts of today will be in the lead. Thank you for inviting me to your Jamboree. God bless you, God bless the Boy Scouts of America, and God bless the United States of America. Thank you all.

REMARKS UPON RECEIVING THE BOY SCOUTS OF AMERICA'S *REPORT TO THE NATION*

FEBRUARY 12, 1990

It is my pleasure to welcome all of you and to participate once again in this tradition that dates all the way back to 1911, when President Taft received the first Boy Scout delegation right here in the White House.

Let me say to all how deeply honored I am to receive this highest award: the Silver Buffalo. I live with a Silver Fox—and now she lives with a Silver Buffalo. But I'm honored because down through the years I've seen what the Boy Scouts mean in the lives of young men. And Scouting is more than learning how to build a campfire or to tie a knot. And Scouting teaches a love of outdoors and appreciation of our environment. It teaches the spirit of serving others, and self-respect. And let me make it pure and simple: It teaches lessons that last a lifetime. And so, when I hear about Boy Scouts that are out there helping the homeless or feeding the hungry or cleaning up our cities and towns or helping other kids stay drug-free, when I hear about boys as young as 8 and 9, Cub Scouts, doing things like that, I see a glimpse of the future—what this nation can be like if we follow the lead of the Scouts.

And I know the Scout slogan is "Do a good turn daily"—and every day you do. And that's why right now, with you here representing the national Boy Scouts organization, I want to recognize the work of the Montana Council of Boy Scouts for an environmental program they call Project Good Turn. In the past 5 years, Project Good Turn has collected over 5,000 tons of trash from all across Montana and involved more than 30,000 young people in the cleanup effort. And the Montana Scouts have made this a real community project, enlisting everyone from the Girl Scouts to the State Highway Patrol and the Montana National Guard. And so, today I take great pleasure in naming Project Good Turn the 65th daily Point of Light, a shining example of the kind of community engagement that makes a difference, the kind we've come to expect from the Boy Scouts of America.

I'm proud to accept this year's report to the Nation, the new edition of the handbook, and to have this opportunity to thank you all for the wonderful works done by the Scouts all across this country. Thank you all very much, and God bless you. Thank you for coming.

REMARKS TO REPRESENTATIVES OF THE
BOY SCOUTS OF AMERICA

FEBRUARY 4, 1991

This has become, appropriately so, an annual event. And I am proud to be now this card-carrying member of the Boy Scouts—and pleased to receive this year's report to the Nation.

I'm also just delighted to have this Desert Storm patch because in my view there's no doubt about the outcome of Desert Storm and no doubt about the reasons why. We're fighting in the Gulf so that this generation of Scouts never has to. And we want to pass on to them the kind of world they deserve—a world of stability and security, peace and justice.

This report that the Scouts have given me is, I am told, full of the good deeds done by our nation's future leaders, from helping the hungry to helping kids stay drug-free. And that's the kind of work that makes the Scouts Points of Light and the leading lights of a new generation.

So, I really wanted to come here to thank you, as representatives of all the Scouts across the Nation, for all the wonderful good deeds you do every single day because in that way you're keeping our country strong.

So, thank you for coming, and thank you for these marvelous souvenirs that I take with me. And God bless you all, and keep up the great work.

Thank you so much.

REMARKS ON RECEIVING THE BOY SCOUTS OF AMERICA'S *REPORT TO THE NATION*

February 10, 1992

Since 1911 with President Taft, every President ... has received the Boy Scout *Report to the Nation*. And I am again proud to receive it this year. The Scout slogan is "Do a good turn daily." This report represents the great and heroic deeds done by our Nation's future, from feeding the hungry to helping kids stay drug-free. I listened to those five goals, and clearly we should all be working to achieve those goals.

Boy Scouts and Scout initiative have been recognized as what we call daily Points of Light for serving others and making positive differences, for example, the members of Boy Scout Troop 4 of Ann Arbor, Michigan. These Scouts made community service central to their mission, providing companionship to our elderly, beautifying the grounds of the elderly homes, as well as working with the hungry and those afflicted by drugs.

So I just mentioned one example; there are many, many more that I could point to. I want to thank all of you for the good turns done by the Scouts throughout the United States; thank each of you, those who have been singled out for personal heroism. It sets a wonderful example to young and old alike.

So for me, this is a very nice interlude, and I'm just delighted to see you all back here. I remember that marvelous encampment in Virginia. I hope someday I'll get to come back. It's good to see you guys.

Thanks for coming.

REMARKS TO THE 1997 NATIONAL BOY SCOUT JAMBOREE IN BOWLING GREEN, VIRGINIA

JULY 30, 1997

Thank you very much. Are those Arkansas flags I see back there? Thank you for waving them.

It's a great privilege for me to be here to celebrate the 60th anniversary of the first national Scout jamboree, a pleasure to serve and an honor to serve as your honorary president. As has already been said, ever since 1910, when William Boyce founded the Boy Scouts of America, every President has proudly served as your honorary president, for every president has recognized what a great contribution Scouting has made and is making to the character of our young people and, therefore, to the character and future of the United States of America.

I, like many members of our administration, was exposed to Scouting at a young age. I began as a Cub Scout in Hot Springs, Pack 1, Ramble Elementary School, Ouachita Area Council. And those are the guys that are waving those flags back there. So don't boo them too hard. They're just sticking up for one of their own.

When I was preparing to come out here to visit you, I was reminded of how the Boy Scouts got its start in our country as the result of a good turn. I reviewed once again the classic story of how William D. Boyce lost his way in a dense London fog and received help from a British Scout who refused to accept a tip. Just think about how that one good turn set in motion millions upon millions of other good turns over the years.

You may know that last April, I and all former presidents and General Colin Powell sponsored a presidents' service summit in Philadelphia. At that summit, we said that we wanted every young person in America—every single one—to have the benefit of five things: a safe childhood, a healthy childhood, a childhood with a good education, a childhood with an adult mentor, and the chance for every child, himself or herself, to serve in every community in the country. In other words, what we said was we challenged all the adults in America to engage in citizen service, another way of doing a good turn. The Boy Scouts of America, as much or more than any other organization in this country, has answered our call, for the Boy Scouts committed after the presidents' service summit to provide 200 million hours of community service through the year 2000. I thank you for that commitment.

Building community and character is what the Boy Scouts have always been about. So today I ask all of you to help spread the word about doing good turns. All of you here, each in your own way, are future leaders of this country. When you return home from the jamboree, please encourage your classmates and your friends to join you in committing to community service. If every young person in America would give back to their community in the way you do, just imagine what we could do. Imagine how many fewer problems we could have. So many times I have wished that every young person in America had the chance to be a part of Scouting. And tonight I see why, more clearly than ever. So I hope you'll go home and help others to serve and learn the joy that you share by the service you do.

And the next time you recite the Scout Oath, I hope you will remember that it's not just your fellow Scouts, your parents, and the people you know well but your whole Nation that is counting on you. We need you to remain focused on the strong values you learned in Scouting, to remember that character counts and service counts. We need you if we're going to build our communities and bring our people together across all the lines that divide us. We need you if we're going to lead our country into the 21st century still the world's strongest force for peace and freedom and democracy and prosperity. We need you if we're going to have a country where every person, without regard to race or station in life, who is responsible enough to work for it, can live out his or her dreams. We need you to keep this country coming together and coming ever closer to the ideals on which we were founded: that we are one Nation under God, all created equal. We have to work harder and harder and harder to build that one America, strong and united and good.

Over 150 years ago, the astute French observer Alexis de Tocqueville said, "America is great because America is good." You help to keep America good, and

I know you will throughout your lives. Thank you for what you do. Thank you for what you are. And thank you for what you will become.

Good luck, and God bless you all.

GEORGE W. BUSH

VIDEOTAPED REMARKS TO THE BOY SCOUTS OF AMERICA'S NATIONAL JAMBOREE

JULY 30, 2001

Hello, Boy Scouts, and thanks for this opportunity to send a word of greeting to your National Jamboree. Let me also thank General Colby Broadwater and the fine men and women of Fort A.P. Hill for hosting this event.

I'm so sorry the weather didn't allow me to join you in person, but I wanted to say a few words to the Scouts and Scoutmasters who have come to this jamboree from all across the country.

It is those values that are such an important part of Boy Scouts. And I want to thank the adults here who have shown good values, who have taken the responsibility upon yourself to build the wisdom and character of our young people. And the Scoutmasters of America accept this responsibility every day. I want to thank all the Scoutmasters who set a good example and help Scouts learn the values that give direction to their lives.

When you join a Scout troop and put on the Boy Scout uniform, you, too, make a statement. Like every uniform, yours is a symbol of commitment. It is a sign to all that you believe in high standards and that you are trying to live up to them every single day. As you do that, you bring credit to the Scout uniform and credit to your country. And I want you to know your country is proud of you.

Many of you have been to Washington this past week, maybe for the first time. You know, it's interesting, one of my predecessors, President Gerald Ford, saw Washington for the first time a few years after he became an Eagle Scout.

Back then, in the thirties, Scouts helped collect food and clothing for people suffering from the Great Depression.

In our own time, you all have taken the lead in the fight against drug abuse. In Texas, Boy Scouts were among the first to take up a reading challenge that I set. All across America, Boy Scouts are doing good turns daily. And every time you do a good turn, this becomes a better country. There are needs in every community, and those needs can be met one heart, one soul at a time.

You can make a difference for America by the life you lead and the lives you serve. Times and challenges change, yet the values of Scouting will never change. Scouts of any era would recognize every word that you live by today, because those words have always defined Scouting. The goodness of a person and of the society he or she lives in often comes down to very simple things and words found in the Scout Law. Every society depends on trust and loyalty, on courtesy and kindness, on bravery and reverence. These are the values of Scouting and these are the values of America.

What you have learned in Scouting will see you through life. In good times and difficult ones, the Scout motto will always help you: Be Prepared. And whatever you do, the Scout Oath will always guide you: On your honor, do your best.

I thank every Scout and Scoutmaster for being a part of this great organization and for being a part of this successful jamboree. May God bless you all, and may God bless the United States of America.

REMARKS TO THE NATIONAL SCOUT JAMBOREE AT FORT A.P. HILL, VIRGINIA

JULY 31, 2005

Here at the 16th National Scout Jamboree, you're carrying on a tradition that dates back almost seven decades. President Franklin Roosevelt came to the first jamboree in 1937. I don't think he rode in the same kind of helicopter I did, though. You know, I was looking forward to coming last week, but the thunderstorms got in the way. So I appreciate the rain check. It's a fantastic sight to look out on more than 30,000 young men wearing the uniform of the Boy Scouts.

At this base there are Scouts from all 50 States plus Puerto Rico, Guam, the Virgin Islands, and countries from all around the world. As a former Cub

Scout from Midland, Texas, I'm especially glad to be here with the Texas Scouts. Sounds like you brought a big delegation this year.

Coming to this jamboree gives me great confidence in the future of our Nation. For nearly 100 years, Boy Scouts have set a high standard of service and duty to God and country. Millions of Americans have pledged the Scout Oath, "On my honor, I'll do my best." And through the generations, Scouts have made America a stronger and better nation.

Scouts have excelled in fields from science to business to education to the arts. Scouts have earned Olympic Gold Medals, Nobel Prizes, and Academy Awards. Thousands of Scouts have shown the highest form of patriotism, by going on to wear the uniform of the United States military.

The first Scout Jamboree was held in Washington, DC, and Scouts have felt at home in the Nation's Capital ever since. More than half of the current members of the United States Congress participated in the Scouts. One of the Capital's most famous Scouts is President Gerald Ford. He first saw Washington just a few years after he earned his Eagle badge and eventually became the first Eagle Scout to call the White House his home.

As president, I have the privilege to work with Scouts every day. When I come to the Oval Office in the morning, the first person I see is a Scout, my Chief of Staff, Andy Card from the State of Massachusetts. Down the hall is Vice President Dick Cheney, a Boy Scout from Casper, Wyoming. And across the river at the Pentagon sits an Eagle Scout from Illinois who Americans count on to "be prepared"—Secretary of Defense Donald Rumsfeld.

These Scouts have a lot of things in common, and one of the most important is that they all benefited from the influence of a caring adult early in their lives. Across America, Scoutmasters and volunteers devote long hours to building the knowledge and integrity of our Scouts. It's not always an easy job. When I was a Cub Scout, my mother was our den mother. It's about the time her hair turned white. I want to thank the Scoutmasters of America and the volunteer Scouters for taking the time to care. I want to thank you for your leadership and thank you for setting such a good example for a new generation of Scouts.

When you join a Scout troop and put on the Boy Scout uniform you make a statement. Your uniform is a sign that you're a certain kind of citizen, trustworthy, loyal, helpful, friendly, courteous, kind, obedient, cheerful, thrifty, brave, clean, and reverent. These are the values of scouting, and they're important values for America. By working to live up to them, you're bringing great credit to yourselves and to our Nation.

Coming to this jamboree is a great way to practice the values of Scout Law. And when you get back home, there are a few lessons you might keep in mind. The first one is one you've probably heard before, and it's one of the most valuable lessons I've learned: Listen to your mother. I didn't have much choice. Mom always has a way of speaking her mind. When I paid attention, I benefited. And that's how it still works. Listen, you may not always agree with your mother, but think of it this way: The first voice you heard is always worth listening to.

Second, always remember where you come from and what you believe. At times you may come across people who say that moral truth is relative or call a religious faith a comforting illusion. They may question the values you learn in Scouting. But remember, lives of purpose are constructed on the conviction there is right, and there is wrong, and we can know the difference.

In the years ahead, you will find that indifferent or cynical people accomplish little that makes them proud. You'll find that confronting injustice and evil requires a vision of goodness and truth. You'll find that many in your community, especially those younger than you, look to you as an example of conduct and leadership. For your sake and for the sake of our country, I hope you'll always strive to be men of conviction and character.

Finally, your life will grow in meaning when you serve a cause greater than yourself. There's a wise saying: We make a living by what we get; we make a life by what we give. That truth is expressed well in the Scout slogan: Do a good turn daily. When you help someone in need, you're making America more hopeful, one heart and one soul at a time. And you're answering the call to love a neighbor just like you'd like to be loved yourself.

Every day, every day Scouts are showing that the greatest strength of America lies in the hearts and souls of our citizens. Through your Good Turn for America initiative, Scouts have given more than 1.4 million hours of volunteer service this year alone. In Nebraska, Scouts have made more than 11,000 pocket-size flags to send to troops serving overseas. In California, Boy Scouts donated money they raised for summer camps to help victims of the tsunami in Asia. In Louisiana, Scouts collected five tons of food to donate to a food bank. In Florida, Boy Scouts and Cub Scouts worked together to clean up the roads before the Super Bowl. And right here at the National Jamboree, Scouts are working with Habitat for Humanity to build a home for a Virginia family in need. On behalf of a grateful nation, I thank the Boy Scouts for serving on the frontline of America's armies of compassion.

The Boy Scouts are recognizing our call to service with a special honor. I was pleased to accept the Good Turn for America award on behalf of the millions of volunteers all across our country who are helping this country be a hopeful place. By making a commitment to service, to integrity, and to good citizenship, all of you are showing your gratitude for the blessings of freedom.

You also understand that freedom must be defended, and I appreciate the Scouts' long tradition of supporting the men and women of the United States military. Your generation is growing up in an historic time, a time when freedom is on the march. And America is proud to lead the armies of liberation. I believe we're laying the foundations of peace for decades to come.

And that's not the only reason I'm optimistic about the decades ahead, because I'm standing in front of America's future leaders. When you follow your conscience and the ideals you have sworn as a Scout, there is no limit to what you can achieve for our country. Continue to make right choices in life. Continue to set high standards. Continue to be a leader.

Thanks for hosting me tonight. May God bless you all, and may God continue to bless the United States of America.

BARRACK OBAMA

LETTER OF CONGRATULATIONS ON
BSA'S 100TH ANNIVERSARY

FEBRUARY 4, 2010

I send greetings to all those celebrating the 100th anniversary of the Boy Scouts of America.

Our Nation's future depends on how well we educate the next generation of leaders. By building a strong foundation of service, character, and active learning, we can open doors of opportunity for our children and secure a brighter future for our country.

For 100 years, the Boy Scouts of America has striven to prepare young men for the world they will inherit, and former Boy Scouts have reached the highest levels in every sector of American life. From members of Congress to CEOs, professors to professional athletes, the Americans have written their own chapter in our Nation's story.

As you look back on your accomplishments and enter the next century of Scouting, I wish you all the best.

PRESIDENTIAL ADDRESS TO THE 2010 NATIONAL SCOUT JAMBOREE

BOWLING GREEN, VIRGINIA, JULY 28, 2010

Hello Everybody,

I wanted to send my greetings to everyone taking part in the National Scout Jamboree at Fort A.P. Hill, to congratulate you on the 100th anniversary of the Boy Scouts of America. I hope you've all enjoyed this year's festivities. You know, for a century, Scouts just like you have served your communities and your nation in ways both large and small. During World War II, Scouts played a vital role in supporting the war effort at home by running messages and selling war bonds. Some our nation's greatest heroes have worn the Scout uniform, including 11 of the 12 men who have walked on the moon.

Today, Scouts across the country continue the tradition of collecting food for those in need, improving our neighborhoods, and reaching out to those less fortunate. That service is worth celebrating, but there is still more to do. Even though we face a different set of challenges today than we did a hundred years ago, they are no less important. Into the years ahead, we're going to depend upon you, the next generation of leaders, to move America forward. So I hope that all of you will carry the lessons you've learned in Scouting with you for the rest of your lives. And I hope that when you are called upon to help write the next great chapter of the American story that you'll uphold the best of the Scouting tradition and respond with enthusiasm, skill, and determination. Congratulations again on your first hundred years. I'm sure the next hundred will be even better.

APPENDIX A

A Sampling of Historical BSA Pilgrimages

T HE BOY SCOUTS OF AMERICA (BSA) is an organization steeped in tradition. Since its founding in 1910, Scouting's leaders have encouraged visits to the burial sites of great Americans through organized pilgrimages.

Although some have been to the graves of national Scouting fathers like BSA co-incorporator, William D. Boyce, and BSA co-founder, Daniel Carter Beard, most have been to the final resting places of our past presidents.

Historically, presidential tombs always have drawn legions of visitors annually. Today, summer family vacations may include visits to these sites as educational opportunities for children. As an organization, BSA managers agree and have sponsored many annual presidential pilgrimages, even one since 1911.

The Valley Forge Pilgrimage

The first presidential pilgrimage was made over the Memorial Day weekend in May 1911 and attended by four hundred local Scouts from the Philadelphia area. It celebrated the sacrifices of Revolutionary War patriots during the Valley Forge winter of 1777-1778 under General George Washington. As such, the Valley Forge Pilgrimage was the first mass assemblage of its kind for Scouts.

"Scoutcraft in many of its details was gone through," *Boys' Life* magazine reported in July 1911. "First aid was given to two visitors who were overcome by the heat."

By 1913, the date had changed to February 22 – President Washington's birthday.

"In spite of severe cold and stormy weather, a large number of Delaware and Montgomery County Scouts turned out for a 'Pilgrimage' to Valley Forge," reported *Boys' Life*. "They had the fun of cooking their luncheons on the woods in the same place where the Revolutionary soldiers cooked theirs, and they ended the day very happily with a service at the Memorial Chapel at Valley Forge." As a service project, Scouts agreed to help build a large hall behind the chapel for their use at future Valley Forge pilgrimages.

This tradition continues today and is the oldest Scouting Pilgrimage still in existence, having evolved into the annual Valley Forge Pilgrimage and Encampment hosted by the Cradle of Liberty Council based in Philadelphia. Scouts experience weekend camping in the same frozen conditions that their patriot ancestors survived more than 235 years earlier.

"The theme is always an historical perspective from the American Revolution and Washington's winter Troop Encampment at Valley Forge," recalled a member of Boy Scout Troop 19.

Theodore Burnett Jr. speaks at BSA's first Theodore Roosevelt Pilgrimage in 1920.

Each year, one of Washington's soldiers is honored as the patron of the celebration. Scouts receive lessons in "drilling, artillery, musket and rifle demonstrations" as well as critical roles taken by American Indians during the conflict.

By 1924, BSA's premier George Washington themed pilgrimage had expanded beyond Valley Forge to encompass his tomb at his beloved Mount Vernon home in Alexandria, Virginia. And a few years later, a BSA pilgrimage sprung up at Washington's military encampment over the winter of 1779-1780 at Morristown, New Jersey – now known as the Morristown National Historical Park.

The Theodore Roosevelt Memorial Pilgrimage

Chief Scout Citizen and former president of the United States, Theodore Roosevelt, was a hero to Boy Scouts and youth across the nation. When he died in January 1919, Scouting managers sought to enshrine his memory through the planting of Roosevelt Memorial Trees using seeds supplied by the walnut tree overlooking at his gravesite in Oyster Bay, Long Island, New York.

Then in 1920 a Roosevelt admirer named Theodore E. Burnett Jr. organized a so-called "Roosevelt Pilgrimage" for Boy Scouts to the president's gravesite and Scout Commissioner Daniel Carter Beard led a small contingent of boys from the area. Its popularity and success prompted Chief Scout Executive James E. West to make the Roosevelt Memorial Pilgrimage an annual event.

And from a small gathering of Scouts in 1920, attendance rose to more than 6,000 pilgrims a decade later. Over the next thirty years, the special Scout memorial program expanded to include patriotic songs, recitations, and speeches, which even the stodgy *New York Times* diligently reported on into the early 1950s:

The New York Times

October 29, 1921

OYSTER BAY, L.I.—Eulogizing the late Colonel Theodore Roosevelt as an American and a true Scout, more than a thousand members of the Boy Scouts of America paid tribute at his grave this afternoon at Youngs Memorial

Cemetery. They presented an impressive scene kneeling in silent prayer at the close of the exercises.

The Scouts, who came from all parts of Long Island, New Jersey, Brooklyn and Manhattan, under the leadership of Colonel Daniel Beard, National Scout Commissioner and an old friend of the late president, made their second annual pilgrimage to the grave.

Headed by a band, the boys marched to the cemetery with members of the Camp Fire Club of America. Hundreds of spectators followed the boys, all uncovering as the band played "The Star-Spangled Banner."

At the grave Colonel Beard then made a short address telling of the late president's Americanism and his pleasure at being made honorary president of the Scout organization. Colonel Beard urged the boys to follow the life of the Colonel and lead good clean lives. Dr. [Charles A.] Eastman declared that Colonel Roosevelt was a "red-blooded American" whose memory would live forever.

Following taps, fifty boys, one by one passed the grave, dropping wreaths. The Oath of the Scouts was then repeated, and at its conclusion Colonel Beard, kneeling, placed the wreath on the grave while the Scouts and hundreds of spectators knelt in a brief silent prayer.

The local council in Nassau County, Long Island, New York, now known as the Theodore Roosevelt Council, has a special way of honoring this great American. Since 1973 its members have presented the Chief Scout Citizen Award to a community supporter who has had a positive impact on Scouting.

The Scouts themselves have another way to honor him: when they gather around the campfire at Camp Wauwepex at the Schiff Scout Reservation in Wading River, New York, there is always an empty seat in the council ring, forever reserved for Theodore Roosevelt.

Theodore Roosevelt's 150th birthday was celebrated with a Roosevelt Memorial Pilgrimage organized by BSA's Northeast Region and the Theodore Roosevelt Council. Festivities included a parade led by Rough Riders on horseback and speakers that included great-grandson Tweed Roosevelt, along with local Theodore Roosevelt impersonator, Thomas Foote. The celebration began with the laying of a wreath at Colonel Roosevelt's gravesite in Youngs Memorial Cemetery followed by the Pilgrimage to Roosevelt's home a few miles away at Sagamore Hill.

The Harding Memorial Pilgrimage

The untimely death of President Warren G. Harding in 1923, a man known to "Roaring '20s" Scouts as "Our Friend," shocked and saddened the Boy Scouts of America. Harding's memory was especially strong in his hometown of Marion, Ohio. Beginning on what would have been his 67th birthday in November 1932, local Scouts began a Harding Memorial Pilgrimage to the tomb of the former president and first lady.

"Four hundred Scouts of Councils in the vicinity of the Harding Memorial in Marion, Ohio, marched in the first pilgrimage to the shrine of the late president," recounted *Boys' Life* in their February 1933 issue. "A throng of four thousand witnessed the ceremonies conducted by Region 4 of the Boy Scouts of America last October."

Today, now organized by the Harding Area District in the Heart of Ohio Council, some 500 Scouts gather at the Marion Grant Middle School at 420 Presidential Drive and begin the two mile parade route to the 103-foot in diameter, 53-foot high, circular Harding Memorial bounded with a series of Roman style columns.

BSA Scouts and Leaders participate in the annual Harding Memorial Pilgrimage in Marion, Ohio.

The U.S. Grant Pilgrimage

The year 1955 brought to Galena, Illinois a pilgrimage that celebrated the life and achievements of the Civil War Union commanding general and president of the United States, Ulysses S. Grant. The celebration, first envisioned by Mrs. Virginia Carroll and Mrs. Ruth Turner, was a weeklong event that kicked off on Saturday, April 23. The pilgrims visited all local Grant historical sites, attended the opening of the Grand Army of the Republic Post, and had tea at the Galena Library. Present that day were 44 Boy Scouts from thirty-seven different troops in three states. Today, the event is hosted by the local Blackhawk Area Council of the Boy Scouts of America.

Although attendance topped out at about 10,000 in 1983, public participation has remained steady since, with annual themes like "U.S. Grant and the Galena Generals" in 1975, "Saluting the Armed Forces" in 1979, and "Understanding the Past, Embracing the Future" in 2011, that have contributed to regional interest.

Recent celebrations have included a VIP Scavenger Hunt in which pilgrims have to do activities like finding the homes of prominent individuals in and around Galena, making a trail hike with questions about historically important sites around the town, and going on a GPS Hike to marked sites.

One prominently marked location is the statue of President Abraham Lincoln a short drive to the east in Freeport, Illinois, on the site of the famous August 27, 1858 debate between Lincoln and Stephen A. Douglas during an Illinois election for U.S. senator.

The Mount Rushmore Pilgrimage

Since 1938 when a mere 450 Scouts and leaders trekked to the Mount Rushmore National Historic Site in the Black Hills of South Dakota, thousands more have made that same hike. Attendees in those first years witnessed the progress of sculptor Gutzon Borglum as he blasted Theodore Roosevelt's face into the granite to complete the massive monument to U.S. presidents George Washington, Thomas Jefferson, Abraham Lincoln and Roosevelt.

Nowadays, about a thousand Scouts and Scouters arrive at the monument aboard a shuttle from their nearby campsites for an awards ceremony in the amphitheater at the base of the Rushmore monument. Afterward, they hike back along one of four trails, each named in honor of one sculpted president that rambles through the ponderosa pines and aspen trees of the Norbeck Wildlife Preserve, Custer State Park, Black Elk Wilderness, and the Black Hills National Forest. With the shortest path extending about seven miles, the longest measures fifteen. And only one trail has no water source on it—the one named for Roosevelt, our greatest conservationist president.

Recent additions include weekend camping at the nearby Crazy Horse Memorial with a master of ceremonies and a jamboree-style atmosphere at the Rushmore monument.

A BSA bugler blows Taps at the Mount Vernon Pilgrimage in 1922.

Sadly, not all presidential pilgrimages have withstood the test of time.

The Chester A. Arthur Scouting Pilgrimage in Albany, New York, the John Adams Pilgrimage in Quincy, Massachusetts, and the Andrew Jackson Pilgrimage to his Hermitage home outside of Nashville, Tennessee did not outlive the 1920s. Scouting pilgrimages to statues of Lincoln in Michigan and New Jersey did not outlive the 1940s.

The Lincoln Pilgrimages

However, beginning in 1936 and continuing for at least six years, Scouts trekked to the Lincoln statue in Muskegon, Michigan, in celebration of Lincoln Day. Now sponsored by the Michigan Crossroads Council (formerly sponsored by the Muskegon Council and the Gerald R. Ford Council), the celebration features a guest speaker in front of the memorial.

Also, the Hudson Council—now the Northern New Jersey Council— once hosted a ceremony at their Lincoln statue in Jersey City.

As such, Lincoln remains the most popular president for a pilgrimage. The most important such pilgrimage—and the largest one-day annual event in the country—is a pilgrimage to Lincoln's Tomb in his hometown of Springfield, Illinois. Now hosted by the Abraham Lincoln Council, this pilgrimage has been made annually since 1946.

Every year, thousands of Scouts and their leaders gather with American flags at Lincoln's Tomb for patriotic songs and tributes to the Great Liberator, followed by a march to the Old State Capital building downtown. Optional hikes include a visit to the Oak Ridge War Memorials and cemetery, walking the Lincoln Trail in the steps of its namesake, as well as trekking the Heritage Trial to Lincoln's Law Office, home, and family church.

Another Lincoln Pilgrimage started up in Fort Wayne, Indiana in 1934. Sponsored by the Anthony Wayne Area Council each February 12 on Lincoln's birthday, hundreds of Scouts and Scouters from northeast Indiana gather to place a wreath at the base of the Lincoln statue, listen to re-enactors deliver Lincoln speeches, and march to the local Lincoln Museum.

The Lincoln Pilgrimage in Redlands, California began in 1940. Founded by a wealthy resident as a result of his son's interest in the martyred president, Robert Watchorn "funded the memorial shrine to Lincoln to be built in his adopted city." Dedicated in memory of his son, Emory, who died of wounds received in the First World War, the centerpiece of the memorial is a marble bust of Lincoln created by sculptor George Grey Barnard.

At this annual event, attendance topped out in 1976 with some 2,500 pilgrims marching. Today the event draws about half that number, but includes other youth development organizations like the Girl Scouts of the USA.

Another Lincoln Pilgrimage was begun in Detroit, Michigan, in 1953. Today, it is hosted by the Michigan Crossroads Council (formerly the Great Lakes Council). Organized and run by BSA's honor camper chapter of the local Order of the Arrow, Migishi Opawgan Lodge 162, as a council-wide service project. The pilgrimage features festivities at a local Scout camp on Lincoln's Birthday each February.

The Gettysburg Reunion Service Project

But perhaps the most interesting pilgrimage was the one that sprang from BSA's earliest and most important service project - the Gettysburg Reunion of 1913 (and eventually the 1938 reunion). At them, Gettysburg battle veterans from both the Union and Confederacy reunited, where they relived their heroism at the nation's most famous and revered Civil War battlefield. Now at peace with each other, these aging warriors came together at the 50th and 75th Great Reunions in Gettysburg, Pennsylvania, with the Boy Scouts of America serving as their devoted aides-de-camp.

Observed one scribe of the 1913 event: "On historic ground, 500 boys have a notable experience which brings renown to Scouting." Scouts were reported to have helped the ancient veterans through the camps to places of interest, administering first aid to those overcome by dehydration and heat exhaustion.

During the 1938 Reunion (the last such gathering), President Franklin D. Roosevelt dedicated the Peace Memorial on those hallowed grounds and delivered a stirring speech thanking the attending veterans for their leadership, bravery, and devotion to country. At each Reunion, participating Scouts received a medal of thanks from BSA—a much valued gift over the years.

Not only did the Scouts' work help the veterans, but it made BSA recognizable and beloved on a national stage. This was their first and largest service project in its brief history, but the 1913 event was its most important in showcasing Scouting values.

In 1939, the York Adams Council formalized a new annual gathering of Scouts at the Gettysburg National Battlefield by sponsoring the first Gettysburg Pilgrimage for the Boy Scouts of America. Occuring for the next thirty years, this event attracted thousands of Scouts and leaders to Pennsylvania to pay homage to the soldiers that fought in the Civil War and revisit the location of Lincoln's 1863 Gettysburg Address, considered by many to be the greatest speech ever delivered in American history.

Today, the newly formed New Birth of Freedom Council, which incorporates the old York-Adams Council, supports the Gettysburg Historic Trail award. It attracts Scouts from across America traveling to Gettysburg throughout the year. Run in co-operation with the National Park Service, this program allows all levels of Scouts to hike the battlefield and earn the patch, segments, and uniform medal. The trip includes a visit to Eisenhower's Farm, the former World War II commander and president's retirement home at Gettysburg, that symbolizes the completion of the historic trail.

APPENDIX B

Funeral of a President

"In our darkest hour, what America needed most was an Eagle Scout, to bring back to our nation's highest office honor and integrity . . . such was found in President Gerald R. Ford."

MICHAEL D. SULGROVE
Eagle Scout and former Scout Executive,
GERALD R. FORD COUNCIL, BOY SCOUTS OF AMERICA

GIVING HONORABLE AND SELFLESS SERVICE to others is the "gold standard" of American Scouting. When applied, lives and situations change for the better. And perhaps, no one knew this better than President Gerald R. Ford—America's Eagle Scout President—who internalized the Scout Oath and Law, and applied them each in high executive office.

After assuming the presidency during a national crisis—the Watergate scandal—Ford was seen as the "Healer-in-Chief" due to his duty-driven way of living his life. He had to help the country rebound from dishonor in the Oval Office and to do so, he called upon his Scouting values – the same ones to which he had pledged his honor as a lad when receiving Scouting's highest accolade, the Eagle Scout medal.

Years later as a 90-year-old former president, an exemplar of Scouting excellence, and the new namesake of his childhood BSA council in Grand Rapids, Michigan, Ford contacted its Scout Executive, Michael D. Sulgrove, with an idea. President Ford wanted Eagle Scouts to assist in his eventual funeral ceremonies. The President passed away in Rancho Mirage, California on December 26, 2006.

Flown to Washington, DC days later, the presidential funerary casket arrived at Andrew's Air Force Base in Maryland, just outside the nation's capitol from Palm Desert, California, bound for Capitol Hill. The casket was carried up the east steps to the door of the U.S. House of Representatives where his former colleagues paid their last respects. After a few hours, it was moved to the Capitol's grand rotunda for the Lying in State portion of the funeral ceremonies along with visitation by the public.

Among those paying their respects were thousands of members of the National Capital Area Council, both Scouts and their leaders, in full uniform, standing at attention in pairs, and crisply saluting the flag-draped casket.

At the official memorial service held at the National Cathedral, a lone Eagle Scout assisted as an usher in helping to seat the 3,700 invited dignitaries and guests.

"His presidency will be remembered as a time of healing in our land," eulogized former President George H.W. Bush. "To know Jerry was to know a Norman Rockwell painting come to life."

At 2:15 pm on Tuesday, January 2, Ford's body arrived at the Gerald R. Ford International Airport in Grand Rapids, where a motorcade began its trek to the Gerald R. Ford Presidential Library and Museum for public viewing. His funeral and interment would be the following day and include a service at the Grace Episcopal Church.

At the end of the route were some 500 Eagle Scouts—reverently saluting their fallen comrade.

Eagle Scouts salute as President Ford's funeral car passes.

Scouting Honors Gerald R. Ford
By Michael D. Sulgrove

We in the Gerald R. Ford Council had been preparing for several years for the role that our Scouts and leaders—in particular our Eagle Scouts—would play in the funeral of a former president of the United States

Since our twelve-county council was the home council of President Gerald R. Ford as a Boy Scout in the 1920s, we were expected to do more during the memorial ceremonies. From the time Air Force One landed at the airport, to the long funeral procession to the Gerald R. Ford Presidential Library and Museum, every mile was filled with the citizens of our Nation, including all parts of Michigan, and most especially from here in Grand Rapids to welcome our hero home to his final resting place at the museum.

Some years earlier, President and Mrs. Ford shared their desire that a "few" Eagle Scouts be a part of his funeral ceremonies. They had two specific requests; Eagle Scouts were to be at the final turn from Pearl Street to the Presidential Library, and secondly, young Eagle Scouts would lower his United States flag at the museum after the thirty day mourning period had passed.

To participate in this final Scout Salute - every Eagle Scout (regardless of age) had to be currently registered with the Boy Scouts of America, agree to wear a full and current Boy Scout uniform, and lastly, proudly wear their Eagle Scout medal upon their left uniform pocket.

When Distinguished Eagle Scout and 38th president of the United States Ford died on December 26, 2006, plans were executed to honor him in California, in Washington D.C., and here in Western Michigan. Within hours of notification that the dear President had passed away, our Scout leaders put those long prepared plans into motion. The word was sent out.

Far and wide went the call for Eagle Scouts. The "few" that President Ford requested was quickly becoming hundreds. The crowd of Eagle Scouts wanting to be a part of this Eagle Scout Honor Guard was growing. At 500 Eagle Scouts a U.S. Secret Service agents asked me (as the Council Scout Executive/CEO) to stop the list. There was no doubt, based on the number of Eagle Scouts we turned away that we could have had 1,000 there.

On Tuesday January 2, 2007, our Eagle Scout Honor Guard gathered at the De-Vos Family Center for Scouting to report in, they received their wrist band (the

only way to control who was permitted with us), had a uniform inspection, and posed for a group photo. Soon, we boarded school busses and headed for Pearl Street. The Grand Rapids Police Department and the U.S. Secret Service cleared the Pearl Street and Museum road corner so our Eagle Scouts could stand. We filled over two hundred yards of street corner—many Eagle Scouts deep.

Earlier, I had shared with my Council staff and volunteers that when advised by the Secret Service that the funeral vehicles are turning off US 131, all Eagle Scouts (aged 15-86) are instructed to remove their winter coats, stand at attention, and give a crisp Scout salute to all vehicles in the procession.

As the cortege passed, Mrs. Ford waved to our Honor Guard with both a smile and tears. Son Steve Ford saluted our Eagle Scouts. I was so very proud of all of them! They stood in the Michigan cold in January for over an hour just to salute an American hero – our hero.

Throughout the procession, tens of thousands of people attended including thousands of Cub Scouts, Boy Scouts, Venturers, their Scout leaders, and their families. They were Mr. Ford's Scouts, on every corner – standing in salute.

Eagle Scouts pay their last respects to President Ford.

The visitation line to see President Ford's flag draped coffin was tens of thousands of people long. First in line, after the family and special dignitaries, was to be the Chiefs of police and Sheriffs from around Michigan. After watching our Eagle Scout Honor Guard, Grand Rapids Police Chief Harry Dolan asked his fellow officers if the "Eagle Scouts shouldn't go first."

So we did.

No one instructed the Eagle Scouts to remove their winter coats at the lobby (it was a mountain of jackets) nor to stand silently in line, nor to stand at attention two to four at a time—with their Boy Scout Salute before the casket.

But they did.

President Gerald Ford's United States flag flew at half-mast for thirty days. As requested, young Eagle Scouts were to take it down for the final time, fold it properly and present it to Mr. Marty Allen, Chairman Emeritus of the Gerald R. Ford Presidential Library and Museum.

We asked the Eagle Scouts and leaders of Troop 271 chartered by the Mayflower Congregational Church to give leadership to this task. For two weeks straight, these teenage boys gathered to practice and practice as they were committed to being 100% perfect in this final flag ceremony.

The late afternoon of January 26, 2007 was a brutally windy and freezing day. Crowds of bundled people had gathered to witness this Flag's last rise and lowering as its final salute to the life and death of West Michigan's favorite son.

With honored guests in their places and Mr. Allen at his post, the local media cameras began rolling as those ten young Eagle Scouts, in perfect Scout uniforms, began performing their long-practiced duties.

At the exact moment, the bugle began to play and the young man selected by his peers to be in charge of this Eagle Scout Honor Guard shouted: "Scout Salute!"

And all around Scouts and leaders snapped to their salute, as did veterans, fire and rescue people, law enforcement officers, dignitaries and guests—all were straight as an arrow.

As you know, an American flag flown at half-mast, must always be raised to the top of its pole before it can be finally lowered and folded. So, with all at full salute, this giant American flag began to slowly move up but it seemed reluctant to rise that final time.

And it was ever so much more reluctant to come down.

Four times that flag "hung up" on its descent—twice by its frozen chain on the pole joints and twice more into the tree branches. But the Eagle Scouts held to their duty (and their salute). After what seemed close to forever (more *like ten minutes) the flag was unhooked, "Two" was called, and the young men began to fold that great flag.*

Once folded, the lead Eagle Scout was to present the heavy, crisply folded, tri-cornered flag to Mr. Allen. Add to it the weight of the frozen moisture in it and the days of grief and pressure placed upon Mr. Allen's shoulders and this flag seemed far too heavy for one man to carry.

Once again, with no word from any adult, and as Mr. Allen seemed to struggle to carry the burden of the flag's weight, Eagle Scouts stepped to his side and helped him to carry on.

Once inside the Gerald R. Ford Presidential Library, Mr. Allen gently laid the flag on a table and called all the Eagle Scouts to him. With tears and a heavy heart Marty said to these young men:

Do not ever forget all that President Ford believed in, stood for, and represented. All the things people have been saying about him these last thirty days, started that night in 1925 when he raised his right hand in the Boy Scout sign and said the Scout Oath for the first time. President Ford was proud to have been a Boy Scout and never forgot what his leaders taught him - and neither should you. You are our nation's future.

Hundreds of Eagle Scouts line the funeral procession route of President Ford.

NOTES

General Sources

National Archives, Boy Scouts of America, Irving, TX (BSA)
David C Scott Personal Collection, Dallas, TX (DCS)
Three Mile River Museum, Narrowsburg, NY (TMR)
Daniel Carter Beard Papers, Library of Congress, Washington, DC (LOC)
John T. Woolley and Gerhard Peters, *The American Presidency Project* [online]. Santa Barbara,
    CA (APP)
Robert W. Peterson Collection, "William Hillcourt Interview File," Macungie, PA (RWP)
Edmund S. Muskie Papers, Bates College Archives, Lewiston, ME (EMP)

Presidential Libraries

Woodrow Wilson Presidential Library, Staunton, VA.
Herbert Hoover Presidential Library and Museum, West Branch, IA.
Franklin D. Roosevelt Presidential Library and Museum, Hyde Park, NY.
Harry S. Truman Library and Museum, Independence, MO.
Eisenhower Presidential Library and Museum, Abilene, KS (EPL).
John F. Kennedy Presidential Library & Museum, Boston, MA (JFK).
LBJ Presidential Library, Austin, TX.
Nixon Presidential Library and Museum, Yorba Linda, CA.
Gerald R. Ford Presidential Library and Museum, Ann Arbor, MI.
Jimmy Carter Library and Museum, Atlanta, GA.
Ronald Reagan Presidential Foundation and Library, Simi Valley, CA.
George Bush Presidential Library and Museum, College Station, TX.
William J. Clinton Presidential Library, Little Rock, AR.
George W. Bush Presidential Library and Museum, Dallas, TX.

Books

Ades, Leslie. *Managing Mavericks: The Art of Sales Management.* New York: McGraw-Hill,
    1992.
Bausum, Ann. *Our Country's Presidents.* New York: National Geographic Society, 2005.
Benson, Michael. *William H. Taft.* Minneapolis, MN: Lerner Publishing Group, 2004.
Benson, Michael. *Bill Clinton.* Minneapolis, MN: Lerner Publishing Group, 2003.
Boger, John Charles. *School Resegregation: Must the South Turn Back?* Chapel Hill, NC:
    University of North Carolina Press, 2005.
Bourne, Peter G. *Jimmy Carter: A Comprehensive Biography from Plains to Post-Presidency.*
    New York: Scribner, 1997.
Boy Scouts of America. *Boy Scout Handbook.* Garden City, NY: Doubleday & Co., 1912).
Boy Scouts of America. *Annual Report of the Boy Scouts of America.* Washington, DC: U.S.
    Government Printing Office, 1961.
Boy Scouts of America. *National and World Jamborees in Pictures.* New York: Boy Scouts of
    America, 1937.
Boy Scouts of America. *Annual Report to the Nation.* Washington, DC: US Government
    Printing Office, 1964.
Boy Scouts of America. *Annual Report to the Nation.* Washington, DC: Government Printing
    Office, 1980.
Boy Scouts of America. *Eighth Annual Report.* New York: Boy Scouts of America, 1919.
Boy Scouts of America. *Annual Report to the Nation.* Washington, DC: U.S. Government
    Printing Office, 1963.

Boy Scouts of America. *Annual Report to the Nation.* Washington, DC: U.S. Government Printing Office, 1960.

Boy Scouts of America. *Annual Report to the Nation.* Washington, DC: U.S. Government Printing Office, 1964.

Boy Scouts of America. *Annual Report to the Nation.* Washington, DC: U.S. Government Printing Office, 1976.

Brands, H. W. *Woodrow Wilson.* New York: Henry Holt & Company, 2003.

Bush, George W. *Decision Points.* New York: Random House, 2010.

Cannon, Lou. *President Reagan: The Role of a Lifetime.* New York: Simon & Schuster, 1991.

Carrier, Thomas J. *Washington DC: An Historical Walking Tour.* Mount Pleasant, SC: Arcadia Press, 1999.

Carter, Hugh Alton and Frances Spatz Leighton. *Cousin Beedie and Cousin Hot: My Life with the Carter Family of Plains, Georgia.* New York: Prentice-Hall, 1978.

Carter, Jimmy. *Sharing Good Times.* New York: Simon & Schuster, 2005.

Clinton, Bill. *Between Hope and History: Meeting America's Challenges for the 21st Century.* New York: Random House, 1996.

Coolidge, Calvin. *Foundations of the Republic,* "Equality of Rights." New York: Charles Scribner's Sons, 1926.

Dallek, Robert. *An Unfinished Life: John F. Kennedy, 1917–1963.* Boston: Little, Brown & Co., 2003.

Davis, Deborah. *Guest of Honor: Booker T. Washington, Theodore Roosevelt, and the White House Dinner That Shocked a Nation.* New York: Atria Books, 2012.

Drinker, Frederick E. and Jay Henry Mowbray. *Theodore Roosevelt: His Life and Work.* Washington, DC: National, 1919.

Ferrell, Robert H. *Harry S. Truman and the Modern American Presidency.* Boston: Little Brown & Co., 1983.

Frum, David. *How We Got Here: The '70s.* New York: Basic Books, 2000.

Harris, David. *The Crisis: The President, the Prophet and the Shah.* New York: Little, Brown & Company, 2004.

Hefley, James C. *Way Back in the "Korn" Fields.* Garland, TX: Hannibal Book, 1994.

Klein, Jonas. *Beloved Island.* Forest Dale, VT: Paul S. Eriksson Publishers, 2000.

Levin, Robert and J. Shawn Landres, eds. *Bill Clinton: The Inside Story.* New York: Shapolsky Publishers, 1992.

Lindenmeyer, Kriste. *A Right to Childhood: The U.S. Children's Bureau and Child Welfare, 1912–46.* Urbana, IL: University of Illinois Press, 1997.

Lurie, Jonathan. *William Howard Taft: The Travails of a Progressive Conservative.* Cambridge, England: Cambridge University Press, 2011.

McIver, Stuart. *Touched by the Sun.* Sarasota, FL: Pineapple Press, 2001.

Memorial Services in the Congress of the United States and Tributes in Eulogy of Lyndon Baines Johnson Late President of the United States. Washington, DC: United States Government, 1973.

Memorial Services in the Congress of the United States and Tributes in Eulogy of Harry S. Truman Late President of the United States. Washington, DC: United States Government, 1973.

Morris, Roger. *Partners in Power: The Clintons and Their America.* New York: Henry Holt & Company, 1996.

Murphy, James W., ed. *Last Speeches of Warren G. Harding Delivered the Course of His Tour from Washington, DC to Alaska and Return to San Francisco June 20 to Aug. 23, 1923.* Washington, DC: U.S. Senate, 1923.

Murray, William D. *The History of the Boy Scouts of America,* New York: The Boy Scouts of America, 1937.

Oakley, Meredith L. *On the Make: The Rise of Bill Clinton.* Washington, DC: Regnery Publishing, 1994.

Peterson, Robert W. *The Boy Scouts: An American Adventure,* New York: American Heritage, 1984.

Pietrusza, David. *Silent Cal's Almanack: The Homespun Wit and Wisdom of Vermont's Calvin Coolidge,* CreateSpace, 2008.

Reagan, Michael. *In the Words of Ronald Reagan: The Wit, Wisdom, and Eternal Optimism of America's 40th President.* New York: Thomas Nelson, 2004.

Reeves, Richard. *President Kennedy Profile of Power.* New York: Simon & Schuster, 1994.

Reis, Mitch. *The Boy Scouts of America During World War I & II.* Windsor, CT: Mitch Reis, 1984.

Russell, Francis. *The Shadow of Blooming Grove-Warren G. Harding In His Times.* Norwalk, CT: Easton Press, 1962.

Scott, David C. and Brendan Murphy. *The Scouting Party: Pioneering and Preservation, Progressivism and Preparedness in the Making of the Boy Scouts of America.* Dallas, TX: Red Honor Press, 2010.

Scott, David C. *We Are Americans, We Are Scouts.* Dallas, TX: Red Honor Press, 2008.

United States Commission of Fine Arts. Washington, DC: US Government Printing Office, 1964.

Vaughn, Stephen. *Ronald Reagan in Hollywood: Movies and Politics.* Cambridge, England: Cambridge University Press, 1994.

Washburn, R. M. *Calvin Coolidge: His First Biography.* Boston: Small, Maynard & Company, 1923.

Werner, M. R. and John Starr. *Teapot Dome.* New York: Viking, 1959.

White, William Allen. *Woodrow Wilson: The Man and His Times.* New York: Houghton Mifflin and Company, 1924.

Magazines/Newspapers/Pamphlets/Broadcast

American Experience: Woodrow Wilson, Public Broadcasting Service, broadcast 2001.

"Austin Scout Meets with Obama, Boehner During DC Visit," *Austin American Statesman.* Feb. 18, 2011.

Boy Scouts of America. *"Boys' Life,"* various issues.

Boy Scouts of America, "The Awards of the Silver Buffalo for Distinguished Service to Boyhood," event brochure, May 13, 1929.

Boy Scouts of America, *Eagle Scout Magazine,* Winter 2009.

Boy Scouts of America, "The Award of the Silver Buffalo, event brochure, 1930.

Boy Scouts of America, "First Annual Meeting Proceedings," Feb. 14, 1911, (BSA)

"Boy Scouts' Campaign," *New York Times,* Nov. 7, 1920.

"Boy Scouts Call on Bush Family for Food Donation," WFAA Television, Dallas, TX.

Dalin, David G., "At the Summit," as quoted in L. Sandy Maisel and Ira Forman, Eds. *Jews in American Politics,* Lanham, MD: Rowman & Littlefield, 2001.

Dallas Morning News, Mar. 4, 1933.

Douglas, William and Tom Fitzgerald, *Kansas City Star,* May 17, 2004.

Eilperin, Juliet and Scott Wilson, "Obama Launches America's Great Outdoors Conservation Initiative," *Washington Post,* Apr. 17, 2010.

Eisenhower, Dwight D., "Radio and Television Address to the American People on the Situation in Little Rock," Sept. 24, 1957.

Herbert Hoover Presidential Library and Museum "Herbert Hoover Biographical Sketch," West Branch, IA.

Hillcourt, Bill, "Hiking with Green Bar Bill, *Boys' Life,* Feb. 1949.

Hubbell, John G. "Exploring—A New Path to a Better America," *Reader's Digest,* Oct. 1970.

Kouri, Samia, "The Jimmy Carter and Ronald Reagan Administrations' Policies Toward Apartheid South Africa: Diverging Rhetoric, Converging Actions," *International Journal of Arts and Science,* 2011.

"Little Sisters of Liberty," *Scouting,* Oct. 2007.

Meroney, John, "Was Ronald Reagan a Secret Snitch?" *Los Angeles Times,* Dec. 12, 2010.

"National President for Venturing Meets President Obama," *Good Things Utah,* Television program, Salt Lake City, UT, Feb. 18, 2011.

New York Times, New York, NY, various issues.

"News of the Day in Pictures," *Washington Post,* May 21, 1927.

"Obama Talks with Bill Clinton," *New York Times,* June 30, 2008.

Ray, Mark, "Eagle Scouts Welcome Gerald Ford Home," *Scouting,* Mar.–Apr. 2007.

Roosevelt, Theodore, "The Philippines: The First Civil Governor," *The Outlook,* New York, Sept. 21, 1901.

Shannon, Margaret, "In All Thy Ways Acknowledge Him: The Funeral for the Healer of a Nation," *Cathedral Age Magazine,* Winter 2006.

Smith, Richard Norton and Timothy Walch, "The Ordeal of Herbert Hoover," *NARA Journal*, Summer 2004, vol. 36, no. 2.

Campbell, Thomas P., "A Best Friend in the White House," *Scouting Magazine*, Mar.–Apr. 2003.

Roberts, William, "Our Number One Webelos Scout," *Scouting*, Jan./Feb. 1980.

Wendell, Bryan, "Heads in the Right Place," *Boys' Life,* Jan.–Feb. 2011.

Witt, Shirley Hill, "Nationalistic Trends Among American Indians," *Midcontinent American Series Journal*, 1965.

Internet

http://www.aaregistry.org/historic_events/view/spokesman-his-people-walter-cohen (accessed Mar. 28, 2011).

http://www.boyandgirlscouts.com/international/update-to-barack-obama-was-a-boy-scout/ (accessed Apr. 2, 2013).

http://www.bridgeboro.com/page4.html (accessed Mar. 15, 2011).

http://www.doctorzebra.com; Mark Sullivan, "Our Times" (accessed Mar. 15, 2011).

http://www.dol.gov/oasam/programs/history/dolchp07.htm (accessed June 7, 2011).

http://domemagazine.com/features/cov011612 (accessed June 7, 2011).

http://www.eeoc.gov/eeoc/history/35th/thelaw/eo-8802.html (accessed Apr. 14, 2011).

http://www.ExtraMile.us (accessed July 31, 2011).

http://www.Fitness.gov (accessed June 9, 2011).

http://www.GoodTurnForAmerica.org (accessed July 7, 2011).

http://www.Habitat.org (accessed July 7, 2011).

http://www.hardingareadistrict.org (accessed June 6, 2011).

http://www.history.com/this-day-in-history/wilson-nominates-brandeis-to-the-supreme-court (accessed Mar. 20, 2011).

Horton, Frank Reed, "The Story Behind the Founding," www.apo.org (accessed Aug. 20, 2011).

http://www.iptv.org (accessed Apr. 3, 2011).

Johnson, Krista, "George H.W. Bush: Domestic Policy," at http://www.highbeam.com/topics/george-hw-bush-domestic-policy-t10116 (accessed July 25, 2011).

http://www.legion.org/boysnation/about (accessed Aug. 1, 2011).

http://www.legion.org/boysnation/stateabout (accessed Aug. 2, 2011).

http://www.Lincoln-highway-museum.org (accessed May 25, 2011).

National Review Online, "Knowing a Good Man When You See One," Jay Nordlinger at http://www.nationalreview.com/corner/181220/knowing-good-man-when-you-see-one/jay-nordlinger (accessed June 29, 2011).

http://www.PointsOfLight.org (accessed July 30, 2011).

http://preserveamerica.gov (accessed Mar. 26, 2013).

http://www.presidents challenge.org (accessed Apr. 4, 2013).

http://www.prosperousamerica.org/library/testimony/jeff_faux_testimony_on_industrial_policy_and_national_security_20100924289.html (accessed May 25, 2011).

Public Papers of the Presidents: Administration of George W. Bush 2004, p. 2443, "Remarks in Hobbs NM, Oct. 11, 2004" (accessed Mar. 26, 2013).

http://"Remarks Delivered at Ford's Funeral at the National Cathedral," www.washingtonpost.com/wp- dyn/content/article/2007/01/02/AR2007010200418.html (accessed, July 5, 2011)

http://www.scouting.org/sitecore/content/Home/BSAFit.aspx (accessed Apr. 2, 2013).

http://www.ScoutingNews.org (accessed July 30, 2011).

http://www.SeniorScoutingHistory.org (accessed June 3, 2011).

Steel, Ronald, *Walter Lippman and the American Century* (Boston: Little Brown & Co., 1980).

http://www.helium.com/items/580881-the-civil-works-administration-during-the-great-depression (accessed Apr. 2, 2011).

http://suite101.com/article/helen-herron-taft-a93346 (accessed Mar. 18, 2011).

http:// www.tmrmuseum.org (accessed Apr. 24, 2011).

Train, Brian R., "Hooverville, Bonus Marcher, General Smedley Butler," at http://www.arete-designs.com/southernprimer/hoover.html (accessed Mar. 25, 2013).

Unites States National Archives and Records Administration at www.archives.gov (accessed Apr. 24, 2011).

http://www.usgrantpilgrimage.org/1usgrantpilgrimage/index.php?option=com_
    content&view=article&id=54&Itemid=59 (accessed June 6, 2011).
Veronese, Keith, "Franklin Delano Roosevelt Probably Didn't Have Polio After All," at
    http://io9.com/5958933/franklin-delano-roosevelt-probably-didnt-have-polio-after-all
    (accessed May 27, 2013).
http://www.whitehouse.gov "New Freedoms Initiative," Feb. 1, 2001 (accessed Mar. 26,
    2013).
http://www.wildlifepartners.org (accessed Mar. 26, 2013).

Correspondence

Dwight D Eisenhower to Gov. James F. Byrnes, Aug. 14, 1953, PL.
Dwight D. Eisenhower to King, Oct. 7, 1957, EPL.
Warren G. Harding, letter, "Jewish Home in Palestine," June 1, 1921.
Martin Luther King, Jr to Eisenhower, telegram, Sept. 25, 1957, EPL.
Theodore Roosevelt to J. C. Martin, Nov. 6, 1908.

Speeches and Interviews

Jimmy Carter, "Inaugural Address," Jan. 20, 1977.
Dwight D. Eisenhower, "State of the Union Address, Feb. 2, 1953, EPL.
Warren G. Harding, address, Birmingham, AL, Oct. 26, 1921.
Robert Higginbotham, phone interview, Mar. 22, 2013.
Herbert Hoover, address, Washington, DC, Apr. 7, 1931.
Lyndon B. Johnson, "Statement About Desegregation of Elementary and Secondary
    Schools," Mar. 24, 1970.
Paul Johnston, interview, Feb. 28, 2013.
Barack Obama, address, Washington DC, Apr. 16, 2010.
Barack Obama, memorandum for the Sec of Interior, Washington, DC, Apr. 16, 2010.
Barack Obama, "Remarks by the President on America's Great Outdoors Initiative,"
    Washington, DC, Feb. 16, 2011.
Barack Obama, address, Washington, DC, Apr. 16, 2010.
Ronald Reagan, speech, Orlando, FL, Mar. 8, 1983).
Woodrow Wilson, "Address in Favor of the League of Nations," Sept. 25, 1919.

REFERENCES

Note: The following chapter sources are listed in the order in which they were cited.

Introduction

Robert W. Peterson, *The Boy Scouts: An American Adventure*, New York: American Heritage, 1984, pp. 2–10.

Robert W. Peterson Collection, "William Hillcourt Interview File," Macungie, PA.

William D. Murray, *The History of the Boy Scouts of America*, New York: The Boy Scouts of America, 1937, pp. 39–40.

David C. Scott and Brendan Murphy, *The Scouting Party: Pioneering and Preservation, Progressivism and Preparedness in the Making of the Boy Scouts of America*, Dallas, TX: Red Honor Press, 2010.

Chapter 1—Theodore Roosevelt

Boys' Life, Sept. 1916, p. 23.

Boys' Life, Feb. 1921, p. 28.

David C. Scott, *We Are Americans, We Are Scouts*, Dallas, TX: Red Honor Press, 2008.

Frederick E. Drinker and Jay Henry Mowbray, *Theodore Roosevelt: His Life and Work*, Washington, DC: National, 1919.

Boys' Life, Oct. 1936, p. 18.

http://www.bridgeboro.com/page4.html (accessed Mar. 15, 2011).

Deborah Davis, "Guest of Honor: Booker T. Washington, Theodore Roosevelt, and the White House Dinner That Shocked a Nation, New York: Atria Books, 2012.

David G. Dalin, "At the Summit," as quoted in L. Sandy Maisel and Ira Forman, Eds. *Jews in American Politics*, Lanham, MD: Rowman & Littlefield, 2001, pp. 31, 33.

Theodore Roosevelt to J. C. Martin, Nov. 6, 1908.

Boys' Life, May 1915, p. 37.

Boys' Life, July 1916, p. 28.

Chapter 2—William Howard Taft

Boys' Life, Nov. 2008, p. 8.

www.doctorzebra.com; Mark Sullivan, "Our Times" (accessed Mar. 15, 2011).

Michael Benson, *William H. Taft*, Minneapolis, MN: Lerner Publishing Group, 2004.

Theodore Roosevelt, "The Philippines: The First Civil Governor," *The Outlook*, New York, Sept. 21, 1901, p. 166–7.

Jonathan Lurie, *William Howard Taft: The Travails of a Progressive Conservative*, Cambridge, England: Cambridge University Press, 2011, p. 50.

Kriste Lindenmeyer, *A Right to Childhood: The U.S. Children's Bureau and Child Welfare, 1912–46*, Urbana, IL: University of Illinois Press, 1997, p. 30.

http://suite101.com/article/helen-herron-taft-a93346 (accessed Mar. 18, 2011).

"First Annual Meeting Proceedings," Feb. 14, 1911, BSA National Archives, Irving, TX.

"News of the Day in Pictures," *Washington Post*, May 21, 1927.

Chapter 3—Woodrow Wilson

Boys' Life, Mar. 1924, p. 3.

Boys' Life, Nov. 1924.

H. W. Brands, *Woodrow Wilson*, New York: Henry Holt & Company, 2003, pp. 3–25.

http://www.history.com/this-day-in-history/wilson-nominates-brandeis-to-the-supreme-court (accessed Mar. 20, 2011).

William Allen White, *Woodrow Wilson: The Man and His Times*, New York: Houghton Mifflin and Company, 1924, p. 15.

American Experience: Woodrow Wilson, Public Broadcasting Service, broadcast 2001.

Woodrow Wilson, "Address in Favor of the League of Nations," Sept. 25, 1919.

Boys' Life, Apr. 1917, p. 27.

Boys' Life, Apr. 1913, pp. 2–4.

"Boy Scouts' Campaign," *New York Times*, Nov. 7, 1920.

Boys' Life, June 1919, pp. 3, 29.

Woodrow Wilson Presidential Library & Archives, Staunton, VA.

Boy Scouts of America, *Eighth Annual Report to the Nation*, New York: Boy Scouts of America, 1918.

New York Times, Nov. 5, 1920.

Boys' Life, Nov. 1932, p. 20.

Chapter 4—Warren G. Harding

Boys' Life, Oct. 1923, pp. 24, 35.

Boys' Life, May 1921.

http://www.aaregistry.org/historic_events/view/spokesman-his-people-walter-cohen (accessed Mar. 28, 2011).

Warren G. Harding, letter, "Jewish Home in Palestine," June 1, 1921.

Warren G. Harding, address, Birmingham, AL, Oct. 26, 1921.

Boys' Life, Aug. 1923, p. 34.

Boys' Life, Oct. 1923, p. 50.

Boys' Life, Feb. 1933, p. 50.

Boys' Life, May 1921, p. 2.

New York Times, Aug. 28, 1921.

Boys' Life, Apr. 1922, p. 28.

Francis Russell. *The Shadow of Blooming Grove-Warren G. Harding In His Times*, Norwalk, CT: Easton Press, 1962, pp. 520–1.

M. R. Werner and John Starr, *Teapot Dome,* New York: Viking, 1959, pp. 316–7, 328–9.

James W. Murphy, ed., *Last Speeches of Warren G. Harding Delivered the Course of His Tour From Washington, DC to Alaska and return to San Francisco June 20 to Aug. 23, 1923*, Washington, DC: US Senate, 1923.

Chapter 5—Calvin Coolidge

Murray, p. 312.

"National Conference of Outdoor Recreation," *Boys' Life*, Aug. 1924, p. 56.

Stuart McIver, *Touched by the Sun*, Sarasota, FL: Pineapple Press, 2001, pp. 31–2.

Ann Bausum, *Our Country's Presidents*, New York: National Geographic Society, 2005.

Leslie Ades, *Managing Mavericks: The Art of Sales Management*, New York: McGraw-Hill, 1992.

James C. Hefley, *Way Back in the "Korn" Fields*, Garland, TX: Hannibal Book, 1994.

R. M. Washburn, *Calvin Coolidge: His First Biography*, Boston: Small, Maynard & Company, 1923.

David Pietrusza, *Silent Cal's Almanack: The Homespun Wit and Wisdom of Vermont's Calvin Coolidge*, CreateSpace, 2008.

Calvin Coolidge, *Foundations of the Republic*, "Equality of Rights," New York: Charles Scribner's Sons, 1926, p. 72.

Boys' Life, Oct. 1923, p. 5.

Boys' Life, Oct. 2000.

"The Awards of the Silver Buffalo for Distinguished Service to Boyhood," program, Boy Scouts of America, May 13, 1929.

BSA National Archives, Irving, TX.

Boys' Life, Feb. 1929, p. 16.

Boys' Life, Oct. 1923, p. 5.

John T. Woolley and Gerhard Peters, *The American Presidency Project*, Santa Barbara, CA, http://www.presidency.ucsb.edu/ws/?pid=24184 (accessed, Mar. 31, 2011).

Chapter 6—Herbert Hoover

www.iptv.org (accessed Apr. 3, 2011).

"Herbert Hoover Biographical Sketch," Herbert Hoover Presidential Library & Museum, West Branch, IA.

Shirley Hill Witt, "Nationalistic Trends Among American Indians," *Midcontinent American Series Journal*, 1965, p. 57.

Mitch Reis, *The Boy Scouts of America During World War I & II*, Windsor, CT: Mitch Reis, 1984, pp. 3–20.

Murray, pp. 121–2.

"Boy Scouts of America History," Apr.16, 1917, BSA National Archives, Irving, TX.

Boy Scouts of America, *Eighth Annual Report*, New York: Boy Scouts of America, 1919, p. 28.

Brian R. Train, "Hooverville, Bonus Marcher, General Smedley Butler," at http://www.arete-designs.com/southernprimer/hoover.html (accessed Mar. 25, 2013).

Boys' Life, June 1920, p. 30.

Address, Washington, DC, Apr. 7, 1931.

"Richard Norton Smith and Timothy Walch, "The Ordeal of Herbert Hoover," *NARA Journal*, Summer 2004, vol. 36, no. 2.

Boys' Life, Aug. 1954.

"The Award of the Silver Buffalo, program, 1930.

John T. Woolley and Gerhard Peters, *The American Presidency Project*, Santa Barbara, CA, at http://www.presidency.ucsb.edu/ws/?pid=24184 (accessed, Apr. 3, 2011).

Chapter 7—Franklin D. Roosevelt

Ronald Steel, *Walter Lippman and the American Century*. Boston: Little Brown & Co., 1980.

http://www.helium.com/items/580881-the-civil-works-administration-during-the-great-depression (accessed Apr. 2, 2011).

Thomas P. Campbell, "A Best Friend in the White House," *Scouting Magazine*, Mar.–Apr. 2003.

Dallas Morning News, Mar. 4, 1933, Sect. 2 , p. ??.

http://www.eeoc.gov/eeoc/history/35th/thelaw/eo-8802.html (accessed Apr. 14, 2011).

Boys' Life, May 1933, pp. 5–6.

Boys' Life, Aug. 1921, p. 1.

Keith Veronese, "Franklin Delano Roosevelt Probably Didn't Have Polio After All," at http://io9.com/5958933/franklin-delano-roosevelt-probably-didnt-have-polio-after-all (accessed May 27, 2013).

Jonas Klein, *Beloved Island* (Forest Dale, VT: Paul S. Eriksson Publishers, 2000) p. 108.

National Archives, Boy Scouts of America, Irving, TX.

National and World Jamborees in Pictures, New York: Boy Scouts of America, 1937, pp. 15–45.

Reis, pp. 15–45.

Unites States National Archives and Records Administration at www.archives.gov (accessed Apr. 24, 2011).

Three Mile River Scout Museum, Narrowsburg, New York at www.tmrmuseum.org (accessed Apr. 24, 2011).

John T. Woolley and Gerhard Peters, *The American Presidency Project*, Santa Barbara, CA at http://www.presidency.ucsb.edu/ws/?pid=24184 (accessed, Apr.7, 2011).

Chapter 8—Harry S. Truman

Memorial Services in the Congress of the United States and Tributes in Eulogy of Harry S. Truman Late President of the United States (Washington, DC: United States Government, 1973) p. 115.

Harry S. Truman Presidential Library and Museum, "Presidential Appointments Calendar" at http://www.trumanlibrary.org/calendar/main.php?currYear=1950&currMonth=6&currDay=30 (accessed May 3, 2011).

Robert H. Ferrell, *Harry S. Truman and the Modern American Presidency* (Boston: Little Brown & Co., 1983).

John T. Woolley and Gerhard Peters, *The American Presidency Project*, Santa Barbara, CA at http://www.presidency.ucsb.edu/ws/?pid=24184 (accessed, Apr.7, 2011).

Harry S. Truman Presidential Library and Museum, Papers, June 8, 1948, May 10, 1950.

"Little Sisters of Liberty," *Scouting*, Oct. 2007.

Harry S. Truman Presidential Library, "President's Personal Files" (PPF1-F) Box 16 "Address at the Boy Scout Jamboree Valley Forge, Penn 6/30/50."

Chapter 9—Dwight D. Eisenhower

Boys' Life, Apr. 1945, cover.

Peterson, pp. 25–65.

Boys' Life, Mar. 1945, p. 35.

Reis, pp. 15–45.

www.Lincoln-highway-museum.org (accessed May 25, 2011).

Boys' Life, Feb. 1946, p. 3.

Dwight D. Eisenhower, "State of the Union Address, Feb. 2, 1953 (EPL).

Eisenhower to Gov. James F. Byrnes, Aug. 14, 1953 (PL).

"Radio and Television Address to the American People on the Situation in Little Rock," Sept. 24, 1957.

Martin Luther King Jr. to Eisenhower, telegram, Sept. 25, 1957, (EPL).

Eisenhower to King, Oct. 7, 1957 (EPL).

Chapter 10—John F. Kennedy

Annual Report of the Boy Scouts of America, Washington, DC: U.S. Government Printing Office, 1961, p. 5.

Boys' Life, Mar. 1961, p. 26.

http://www.jfklibrary.org/Research/Ready-Reference/JFK-Miscellaneous-Information.aspx (JFK).

Robert Dallek, *An Unfinished Life: John F. Kennedy, 1917–1963*, Boston: Little, Brown & Co., 2003, pp. 292–293, 580.

Richard Reeves, *President Kennedy Profile of Power,* New York: Simon & Schuster, 1994, p. 433.

Boys' Life, Feb. 1964, p. 18; Aug. 1964, p. 15.

Annual Report of the Boy Scouts of America, Washington, DC: US Government Printing Office, 1963, p. 1–4.

http://www.prosperousamerica.org/library/testimony/jeff_faux_testimony_on_industrial_policy_and_national_security_20100924289.html (accessed May 25, 2011).

John T. Woolley and Gerhard Peters, *The American Presidency Project*, Santa Barbara, CA at http://www.presidency.ucsb.edu/ws/?pid=24184 (accessed, May 21, 2011).

Chapter 11—Lyndon B. Johnson

Memorial Services in the Congress of the United States and Tributes in Eulogy of Lyndon Baines Johnson Late President of the United States, Washington, DC: United States Government, 1973, p. 192.

Boy Scout Handbook, Garden City, NY: Doubleday & Co., 1912, p. 173.

Boys' Life, May 1913, p. 19.

Annual Report to the Nation, Washington, DC: US Government Printing Office, 1960, pp. 6–7.

United States Commission of Fine Arts, Washington, DC: US Government Printing Office, vol. 18, p. 40.

Boys' Life, Dec. 1988, p. 42.

Thomas J. Carrier, *Washington DC: An Historical Walking Tour,* Mount Pleasant, SC: Arcadia Press, 1999, p. 95.

Annual Report to the Nation, Washington, DC: US Government Printing Office, 1964, pp. 30–1.

John T. Woolley and Gerhard Peters, *The American Presidency Project*, Santa Barbara, CA at http://www.presidency.ucsb.edu/ws/?pid=24184 (accessed, May 29, 2011).

Chapter 12—Richard M. Nixon

Edmund S. Muskie Papers, Bates College Archives, Lewiston, ME, "Nixon Misc. file, 1971, 1st Session, 92nd Congress."

John G. Hubbell, "Exploring—A New Path to a Better America," *Reader's Digest*, Oct. 1970.

www.SeniorScoutingHistory.org (accessed June 3, 2011).

Louis Sabin, "The Prospectors of Project SOAR," *Boys' Life*, May 1971, pp. 36–7.

"Scouting," *Boys' Life*, July 1970, pp. 18–9.

"Statement About Desegregation of Elementary and Secondary Schools," Pres. Lyndon B. Johnson, Mar. 24, 1970.

John Charles Boger, *School Resegregation: Must the South Turn Back?* Chapel Hill, N.C: University of North Carolina Press, 2005, p. 6.

http://www.dol.gov/oasam/programs/history/dolchp07.htm (accessed June 7, 2011).

Paul Delaney, "Nixon Plan for Negro Construction Jobs Is Lagging," *New York Times*, July 20, 1970, p. 1.

David Frum, *How We Got Here: The '70s* , New York: Basic Books, 2000, p. 246.

Martin Cohen, "The BSA Project SOAR Continues to Sweep the Nation" *Boys' Life*, Apr. 1973, p. 18.

John T. Woolley and Gerhard Peters, *The American Presidency Project*, Santa Barbara, CA at http://www.presidency.ucsb.edu/ws/?pid=24184 (accessed, June 1, 2011).

Chapter 13—Gerald R. Ford

Gerald R. Ford Presidential library & Museum, Ann Arbor, MI.

Boys' Life, Sept. 1976, pp. 54–5, June 1976, pp. 52–3.

http://domemagazine.com/features/cov011612 (accessed June 7, 2011).

Annual Report to the Nation, (Washington, DC: US Government Printing Office, 1976, pp. 5–6.

www.Fitness.gov (accessed June 9, 2011).

"Presidential Sports Award," *Boys' Life*, Sept. 1976, p. 88.

John T. Woolley and Gerhard Peters, *The American Presidency Project*, Santa Barbara, CA at http://www.presidency.ucsb.edu/ws/?pid=24184 (accessed, June 3, 2011).

Chapter 14—Jimmy Carter

Jimmy Carter Presidential Papers, p. 787 (CPL).

Jimmy Carter, *Sharing Good Times,* New York: Simon & Schuster, 2005, p. 33.

Jimmy Carter, "Inaugural Address," Jan. 20, 1977.

Samia Kouri, "The Jimmy Carter and Ronald Reagan Administrations' Policies Toward Apartheid South Africa: Diverging Rhetoric, Converging Actions," *International Journal of Arts and Science*, 2011.

Boys' Life, Nov. 1977, p. 6.

William Roberts, "Our Number One Webelos Scout," *Scouting*, Jan./Feb. 1980, p. 31.

Annual Report to the Nation, Washington, DC: US Government Printing Office, 1980, p. 12.

"Skill Award: Conservation," *Boys' Life*, Oct. 1977, p. 53.

"Green Heroes," *Boys' Life*, Dec. 2008, p. 26.

www.Habitat.org (accessed July 7, 2011).

www.GoodTurnForAmerica.org (accessed July 7, 2011).

Hugh Alton Carter and Frances Spatz Leighton, *Cousin Beedie and Cousin Hot: My Life with the Carter Family of Plains, Georgia,* New York: Prentice-Hall, 1978, p. 82.

David Harris, *The Crisis: The President, the Prophet and the Shah,* New York: Little, Brown & Company, 2004, p. 54.

Peter G. Bourne, *Jimmy Carter: A Comprehensive Biography from Plains to Post-Presidency,* New York: Scribner, 1997, p. 90.

John T. Woolley and Gerhard Peters, *The American Presidency Project*, Santa Barbara, CA at http://www.presidency.ucsb.edu/ws/?pid=24184 (accessed, Jul. 3, 2011).

Chapter 15—Ronald Reagan

Michael Reagan, *In the Words of Ronald Reagan: The Wit, Wisdom, and Eternal Optimism of America's 40th President,* New York: Thomas Nelson, 2004, pp. 5–25.

Eagle Scout Magazine, Winter 2009, p. 8.

Boys' Life, Nov. 1982, p. 6.

Phone Interview, Robert Higginbotham, Mar. 22, 2013.

Interview, Paul Johnston, Feb. 28, 2013.

Stephen Vaughn, *Ronald Reagan in Hollywood: Movies and Politics* (Cambridge, England: Cambridge University Press, 1994).

John Meroney, "Was Ronald Reagan a Secret Snitch?" *Los Angeles Times,* Dec. 12, 2010.

Lou Cannon, *President Reagan: The Role of a Lifetime*, New York: Simon & Schuster, 1991, p. 804.

Speech, Orlando, FL, Mar. 8, 1983.

Ben Love, "Just Say No," *Boys' Life*, Mar. 1987, p. 38.

http://www.Lincoln-Highway-Museum.org (accessed Jul. 15, 2011).

Deborah Hart Strobe, *The Reagan Presidency,* p. 573.

John T. Woolley and Gerhard Peters, *The American Presidency Project*, Santa Barbara, CA at http://www.presidency.ucsb.edu/ws/?pid=24184 (accessed, July 7, 2011).

Chapter 16—George H.W. Bush

George H. W. Bush, Presidential Papers, Mar. 28, 1989.

http://millercenter.org/president/bush/essays/biography/4 (accessed Jul. 25, 2011).

Krista Johnson, "George H.W. Bush: Domestic Policy," at http://www.highbeam.com/topics/george-hw-bush-domestic-policy-t10116 (accessed July 25, 2011).

http://www.PointsOfLight.org (accessed July 30, 2011).

http://www.ScoutingNews.org (accessed July 30, 2011).

http://www.ExtraMile.us (accessed July 31, 2011).

George H. W. Bush Presidential Library.

John T. Woolley and Gerhard Peters, *The American Presidency Project*, Santa Barbara, CA at http://www.presidency.ucsb.edu/ws/?pid=24184 (accessed, Jul. 25, 2011).

Chapter 17—William J. Clinton

"Obama Talks with Bill Clinton," *New York Times*, June 30, 2008.

http://www.legion.org/boysnation/about (accessed Aug. 1, 2011).

http://www.legion.org/boysnation/stateabout (accessed Aug. 2, 2011).

Roger Morris, *Partners in Power: The Clintons and Their America,* New York: Henry Holt & Company, 1996.

Meredith L Oakley, *On the Make: The Rise of Bill Clinton,* Washington, DC: Regnery Publishing, 1994.

Robert Levin and J. Shawn Landres, ed., *Bill Clinton: The Inside Story,* New York: Shapolsky Publishers, 1992.

Bill Clinton, *Between Hope and History: Meeting America's Challenges for the 21ˢᵗ Century*, p. 312.

www.WhiteHouse.gov, Aug. 1, 2000 (accessed Apr. 20, 2011).

Michael Benson, *Bill Clinton*, Minneapolis, MN: Lerner Publishing Group, 2003.

Frank Reed Horton, "The Story Behind the Founding," www.apo.org.

John T. Woolley and Gerhard Peters, *The American Presidency Project*, Santa Barbara, CA at http://www.presidency.ucsb.edu/ws/?pid=24184 (accessed, July 25, 2011).

Chapter 18—George W. Bush

National Review Online, "Knowing a Good Man When You See One," Jay Nordlinger. http://www.nationalreview.com/corner/181220/knowing-good-man-when-you-see-one/jay-nordlinger.

George W. Bush, *Decision Points*. New York: Random House, 2010, p. 7.

www.whitehouse.gov "New Freedoms Initiative" Feb. 1, 2001 (accessed Mar. 26, 2013).

Public Papers of the Presidents: Administration of George W Bush, 2004, p. 2443, "remarks in Hobbs NM, Oct. 11, 2004."

William Douglas/Tom Fitzgerald; *Kansas City Star*, May 17, 2004.

http://www.preserveamerica.gov/news-08paawards.html).

http://www.wildlifepartners.org.

"Boy Scouts Call on Bush Family for Food Donation," WFAA Television, Dallas, TX.

John T. Woolley and Gerhard Peters, *The American Presidency Project*, Santa Barbara, CA at
http://www.presidency.ucsb.edu/ws/?pid=24184 (accessed, Aug. 4, 2011).

Chapter 19—Barack H. Obama

Barack Obama, address, Washington, DC, Apr. 16, 2010.
Barack Obama, memorandum for the Sec of Interior, Washington, DC, Apr. 16, 2010.
Barack Obama, "Remarks by the President on America's Great Outdoors Initiative,"
Washington, DC, Feb. 16, 2011.
Barack Obama, address, Washington, DC, Apr. 16, 2010.
"Obama Talks with Bill Clinton," *New York Times,* June 30, 2008.
http://www.boyandgirlscouts.com/international/update-to-barack-obama-was-a-boy-scout.
Eilperin, Juliet and Scott Wilson, "Obama Launches America's Great Outdoors Conservation
Initiative," *Washington Post*, Apr. 17, 2010.
"Austin Scout Meets with Obama, Boehner During DC Visit," *Austin American Statesman,*
Feb. 18, 2011.
"National President for Venturing Meets President Obama," *Good Things Utah,* Television
program, Salt Lake City, UT, Feb. 18, 2011.
John T. Woolley and Gerhard Peters, *The American Presidency Project*, Santa Barbara, CA at
http://www.presidency.ucsb.edu/ws/?pid=24184 (accessed, Aug. 4, 2011).

Appendix A

Boys' Life, July 1911, 29; Robert Peterson "Testing Time at Valley Forge" *Boys' Life*, Nov.–
Dec. 2003.
Boys' Life, Apr. 1914, 23.
http://www.t30bcc.org/vf2009/index.html).
http://www.troop19.org/photos2010/ValleyForge/VF.html).
Bill Hillcourt,"Hiking with Green Bar Bill, *Boys' Life*, Feb. 1949, p. 20; "nat council official
news" bl ap 1924, p. 43).
David C. Scott, *We Are Americans, We Are Scouts*, Dallas, TX: Red Honor Press, 2008, pp.
125–165.
http://www.troop45mineola.org/index_files/Page767.htm.
Boys' Life, Feb. 1933, p. 50.
Boys' Life, Mar. 1939, p. 40.
http://www.hardingareadistrict.org.
http://www.usgrantpilgrimage.org/1usgrantpilgrimage/index.php?option=com_
content&view=article&id=54&Itemid=59.
Bryan Wendell, "Heads in the Right Place", *Boys' Life*, Jan.–Feb. 2011.
Norman Sklarewitz, "Mount Rushmore Turns 50," *Boys' Life*, June 1991, pp. 40–1. http://
www.munchmaster.com/troop7/pilgrimage.html.
Black Hill Area Council, "Your Leaders' Guide to the 70th Mount Rushmore Pilgrimage,
brochure.
Boys' Life, Apr. 1924, p. 43.
James E. West, "The Scout World," *Boys' Life*, May 1941, p. 21.
"Numbers," *Boys' Life,* Oct. 2001, p. 10.
http://lcweb2.loc.gov/gidlib/legacies/CA/200002746.html.
"The Scouts at Gettysburg," *Boys' Life,* Sept. 1913, p. 16.

Appendix B

"President Ford's Funeral Schedule," http:// www.foxnews.com/printer_friendly_
story/0,3566,239860,00.html (accessed July 25, 2013).
Mark Ray, "Eagle Scouts Welcome Gerald Ford Home," *Scouting*, Mar.–Apr. 2007.
Margaret Shannon, "In All Thy Ways Acknowledge Him: The Funeral for the Healer of a
Nation," *Cathedral Age Magazine*, Winter 2006.
"Remarks delivered at Ford's funeral at the National Cathedral," at http://www.
washingtonpost.com/wp-dyn/content/article/2007/01/02/AR2007010200418.html
(accessed July 25, 2013).

INDEX

ACKNOWLEDGMENTS

AS WITH ANY LARGE BOOK PROJECT, I did not work in a vacuum. In fact, it took a small army to gather the needed research material for its production.

First, I must thank the outstanding archivists at the presidential libraries, each of whom went out of their way to assemble copies of speech texts and images. They were: Peggy L. Dillard at the Wilson library, Lynn Smith and the Hoover library, Karen Anson at the Franklin Roosevelt library, Pauline Testerman at the Truman library, both Herb Pankratz and Kathleen A. Struss at the Eisenhower library, Stephen Plotkin at the Kennedy library, Margaret Harman at the Johnson library, Ryan Pettigrew, Jason Schultz, and Pamela Eisenberg at the Nixon library, David Horrocks, Timothy M. Holtz, and Nancy Mirshah at the Ford library, Polly Nodine at the Carter library, Michael Pickney at the Reagan library, Bonnie Burlbaw at the George H.W. Bush library, Herbert Ragan at the Clinton library, and Jodie Steck at the George W. Bush library.

To Steven Price, archivist for the Boy Scouts of America, and Christy Batchelor, archivist for Pearson Education, I offer my gratitude for your gathering of presidential Scouting images from your plentiful photo banks. To Nancy Burke and Carolyn Herter Stalder of Pack 19 in Dallas, Texas, I thank you very much for allowing me to use your story and images from your incredible meeting with President George W. Bush. To my manuscript fact checkers, Deputy Chief Scout Executive Gary Butler, Glenn A. Adams president of the National Eagle Scout Association, C. William Steele, the director of BSA's Alumni Association, De Tan Nguyen, director of Multicultural Markets, and National BSA volunteer and Scoutmaster Michael R. Bradle, I offer my sincere thanks for your time and appreciate your suggestions for improvement.

I thank former Scout Executive Michael D. Sulgrove for his stirring testimony on the funeral of Gerald Ford – being a magnificent firsthand account for this book. To my production team of Matthew Land, Pam Blackmon, and the entire staff of Publications Development Company, I could not have done it without your excellent work. To my magnificent photo editor, John K. Shipes, you're the BEST at your craft 'ole buddy.

And finally, I thank my friend and presidential scholar, Doug Brinkley, for taking time out of his busy schedule to scribe an outstanding Foreword for my book.

PHOTO CREDITS

George Bush Library (TX) 186, 187, 189

George W. Bush Presidential Library (TX) 204, 207, 208

William Clinton Presidential Library (AR) 195, 196, 198

Dwight D. Eisenhower Presidential Library (KS) 111, 115

Gerald R. Ford Presidential Library (MI) 155, 156 (top), 156 (right), 157, 336, 338, 340

William "Green Bar Bill" Hillcourt Trust (TX) 98

Charles Holmes Collection (TX) 110

John F. Kennedy Presidential Library (MA) 122, 123, 126, 127, 194,

Library of Congress (DC) vi, xiv, 9, 16, 18, 28, 32, 35, 36, 42, 44, 45, 50, 58, 61, 62, 65, 66, 72, 75, 76, 78, 84, 91,

Michael R. Marks Collection (PA) 220

National Archives, Boy Scouts of America (TX) xviii, 5, 7, 19, 21, 30, 31, 46, 47, 74, 144, 145, 146, 148, 159, 166, 168, 188, 210, 216, 218, 220, 221

Ronald Reagan Foundation (CA) 177, 178, 180,

Franklin D. Roosevelt Presidential Library (NY) 85, 89, 90

Theodore Roosevelt Collection, Harvard College (MA) 4

David C. Scott Collection (TX) xvii, xx, 49, 63, 73, 109, 134, 135, 137, 138, 154, 156 (bottom), 158, 161, 176, 326, 331,

Carolyn Herter Stalder Collection (TX) 209

Harry S. Truman Presidential Library (MO) 99, 102, 103

Diane Watson/Marion Area Convention & Visitors Bureau (OH) 329

ABOUT THE AUTHOR

DAVID C. SCOTT is the author of three nationally award winning and best-selling books. *The Scouting Party* (2010) recounts the origins of the Scouting movement. *We Are Americans, We Are Scouts* (2008) fuses the words and stories of President Theodore Roosevelt within the framework of the ideals of the Boy Scouts of America. And *Where Character is Caught* (2013) details the storied history of Dallas' Circle Ten Council, Boy Scouts of America.

A 1981 Eagle Scout, he is a member of the Boy Scouts of America's National Speakers Bank, helped train newly-hired Scout executives as the team lead for BSA's National Volunteer Training Team (2011-2013), and is a 2012 Silver Beaver recipient – the highest award bestowed upon a volunteer by a Scouting council. Also, he is a member of numerous lineal and national patriotic societies that include the Sons of the American Revolution, the Sons of the Republic of Texas, the Jamestowne Society, and the Presidential Families of America, being a 1st cousin (6 generations removed) to President James K. Polk and a 2nd cousin (8 generations removed) to President George Washington.

David has been married to his wife, Aimee, for over twenty-two years. They have four children.

ABOUT
WINDRUSH PUBLISHERS

Founded in Dallas, Texas, WindRush Publishers excels at bringing books of exceptional quality and content to the minds of discriminating readers everywhere. With an eye for excellence we are always on the search for new inspirational and motivational topics by expert authors in a variety of subjects.

With more great books to follow, WindRush remains devoted to producing exciting works designed for audiences of all ages and interests.